Damaged

Damaged

Heartbreaking stories of
the kids trapped in Britain's
broken care system

CHRIS WILD

WITH NIKKI GIRVAN

BLINK
bringing you closer

Published by Blink Publishing
2.25, The Plaza,
535 Kings Road,
Chelsea Harbour,
London, SW10 0SZ

www.blinkpublishing.co.uk

facebook.com/blinkpublishing
twitter.com/blinkpublishing

Paperback – 978-1-911-600-64-0
Ebook – 978-1-911-600-65-7

A CIP catalogue of this book is available from the British Library.

Typeset by seagulls.net
Printed and bound by Clays Ltd, St. Ives Plc

1 3 5 7 9 10 8 6 4 2

This is a work of non-fiction but some names have been changed
to protect the identity of the victims and survivors.

Blink Publishing is an imprint of the Bonnier Publishing Group
www.bonnierpublishing.co.uk

*To everyone who has suffered from trauma,
to my wife and children, to Nikki, Kelly and my Dad*

CONTENTS

A NOTE FROM THE AUTHOR

Sometimes, for real horror to be understood, it needs to be personified.

At first glance, this book contains the tales of 11 broken souls, united by their part in my life.

But these stories are more than that. They are the collective truths of thousands of children whose lives were devastated by the care system. Whose already broken souls were ground down behind the walls of a children's home.

Some grew up to be damaged adults, starting the cycle all over again.

Others never made it that far.

Everything I have written is based on real-life events – both those I witnessed and was a part of and those that I have researched. In places I have merged realities, intertwined stories and added my personal experiences. I have fictionalised names, locations, dates and used artistic licence where appropriate.

This isn't to mislead. It's to protect the identities of vulnerable children and families that are still grieving today. It's to highlight the failings of the care system past and present.

This book is a reflection of true experiences and emotions, the lives of a sad group of broken people connected to each other by their relationship to me. I hope it will speak to your soul in the same way their voices spoke to mine.

Chris Wild x

CHAPTER ONE

An Ordinary Life

'Dad, Dad, look at that,' I said, pointing enthusiastically as we drove past the Furness Drive estate, where the shell of a Volkswagen Golf was engulfed in flames. In the distance sirens wailed and the acrid smell of burning rubber stung my nostrils.

Police cars zipped through the streets, chasing sketchy-looking youths on revving motorbikes. Dad gave an irritated sideways glance as I craned my neck to catch a glimpse of the action. 'Give over, Chris,' he snapped.

But I was entranced; it was like a movie scene, the Wild West, just closer to home. Instead of people running round and panicking, they were circling the crackling fireball, throwing bulging bags of rubbish onto it and transforming it into a huge, rapidly expanding bonfire. There was no fear, just defiance. To a nine-year-old kid on his way to Morrisons with his family it was the most exciting interlude to a Saturday ever.

'Can we move here, Dad?' I whined. 'It's so boring where we live.'

The words had barely escaped my lips when I jolted violently forward, almost head-butting the driver passenger seat in front of me.

Dad had slammed the breaks on hard and was glaring at me through the rear-view mirror.

'You wouldn't last two seconds living here, lad,' he chastised me. 'Take a bloody good look around you. Do you think people want to live in this shithole? They have no bloody choice!'

Tears pricked my eyes and my bottom lip started to quiver. My dad never swore, especially in front of me and my sister Donna.

What had I said wrong?

Whatever it was, I'd really pissed him off. The emotion receptors in my brain went into overdrive, confused by what I'd done and scared by my dad's reaction. I started to cry. Well, I was just a kid after all.

Too upset to speak, I covered my face with my hands and sobbed as his tirade continued.

Then Mum calmly interjected. 'You're scaring him. Dave, leave him alone.'

She knew I didn't like being shouted at, as it was usually her doing the shouting. Dad was always Good Cop.

We drove the rest of the way to the supermarket without anyone saying another word. The silence hung awkwardly in the air until we arrived at the car park and climbed out of the car.

Dad pulled me to one side. 'I'm sorry, son,' he said, hugging me tightly. 'I didn't mean to scare you. It's just that place – it's not a good place.'

I frowned. The cogs in my young brain started to turn, piecing together Dad's reaction and the scene I'd witnessed just a few minutes earlier.

'Why were the boys on motorbikes being chased by police?' I asked, wondering if that was what he meant.

'I've no idea,' he shrugged. 'They're probably from the children's home.'

My ears pricked up. *That sounds exciting.*

'What's a children's home?' I asked, although my brain was already piecing together an idyllic image: *Swallows and Amazons* in the heart of Halifax. A home full of children? Where they had motorbikes and got chased by police? What child wouldn't be intrigued? It sounded like the best game of cops and robbers ever.

The floodgates holding back my childish questions were at bursting point when I noticed my dad's expression, one I'd never seen before. Just for a moment, a veil of sadness seemed to fall over him and dim the light in his eyes.

'It's a place you'll never, ever experience,' he said, then turned away.

End of conversation.

* * *

DAVE

'I promised myself that my kids would never know my life.'

My dad, Dave Cockcroft, was something of a local legend. Although streetwise, he was also renowned for being fair and selfless – a tough man with a kind heart. Walking through the streets of Halifax with him as a kid felt like being escorted around by a celebrity.

'Morning, Dave. How's the family?'

'I owe you a pint, Dave.'

'Your lad's growing up fast, Dave!'

Everyone knew his name and everyone wanted to speak to him. Every conversation was filled with respect and gratitude.

From the moment I was born, his influence and values shaped my life.

But he hadn't been as lucky with his own father, Layton 'Taffy' Thomas, the grandad I never knew.

He had influence on Dad's life all right. But his reputation was altogether less savoury.

They called him 'Taffy' cause he was Welsh. He moved up to Halifax as a solider based at the barracks in the town and he had a reputation from the moment he arrived.

An eye for the ladies and a reputation for spreading his oats.

He was effusive in his approach. Promised women the world to get them into bed. Each one believed they were special, that their story would have a different ending, that they'd get something more than just a one-night stand.

But that was never the case. Certainly not for my nan, Evelyn Wiseman. She was 31 years old when she fell for this Welsh lothario. Within weeks she was pregnant with my dad.

Taffy was gone in a flash at the slightest sniff of responsibility – that was just the kind of man he was – so Nan had to raise Dad on her own.

The times he spoke about her, Dad said she tried her best, but when he was two years old she contracted tuberculosis. She suffered for two years before she died. She was only 35.

As a child, piecing together snippets from conversations between grown-ups and the slurred outpourings of emotion from Dad after a few beers, I learned that Nan's boyfriend, Harold Cockcroft, took care of Dad for a while, that's why he had his name.

But then the pressure got too much. He dropped Dad like a sack of spuds. They all did.

I always wanted Dad to tell me more about his childhood, but he always pretended he had very little memory of it.

'I was passed from foster parent to foster parent,' he revealed one night. 'I was always living in a new house that was never a home. I never even knew who my real dad was until I was a teenager.'

In Dad's eyes he was an orphan, unwanted by the world. So when he ended up in a children's home, full of other 'unwanted bastards', he felt his point had been proven.

'They called it a "care" home, what a joke,' he'd say, shaking his head. 'Cattle market, more like.'

I didn't really understand what he meant at the time. How could I?

All I knew was that Dad found no care there, just pain. The only things he seemed to remember were the haunted faces of the kids that lived there with him, the fights and the fear.

'Terrible things happened behind closed doors there,' he said. 'But no one said anything. Everyone just ignored it, me included.'

Surrounded by my loving family, listening to my dad's words, it was hard to imagine not speaking up.

But then I had people who cared about me.

'There was no one to care about us, so the system could do what it wanted to us,' Dad sighed.

To the system, my dad and all those other broken kids were already dead, subhuman almost.

Dad wanted to be loved. What kid doesn't?

But his surroundings told him he wasn't worth it.

When he wasn't hemmed in by the horrors of the home, he was tearing through the streets with other kids just like him. Fighting, drinking, revelling in the mayhem because it was all they knew.

Despite all of that, Dad was one of the lucky ones. While kids in the home were being raped and abused, he was taken in by a local farmer called Sid Hawkins.

Sid and his family looked after Dad during his teenage years. They gave him work shovelling pig shit in return for a roof over his head and food in his belly.

It was the perfect opportunity to let love in, to be part of something. To be cared for.

But he didn't know how to do that.

He repaid their kindness with rebellion, the feral animal in him fighting against the love they were showing him.

Dad was already broken, accustomed to life on the street. He lied and stole from them, was nothing but trouble.

He was no one's to keep.

Unsurprisingly, they kicked him out in the end.

I think Dad didn't know how to be loved.

He'd lost his mum to TB so young that he never got to know her, never experienced that most primal of bonds.

Like so many care-home kids, he was plagued by his past. So used to being abandoned that he created a self-fulfilling prophecy.

He made it happen, because it was all he knew.

Everything I knew and remembered about Dad told me he wanted to be loved and cared for, but his heart and soul were already broken.

He knew the pain of abandonment and refused to take the risk of feeling that again.

As a youngster there was only one person in his life that he trusted. Baz Fawcett. His best mate and the closest thing he had to family.

At 15, when Dad was living on the streets with a park bench for a bed and newspapers wrapped around him like a makeshift igloo so he wouldn't freeze to death, Baz was the only one who gave a damn.

Dad used to tell us how Baz would sneak him into his house, where he'd feast like a king on whatever was in his parents' kitchen.

Dad reckoned Baz's mum hated him. Thought he was a bad influence.

In many ways she was right. Dad was a scrapper. Small but able to kick some serious arse when he had to.

Over time it became clear that I'd inherited that trait from Dad.

How could he have been any other way? Unlike my sister and me, Dad had to fight through life since the day he was born, because there was no one to fight for him.

Survive or die.

Dad survived. At 16 he got a job and found himself a bedsit. Every day he'd trudge six miles on an empty stomach to a cold, wet slaughterhouse, where he'd spend 15 hours a day covered in blood, breaking the necks of sheep.

'Whatever it took to keep myself off the streets,' he'd say, 'that's what I did.'

Thing was, Dad realised early on that no one else was coming to rescue him. He had to rely on himself.

He was incredibly proud of the fact that that he never once missed a day of that job. He eventually even managed to save up enough to buy a motorbike.

'A rust bucket with peddles,' he'd laugh fondly as he recalled it.

It was barely roadworthy, but it beat walking.

I often wished this part of Dad's story was the turning point, the part where he escaped his past on those two rickety wheels, but he never did.

Dad was born into misfortune.

Even the bike let him down. Driving to work one day, he fell off it and broke his ankle. But he couldn't go to the hospital: his rent was due and he was working cash in hand.

No show, no pay.

Dad had no choice. If he didn't want to end up back on the park bench, wrapped in plastic bags and shivering like a dog, he had to go to work.

I remember being in awe of him as he told me how he'd found a stick, strapped it up to his ankle with his bootlaces like a splint, got back on his bike and rode to work.

Like a superhero, I'd thought, as a young boy listening to the tale. *My dad can overcome anything.*

Truth was that every step that day was like standing on the edge of a knife, shooting pain through Dad's body. He endured it for the whole 15 hours of his shift before he even thought of going to hospital.

But Dad wasn't a hero. I realise that now.

He was a victim, a creature of the system.

He'd been in pain his whole life. A few more hours weren't going to kill him.

It's funny what pain does to you though. It's an emotional trigger.

Dad told me that the pain made him think about things, see things more clearly.

'I was 16 and limping through manure, covered in the blood of livestock I'd killed with my bare hands,' he said. 'I was so angry at the people who had abandoned me and left me to face the world alone. The people I felt were responsible for putting me there.'

He never said it, but I could tell he also cursed himself for not knowing how to accept the love and support that could have saved him.

'I made a promise that day,' Dad said, looking intensely into my eyes. 'If I ever had kids I'd do everything to protect them from the life I had known.'

I remember nodding, but not fully understanding. To me the chances of experiencing a life like that seemed impossible.

After all, I had my dad. He was a superhero and he had decided that the cycle he had witnessed time and again on the streets and in the children's home, where pain bred pain and poverty, would stop with him.

He wanted to make a home – a real home. Do everything in his power to give his children the best start in life.

And do you know what?

He did.

But sometimes a cruel twist of fate can destabilise everything, allowing the shadow of the past to creep back in, and the cycle to begin once again.

* * *

In 1989, I had the most ordinary life going. I lived in an ordinary house with two bedrooms, a slate roof and big bright windows on a nice street, surrounded by other nice, ordinary families going about their daily business.

Like most boys, my dad was my hero, but it wasn't just me who felt that way. It seemed like everyone did. Dad was a small man with the presence of a giant. He worked hard and looked after people, especially his family. He and my mum were childhood sweethearts. He'd been the cock of the town, everyone wanted him, but it was my mum who won his heart. From the moment he met her, he had eyes for no one but her.

We didn't have much, but then no one in my neck of the woods did. My parents and their neighbours on Ripon Terrace were the ordinary working-class folk that Margaret Thatcher's Conservative government had kicked down, leaving them struggling to just make ends meet.

But there were no police chases, no broken families and no cars engulfed in flames – just a row of stone houses with neat front yards, cheerfully painted doors and windows looking out onto an enclosed park, where we all used to play. Each building safely cocooned a family living its own happy ever after. Or so it seemed.

Of course, at that age you never saw your parents crying over a bottle of cheap wine, trying to figure out how to pay the mortgage. You didn't notice the wear and tear on their bodies and souls as they worked like donkeys just to keep a roof over your head. And of course they never told you.

Me and the other kids on the street were oblivious then to the fact that we were all living just above the breadline. Nestled in the beauty and safety of Halifax's green hills, we went to school, played football in the streets, and a game of knock and run occasionally, but always went in for dinner when our mums called us. We were happy.

Playing in the street, watching films at home as a family, going swimming in the local baths with my sister, it was hard to imagine life ever being any different. Until one day when I was 11 years old, everything changed.

It was me who answered the phone that day. 'Hello?'

Nothing could have prepared me for the words I heard next.

'Your dad's dead. Can you put your mum on the phone?' said a voice, twisted with pain. I hardly recognised it as belonging to my Uncle Gary.

'What?' I replied.

'Just get your mum,' he said.

My head swam as I dropped the receiver and stumbled through the house calling my mum's name. A few weeks earlier, Donna caught chicken pox. Then Dad got them too. When he got them they turned to shingles and he'd become really poorly, so he'd been taken into the Bradford Royal Infirmary. I was so young that I didn't understand the severity of it all, but no one seemed too worried. I mean, it *was* only chicken pox after all. Who dies of chicken pox?

As Mum came to the phone I caught a glimpse of the calendar and started to laugh.

1 April 1991.

Sick joke, that. Not really that funny, but nice try all the same. I watched and waited for Mum to react. Laugh and tell him what a horrible joke it was. But she didn't, she just crumpled to the floor.

In that moment, I knew. Dad was gone.

The days and weeks that followed passed in a blur. Family members came and went. Dad's friends dropped in to offer their condolences. I loved those visits. The short-term attention was something else. I was Dave Cockcroft's lad and everyone had a story about his gallantry they wanted to regale me with.

'Remember that awful snow storm in 1986?' said Baz. 'He was out there at the crack of dawn with his shovel, clearing everyone's path. He was always making sure everyone was safe.'

That was Dad all over – a true gent, always looking out for others.

It was probably a way of dealing with their grief, but for me it was more than that. It kept Dad alive for me just that little bit longer.

Truth be told, it was weeks, maybe even months, before I accepted he was gone. I kept thinking that it was all an elaborate prank.

One day, about two weeks after Dad's death, we were walking home from school through the park – Mum had insisted that Donna and I go back to school to restore some sense of normality.

As our house came into view, I spotted a blue Ford Fiesta outside. My heart leapt into my throat. *Dad's car!*

My school bag slipped from my grip and I started to run as fast as I could, blood pounding in my ears so I could barely hear myself screaming.

So Uncle Gary was being a dick. This was all a joke, wasn't it? I bet Dad was back home laughing about it too.

'Dad, Dad, where are you?' I yelled as, propelled by adrenalin and gasping for breath, I burst into the house.

I collided against a wall of silence.

No laughter, no Dad slapping his knee and congratulating Uncle Gary on a top-class prank.

Just deafening silence. Then a guttural cry emerged from the living room, low and from the pit of her stomach. The kind of heart-wrenching noise that only comes from real anguish. It was Mum, sobbing.

I looked up and my grandma was standing at the top of the landing. Behind me, Donna had finally caught up and was standing at the front door, staring into space.

'Your dad's gone, Chris,' she said as she descended the stairs, the creak of each step like a gunshot to my heart as reality once again took aim and fired.

'But his car,' I stuttered, 'it's outside. He must be here. Is he hiding?'

Grandma threw her arms around me and I sank into her, big fat tears rolling down my face and blurring my vision. I felt her whole body rattle as she started to sob too.

Even at the funeral, nothing felt real. As we drove behind the hearse up Haley Hill towards St Bernard's Church, it felt like the whole of Halifax had come out to mourn with us. No one seemed to care about the thoughtlessly parked cars that were spilling out of the car park and blocking the road. Not today.

We were the last ones to enter the church. Dad's coffin was already in place and all I could see was a sea of teary faces that couldn't quite bring themselves to make direct eye contact with us. It was the very first funeral I had ever attended. Why did it have to be my dad's?

Even then, as we chanted, genuflected and bowed our heads, the only prayer I was saying was for this all to be a joke. A Jeremy Beadle wheeze that Mum and Dad had concocted to earn a little extra cash. Childish visions of the priest ripping off a fake beard and a camera crew leaping out of the pulpit danced through my head. I might even have smiled.

But as we moved on to Stoney Royd Cemetery for the burial, hundreds of mourners climbing in procession in the scorching heat up the precipitous hill to where Dad was to be laid to rest, that glimmer of hope began to flicker.

Come on, Dad. If you're joking, you need to wake up now. This is getting serious!

We all sobbed as Mum laid a pile of juicy oranges and four cans of Foster's on the top of Dad's coffin as he was lowered into the grave. The picture of him blowing a kiss that she'd chosen to emblazon his shiny black headstone oversaw the proceedings.

While he'd been in hospital in his medicated coma he only woke up once. He'd asked her to make sure she looked after me and Donna, then their conversation had drifted.

'Not half got a craving for a Foster's,' he'd said. 'And some oranges.'

Mum never guessed then that they'd be the last words he ever said to her.

Dad would have appreciated the touch and Mum knew that.

One by one, people sidled away to the pub for the wake, but I stayed beside Aunty Carol, my dad's sister, and watched as his grave was filled with soil and rubble. I don't know how long we were there but if felt like a very, very long time.

As the last bit of soil was patted down, the flickering flame of hope I'd kept alight for so many weeks was extinguished, leaving an aching void deep inside me.

Nothing would ever be the same again.

I stepped forward and placed a red rose on the gritty, raw earth.

'Goodbye, Dad. I love you.'

CHAPTER TWO

A Broken Family

For a short while, life was quiet. My twelfth birthday came and went without much ceremony. I didn't care. No day was special any more, I just went through the motions, dazed and numb.

Mum breaking down in the street while we were out shopping or visiting family became a regular occurrence. She was too young to be a widow, too young to make sense of what had happened to her world. The pain was tearing her apart.

Before long the numbness wore away and instead I was filled with a searing rage.

Why my dad? Why my family?

I began to lash out, do everything I could to rebel. It was like I was attacking the invisible force that had snatched my dad away from us.

Of course, for a while, people gave me the benefit of the doubt.

Give the lad a break, he's not long lost his dad.

But I didn't stop pushing at the boundaries. I'd pick fights for the hell of it, break things, even got caught smoking weed. Before long I was expelled from school.

Friends and neighbours who had once been so close to us now looked at us as if we were aliens. They couldn't relate to us any more. We were broken. Different.

'Poor family, glad it wasn't my husband,' they'd whisper as we passed.

'I hear she's moved a new man in, very quick that.'

Sympathy with a backhand of suspicion and judgement.

It was true, though. Desperate to find a way out of her grief, Mum fell into the arms of Dad's foster bother, Viv. It can't have been easy, being widowed at the age of 30 with two young kids. She must have needed someone to lean on, a grown-up to share the burden with, especially with me acting up like I was, but God knows why it had to be him.

It was too quick, but that was just the way he planned it.

He slithered into our life like a snake, through the cracks of Mum's pain. Within six months of Dad's death he'd even moved into our family home.

His arrival on our nice, ordinary street changed everything. He wasn't like our neighbours, and now neither were we. We were outcasts.

Everyone could see he was a vulture – everyone except Mum. Days after Dad's funeral he was circling us, beady eyes on the life insurance policy that Dad had set up in case anything ever happened to him.

He was everything that my dad wasn't – violent, manipulative and greedy. He could smell vulnerability and sought out broken women like my mum to meet his own ends. It wasn't long before he got what he wanted.

'We're buying a car lot with Viv's friend Craig,' Mum announced one day, smiling nervously over at him. 'It's a great investment.'

Viv put a controlling hand on her shoulder. 'You can come and work with me, Chris,' he sneered. 'Be part of the business.'

I couldn't imagine anything worse, but what choice do you have at the age of 12? I obliged, but it was just one more thing stoking the flames of fury that had begun to burn inside me.

Working as tea boy and car washer at the lot initiated me into a world I'd never seen before.

I watched from the wings as Viv and his cronies brought stolen cars into the lot and dismantled the parts for cloning. Shifty characters loitered in doorways having hushed conversations and lots of money changed hands. More money than I'd ever seen in my life.

The dark dynamics of the lot and its clientele reminded me of the council estate that Dad had been so keen to keep me away from. I was intoxicated. It just seemed so *alive*.

Violence became a regular occurrence for us almost as soon as Viv came on the scene. If Mum so much as looked at Viv the wrong way, she'd get a swift backhand from him. If the house wasn't tidy enough or tea wasn't on the table, he'd beat her into submission.

I was only a kid, but I couldn't stand by and watch. She was my mum.

'Stop it, Viv,' I'd yell, trying to block the path of his fist as he swung for her.

'Who do you think you are?' he'd hiss, grabbing me by the neck and launching me across the room. Winded, I'd pull myself to my feet.

'Leave her alone,' I'd sob. 'My dad would kill you for this.'

'Well, your dad's not fucking here, is he?' he'd say, grabbing me by the hair and dragging me upstairs to my room as Mum sobbed in a crumpled heap.

He wasn't just physically abusive either. He manipulated Mum and convinced her that she was always in the wrong. She couldn't even put on a nice dress to go out for dinner with him without him calling her a slut.

Before long, Viv convinced Mum to sell the family home and buy a cottage just off Shay Lane and move in with him there. I didn't take her decision well at all.

'You can't do this!' I screamed at her. 'This is our home.'

I knew that living under a new roof with him would give Viv even more power.

'Don't you speak to your mother in that tone,' Viv said, shoving me in the shoulder.

'I know what you're doing,' I yelled, hot tears streaming down my face.

Viv grabbed me and pushed me against the wall.

'So what are you going to do to stop me?' he growled in my ear, a sinister smile on his lips.

He was right, what could I do?

Nothing.

I turned to the streets to escape my crumbling home. Drinking, fighting, taking drugs and stealing became my solace and the streets of Halifax became my playground. In the absence of my family unit, I began to build a new one, made up of shady characters that supplied my new and dangerous habits.

Twelve months after my dad died, I was out roaming the streets with my friend Shane. Our mums had gone to school together and sent us to the same nursery, so we'd known each other for years.

His mum and dad divorced a year before my dad died. Rumour was that his mum was having an affair with a toy boy, whole town knew about it before he did.

To be honest, it was the hottest topic in Halifax until my family clinched top prize for gossip fodder of the year. Shane must have been relieved that I'd gone so spectacularly off the rails after Dad's death.

Although I was a year older than Shane, fate ensured we had lots in common. Not least that we were both angry young boys from broken families. Bored, restless and looking to cause trouble, we'd been out on a shoplifting spree all day.

Pocketing pointless things like batteries and kitchen knives – it wasn't like we needed any of it – we were just doing it for the hell of it. We'd been strutting the streets, chests puffed out with pride at our rebellion, but as the wind and rain rolled down from the hills, we began to hunt for shelter.

'Over here, Chris,' said Shane, pointing to a low window on the side of Akroydon Church, an imposing, abandoned old building that hadn't been used for at least a century.

We smashed through the pane with a brick, covering our skin with our coats as we nudged the shards of glass out of the window frame, before we squeezed our bodies through the gap we'd made. I was twelve years old and there wasn't a pick on me, so it was as effortless as it was reckless.

The pews and altar were still intact and the imposing walls enveloped us in a sense of safety and security as the wind whistled around the building and the rain battered the old stained-glass windows.

'This place is brilliant,' I said, lighting a cigarette and taking a deep drag.

Shane nodded as he exhaled a long plume of smoke into the air and tossed our spoils on to the wooden seats.

We'd found ourselves a top-class hangout; no one would find us here.

Or so I reckoned.

I lost count of how many cigarettes we chained through before our peace and quiet was shattered by an authoritative cry.

'POLICE!' came a booming voice. 'Stay where you are.'

Shane and I looked at each other before our eyes darted around the church looking for possible escape routes, but there were none.

Turns out a resident had spotted us breaking the church window and called the police. Halifax was a small place and there were also a number of shopkeepers who'd made calls about kids going round thieving too. It didn't take much for them to put it all together.

The officers took the pathetic haul and our fags too before they bundled us into the police car waiting outside.

'You'll have to pay for that window too,' one of them barked.

With what? I thought.

I was a kid from a broken home. I had nothing.

A year earlier, I'd have been terrified of turning up on my street in a police car. *What would my dad think?*

Not now. It was like a light had gone out inside me. Didn't even feel a pang of guilt or regret as the squad car rolled down my street, prompting the neighbours to come out of their houses to see what had happened.

To the kids it was all a game, a bit of excitement, but not for their parents.

All those faces that had once been so familiar and sympathetic were contorted with disgust, as they held on tight to their children.

This kind of thing didn't happen on *their* street. Not in this nice part of town.

I sat with my head down in the car as the police officer knocked on my front door. I felt like I was trapped in a bubble as I heard him explain just what had happened.

'I'm so sorry, officer. He's had a hard time, losing his dad and all. He's just acting up,' Mum apologised for me.

'It won't happen again, I promise,' she added.

I raised an eyebrow.

I think that's for me to decide, isn't it?

Eventually the officer returned to the car to get me. The neighbours were still out in force. *Nosey gits.*

I could hear the whispers as I was escorted out of the car and frogmarched up the path to my mum.

'You stay away from that one. You can't play out with him any more,' they hissed.

Mum was stood in the doorway, arms crossed and seething with rage.

'Thank you, officer,' she said dutifully. 'I'll make sure he stays out of trouble.'

Mum waved the officer off, pushed the front door shut and then spun round on her heel. She glared at me for a moment, then her face dropped and she shook her head sadly.

'What were you thinking, Chris?' she said. 'What on earth are you doing, shoplifting?'

I shrugged and looked at the floor. Mum's disappointment seeped through the tiny cracks in my tough façade and crimson rose from my neck up to my cheeks.

Now I was outside of the bubble of the police car, I could tell she was horrified and I hated hearing the shame in her voice.

'I just can't believe it,' she said. 'Can you imagine what your dad would say?'

Those words cut like a knife.

Her voice cracked at the mention of my dad and for a moment my heart sank into my stomach. I knew he'd be embarrassed too.

He'd never talked about it much, but I knew that Dad had been in trouble with the police when he was younger. Maybe it was the emotion and gratitude for having a family to spend it with, or maybe just that fifth can of Foster's, but occasionally, around Christmas time, little snippets of stories from his past would slip out, each one starting and ending in the same way.

'You don't know how lucky you are to be alive,' he'd begin, before opening a door into that mysterious part of his life. The one he kept hidden from us.

No matter how much we begged he'd never get through a full story. It would just end with him wrapping his arms around us and giving a big bear hug as tears streaked down his cheeks. It always broke my heart.

Seeing the tears in Mum's eyes took me right back to those moments, and I swallowed down the lump in my throat.

Dad had long paid his dues for his misdemeanours. He'd put a halo round our surname – round our family – and gave us all something to be proud of.

And here I was, fucking it all up.

This was not the behaviour of a Cockcroft.

But as suddenly as the ripple of sadness and guilt washed over me, it was gone, replaced by a wave of rage.

What did it matter though? He wasn't here any more, was he?

The anger and pain driving my rebellion returned, and within hours I had sneaked out of the house, turning to my new friends – my street family.

They were different to me. Older boys and girls in their late teens and early twenties who'd never known the love and security I'd grown up with, who were born into chaos with violent families that meant the authorities had washed their hands of them.

They were like vampires, hunting the streets for other angry broken creatures to join their pack, or weak victims to feast on, kids like Callum.

Callum was a weird lad who hung round the bus station all the time. He was from a council estate in Siddal, Halifax, that had a reputation for being one of the poorest going, and that was saying something.

He was a penny short of a pound, lived in his own world and took regular beatings from the older kids, who called him 'spaz' and 'retard'. He didn't do anything to rile them up, he was just a vent for their anger, a human punch bag.

The thing about Callum was, even though they all hated him, he'd do anything you asked for a cigarette and never fought back, so that made him useful too.

Whether from the estate or the care home, or fresh out of prison, they were all bound by one thing – an innate lack of fear, because they'd never had anything to lose.

I was one of them now.

What did I have to lose?

Dad was gone, Mum had been beaten down to nothing by the vile creature she'd let into our home, and my sister was a mess too. Like all of us, she was struggling to find a way to cope with life after the loss of the man that had been the centre of all our worlds.

In the weeks and months that followed, my behaviour spiralled out of control. Roaming the streets high as a kite on acid, fighting, shoplifting and helping to burgle houses.

Anything to escape what was happening at home.

Out on the streets I was free. I didn't have to worry about getting bad grades at school, or if Mum could pay the bills. I didn't have to feel helpless as Viv wrapped his hands round Mum's throat, or worry about him coming after me.

On the streets, I was free.

What's more, I felt wanted and useful too.

* * *

'Cocky, here. This window is open,' my mate, Steve Carney, whispered one day as we walked around a local house. We'd heard the people who lived there were away for a few days, so we'd been to see if we could find a way in.

Lucky for us, they had left one of the narrow windows at the top of the pane slightly ajar.

'I'll get in there easy,' I said as Steve used a crowbar to force it open wide enough for me to squeeze my skinny body through.

Steve was about seven years older than me. He was from the Grove Estate in Ovenden and as one of the ringleaders of our group, no one messed with him.

When I was with him, no one messed with me either.

'Get the back door open and we'll get the gear out that way,' he said as I slid effortlessly through the frame. Within seconds I was darting through the house. My heart was racing and adrenalin was pumping round my body. I was thinking about nothing but doing what Steve asked of me.

I wanted him to like me. I wanted him to ask me to help him again.

Soon I was at the back door.

My heart skipped a beat.

The idiots had left the key in the lock.

I smiled as I turned it, slide the bolt across and opened the door.

'Come on,' I hissed excitedly to Steve and the two lads he'd brought with him.

'Great work, Cocky,' Steve said, ruffling my hair as he ran past me. 'Now keep watch.'

Heart still pounding out of my chest, I crouched by the back gate ready to raise the alarm if a nosey neighbour or the police appeared.

Nothing so far…

I could hear rustling and bangs from inside the house, then one by one they whizzed past me, clutching TVs and radios and handfuls of jewellery.

'Get gone, Cocky,' Steve shouted. 'See you back on the estate later.'

We all scattered in different directions. I knew the drill by now.

As I ran I found myself grinning from ear to ear. I felt elated, like I was part of a winning team.

Later that night, stolen goods flogged and cash in hand, Steve treated me like a king. As well as my cut, I was showered with cigarettes and as much beer as I could drink.

I didn't have a care in the world, not as long as I stayed firmly in my street bubble.

Of course, I wasn't always so lucky. We all got caught from time to time.

It wasn't so much the getting caught that bothered me. It was what it meant.

Being taken back to Mum and Viv's.

Each time I was brought home by the police, Mum would beg me to stop hanging out in those parts of town, to stay at home, to try and get back into school.

Then Viv would show up, usually rough me up a bit – and Mum too, for good measure. Resentment and rage burned inside me.

No amount of pleading from Mum could pull me back.

I ran with the street kids now.

Yes, it was dangerous and risky, but it was better than home, which was filled with poison and pain.

*　*　*

Twelve months and six arrests later eventually led to a decision. I was to be taken into care and would be moving into the local children's home, Skircoat Lodge.

It can't have been that much of a surprise to Mum. I was 12 years old with a probation officer, a Youth Offending Team officer, a social worker, a school officer and a big black mark next to my name with all of the authorities.

Who smashed the window? *Chris Cockcroft*.

Who punched you? *Chris Cockcroft*.

Who do you see breaking into the house? *Chris Cockcroft*.

The fact was, it was true. I wore my reputation like a badge of honour.

I didn't identify with the safe, secure world I'd grown up in any more.

I was a street kid and I wanted the world to know that I wasn't someone to be messed with.

I didn't even try to avoid trouble. In fact, I actively went looking for it. I had my status as a tough kid to uphold.

One day, I found myself in the park, squaring up to some kid a couple of years older than me. The adrenalin was pumping, but I wasn't scared. I was revelling in it.

'Who do you think you are, you skinny shit?' he goaded, as a crowd gathered round to absorb the spectacle.

I smirked. It wasn't the first time someone had under-estimated me because of my stature and it wasn't going to be the last.

'I'm fucking Chris Cockcroft,' I said, punching him directly on the nose. 'Who the fuck do *you* think you are?'

The air was blue with expletives as I wrestled him to the floor and hammered blow after blow to his face, causing his nose to burst and blood to spurt everywhere.

The crowd cheered me on as he put me in headlock, but I wiggled free and continued to pummel away at him, ducking and diving out of the way of his swings.

As we lurched at each other, moving back and forth, I suddenly realised I had no idea what had caused the fight. I barely knew who the lad was.

For a split second I felt the anger inside me lower to a simmer.

Why am I doing this?

Then SMACK.

A blow to my ear reignited my rage. I was off like a rocket.

It could have gone on for hours, but suddenly the sound of a siren forced our spectators to scatter.

Shit.

'I'll fucking have you next time,' I threatened, as my opponent turned on his heels. I knew there was no real need for a 'next time'. I'd made my point – even if I didn't know about what.

But I was always on the lookout for the next way to expel the anger and bitterness festering inside me.

My rage at the way my life had been turned upside down.

Whether it was goading someone into a fight or smashing a window just for the hell of it, I became addicted to the feeling of release that it gave me.

In her emotionally fragile state, Mum just couldn't control me, especially not since Viv was controlling her like a puppet master and his puppet. He pulled all of her strings and she was exhausted, a shadow of her former self.

Yet I remember overhearing the conversation between the social worker and Mum and Viv just a few weeks before I entered the home.

'Diane, it's not looking good. He's on their radar,' she said in a hushed tone. 'The juvenile courts will be onto him soon and they will send him away to juvenile detention.'

Mum covered her open mouth with her hand and shook her head in disbelief.

'You can't cope. You have to send him to the children's home.'

Peeking through the banisters at the top of the stairs, I saw a look of horror cross my mum's face.

'No,' she gasped. 'Dave would never have that. It can't happen.'

The discussion circled through Mum's refusal, knowing that it was the last thing my dad would ever want, squaring up to the social worker and Viv's insistence that she couldn't handle me on her own and that she needed to let the authorities take over.

'That way he'll be looked after and you can get a break,' pushed Viv. 'Sort yourself out.'

Like he cares about either of us.

In the end she held her hands up. 'Maybe it's for the best.'

I can still remember Viv's face as he pulled her final string.

'It's the right decision, love,' he said, stifling the victorious grin creeping across his lips.

Broken and defeated, Mum nodded and it was decided.

Now he has her all to himself.

* * *

Arrangements were made and in August 1992 my social worker took me to the home. At the time it didn't feel like a punishment. In fact, it was exciting. It brought back memories of the day we'd seen that burning car on the estate.

They're probably from the children's home. Dad's words echoed in my head.

Perhaps I should have felt scared but instead it all felt like an adventure, like I was being handed a passport to hang out with my mates and cause mayhem whenever I liked.

What I did notice though was that Skircoat Lodge looked nothing like the place I associated the word 'home' with. It had too many heavy doors and windows with thick glass, like 1970s NHS bifocals and dints in the frames, like someone had tried to break in – or out, maybe?

Colourful, but poorly spelled graffiti peppered the ambitiously decorative solid oak fames. I sniggered as I read it.

fuk you, u bastad

Well, you got the sentiment at least.

I was shown around by my social worker. I can't remember her real name – I later found out everyone called her 'The Bear'. I was just mesmerised by the fact she had a wiry beard and looked like Worzel Gummidge – he frightened the life out of me as a child, and she gave me the same creeps as a teenager.

The home, although not welcoming, was like a Tardis. As we stepped through the heavy oak door the building seemed to open up, room after room appearing round each corner.

'This is the communal area,' she said. 'And the bedrooms are here.'

'Will I have my own room?' I asked excitedly.

'No, you'll be sharing,' she replied.

That's cool. I've never had a roommate apart from my sister.

As we made our way round we eventually fell into the shadow of a tall, broad man, who wore a whistle round his neck.

He must be the Boss Man.

'Hello, Chris,' he said in a clipped, baritone voice. 'Welcome to Skircoat Lodge. Make yourself at home.'

So I did. I dropped my bag in the communal kitchen and began shuffling round the corridors to get my bearings, memorising each twist and turn. Each door and loose window frame.

Whether that came from running away from the police or dodging Viv, I knew better than anyone that you had to know your escape routes if you wanted to survive.

Soon, I was introduced to my roommate. My heart sank. There, sat on the bed with a vacant look on his face, was Callum.

'This is—' began the bearded social worker.

'Callum. I know him,' I finished, nodding at him in acknowledgement.

I wasn't happy about it. At 14, he was a couple of years older than me, but had the mental capacity of a ten-year-old, and was always going on about superheroes and comics when all I wanted to talk about was drinking and girls.

I guess he was okay to have a chat and a fag with, though. Plus, he'd been in care most of his life, so he could give me the low-down on how things worked.

The other good thing about Callum was that he acted on demand. He was simple like that, didn't ask any questions, and, as I'd seen on the streets, he'd do anything for a cigarette.

I'd already learned before moving into the home that ciga-rettes were currency, so I made sure I was well stocked up on Regals before entering it.

They were like a fashion statement. If you smoked Regals, it meant you had money. Not a poor bastard on the baccy.

It was all an illusion, though. I'd slipped £20 out of Mum's purse one night when she was drunk, processing what had happened to her family, I guess – or hiding from it.

Twenty quid got you a lot of cigarettes in 1992, but I wish I'd put a bit aside. Callum had the worst case of smelly feet I'd ever experienced. I got through two cans of Lynx a week trying to exterminate the pungent smell.

The lad had issues and questionable hygiene.

But that was my life now.

This was my new 'home'.

*   *   *

CALLUM

'I just wanted people to like me.'

Callum loved comic books, which would be fine for a little boy, but for a teenager round our way it was weird.

Superman, Batman or someone he'd made up, he once told me that he wanted to be a superhero because it meant he'd be loved and respected by everyone.

'And no one would be able to hurt me,' he added.

I guess I'd immediately thought he meant the gangs of lads who roamed the streets like a pack of wolves baying for blood and taking advantage of the weak.

Callum was always a target for them. I lost count of the times he took a beating.

But it turns out, that wasn't the hurt he was trying to avoid. That damage had already happened a long time ago.

He was eight years old when it first happened.

He'd always been a bit different. Lived in his own world and was easily led. Unlike me, or any number of kids I knew, he didn't question much, just went along with things.

He's slow, people would say, *not the full ticket.*

And they were probably right.

Because when his grandad forced himself on him, he didn't know it was wrong.

When his grandad was babysitting him and his six siblings, Callum didn't question it when a gang of his mates came round and paid to 'have a go' with him. Not even as tears of pain streamed down his face while they took turns to rape him.

I often wondered where his parents were while all this was going on. Apparently his dad suffered from bipolar disorder.

When I met Callum, I didn't know what that was. No one talked about depression or mental health then. They barely do now. But I knew it meant he was always ill, hardly had a clue what he was doing, let alone what was happening to Callum.

His grandad must've looked like a saint. Always volunteering to babysit when his dad had a doctor's appointment. To the outside world, he was a doting grandparent, but behind closed doors he was as vicious as a wolf, taking any opportunity to abuse his grandson.

I found out that when Callum was eight years old his grandad had given him a bath.

Not his other siblings.

Just Callum.

'You're my favourite,' he'd told him, wickedly preying on that childish desire to be special and feel loved. As he bathed him, he'd paid special attention to Callum's private parts.

'These bits need to be extra clean,' he'd say, first using a sponge, then rubbing between his legs with his bare hands.

Poor naive Callum believed that he just had a problem with his cleanliness. Until the next time, that is, when he made Callum do the same to him.

It started off with hands. Then he'd 'clean' him with his mouth.

It happened once, then twice, then again and again.

But Callum was just a kid, and a broken and vulnerable one at that.

It seemed so obviously wrong to me, but thinking about it, with Callum's learning difficulties and his dad's illness meaning he was exposed with no protector, how was he to know it wasn't right?

Of course, eventually someone slipped up and social services whisked Callum away to the children's home.

They probably thought they saved him. But they didn't.

The system had already failed him a long time before they leapt on their white horses.

He always told me that the cold was the thing he remembered most about going into care.

'For the first two weeks, I'd get lost going to the showers,' Callum said.

I wasn't surprised, the corridors were like Spaghetti Junction.

'I'd stand shivering and crying until someone found me and took me back to my room,' he finished.

Usually it was Brian, his key worker. I suppose he was one of the better things to happen to Callum. You see, Brian was how a grandad should be – old, sweet and harmless.

I mean, he wasn't warm or emotional or anything. He kept things simple. He had to with the job; he couldn't have favourites.

I knew Callum wished that Brian had been his real grandad.

Brian was a Good Samaritan, not a pervert. He just wanted to help Callum.

At 15, when they started 'semi-independent training' to prepare Callum for adult life outside the home, Brian tried his best to mentor Callum away from the dark towards a happy and prosperous life. But even before he got to the children's home, it was already too late.

A wolf had bitten him and his blood was infected.

I have the same disease as my grandad.

Callum really believed that the abuse meant he'd have an unnatural attraction to children too. He always thought he might as well have been dead.

You see, in his eyes kids from broken homes didn't find happy ever afters, especially not those with sick desires and an address that screamed 'high risk'.

Callum's fate was predetermined.

He knew exactly what he was, and what he would become.

The system wanted to sweep kids like him under the carpet.

Callum humoured him when he asked him what he wanted to be.

'I want to be a superhero,' he'd say. 'I want to save the world from evil.'

Brian would always have an educated response.

'That's not a real job, it's a fantasy,' he'd say kindly. 'I don't think you've thought this through, Callum.'

But Callum was nuts. Broken by the horrors of his past. Brian knew it too, but still he tried. Said he wanted the best for Callum.

But, of course, that's what his grandad said too.

I think through it all, Callum could see the difference between Brian and his grandad.

Brian *did* want the best for him. He thought he could cure Callum. But his grandad only ever did was what was best for himself.

People would use Callum all of his life.

He never did become a superhero.

He ended up becoming a drug addict and a child molester.

He'd get high on whatever drugs he could get his hands on and allow the lines of reality to blur, enabling his dreams of being one of the DC or Marvel heroes to become a reality.

He told me it was the only time he felt special or wanted. But it got him into trouble when his chemical dreams spilled into reality and he'd run around the park naked, near young girls.

Despite what he thought, what the demons in his head told him, Callum wasn't a monster.

He was lonely. He wanted friends, people who liked him. He wanted someone to save him. He was crying out for help, but no one heard him. His superhero obsession was simply a way to create someone who gave a damn about him.

Years after I first met Callum, I learned about what happens to children if they suffer a trauma like he did. It permanently damages the amygdala – the grey matter in your brain that allows you to experience emotion.

Well, Callum's grandad really fucked him up when he abused him.

It took years before Callum had the courage to really face his past. When he peeked behind the curtain, all he found was more pain.

Turns out his grandad had abused his dad too.

A wolf in sheep's clothing.

When I learned that, Callum's dad's sickness made sense. Like Callum, he was living under the shadow of the abuse. The system let him down, and then Callum after him.

Callum didn't hate his dad for letting it happen; Callum didn't hate anyone apart from himself.

Truth is, he didn't stand a chance – none of them did. All five of his siblings ended up in care.

When he left the children's home at 16 he ended up living on the streets. He was picked up by the pack and made into a slave once again. The sad thing is, it wasn't a surprise. Any hope he'd had died when he was eight years old.

To Callum, the streets felt safer. But he knew they weren't for others.

Especially not young girls.

Not with him around.

He once told me about the night he saw her. He was sleeping rough in the park. He described how there were fireworks everywhere. The plumes of light illuminated her beauty.

'I couldn't believe it when she spoke to me. Girls never paid me any attention,' he said.

Of course, Callum felt like a king. Like the superhero he'd always wanted to be.

He told me how innocent she seemed, but that she spoke with words way beyond her years.

'I wanted to show her I liked her, so I leaned in to kiss her,' he told me.

But when she recoiled from his advances, Callum just pushed harder. Forced himself upon her until she slipped away from his grasp.

He didn't realise at the time, but she was scared. Just like he used to be when his grandad and his cronies came round.

Four months after the incident, Callum was held to account for his actions at the local police station, where he was accused of statutory rape.

He didn't even fully understood what that meant, he just knew it was bad.

Why did you do it, Callum?

I just wanted her to like me. I thought she did, he said.

She was only 15 years old. Still a child in the eyes of the law.

Callum was 18.

I thought she was older, he told the police officer. *I liked her. She wasn't mean to me like the older kids who beat me up.*

There was no evidence of sexual intercourse. That's what Callum's defence said. They said he didn't have the mental capacity.

They were probably right. Trauma had damaged Callum irreparably, not that anyone gave a damn.

When he was sniffing glue in the streets as he tried to escape reality, no one helped him. They ignored him. Walked the other way. But when he was high as a kite and running naked around the park, or squatting and shitting on the pavement in broad daylight? They paid attention then.

They called him a nonce and beat him black and blue.

Isolated and lonely, when he desperately tried to forge friendships with younger kids by buying them beer and sweets, they came after him, chanting 'paedo' and pissing on him in the street.

Despite never being convicted, to the town of Halifax Callum was just as guilty as his grandad.

Soon he believed it too.

I heard that he'd told the police that he was a victim of his own misfortune. That he'd been abused and sentenced to life in hell, even before he'd committed any crime of his own.

'But no one sympathises with a paedo, do they?' he told me.

He was convinced he'd become a monster himself.

CHAPTER THREE

A Children's Home

At first I thought the reason that no one spoke much in the home was that the place was so big. The girls' dorm was on one side of the building and the boys' was right on the opposite one. Plus, there were only four of us living there at the time. Must have been a good year for family counselling.

But the longer I stayed, the more it became clear that silence pervaded the home regardless of the number of residents or where they were sleeping. It was a deafening kind of silence. Haunting, with unanswered questions hanging painfully in the air.

Why am I here?

Why did it happen to me?

Why can't I leave?

I knew that the other kids in the home came from bad backgrounds. They were different from me.

I'd known a loving home, with good, solid foundations. All they'd known from birth was fear and abuse in one form or another.

My housemates at the home, along with Callum, were two girls around 15 years old, a good few years older than me.

One of the girls, Claire, was stunning. Perfectly groomed with developing curves that a lad like me, teetering on the cusp of puberty, found impossible to ignore.

She was beautiful, but she was stuck up too. Looked down her nose at everyone and sucked up to the Boss Man all the time. He loved her and so did all the other male staff. She didn't seem like a care-home kid.

Her hair was glossy and manicured and her dark skin was flawless. She stank of privilege and she never spoke about her background.

She barely spoke at all.

The other girl, Lottie, was the polar opposite. She was boyish, ballsy and everyone knew about her background. She came from a tough family who were renowned for their criminal activities in the town. You really didn't mess around with them.

Any conversations we had were always in private. Whispered in corridors or spoken in the streets after we'd tried to run away from the home.

It wasn't like at school, where you chatted about football or what you did at the weekend, the conversations had a darker edge.

What kind of drugs have you taken?

How many times have you been arrested?

That was the thing about care-home kids. They had reputations that preceded them and sordid family expectations to live up to. So they fabricated and elaborated stories, creating a persona that made people fear or admire them, so people didn't try to fuck with them.

Even then I knew it wasn't real. It was a coping mechanism, a way to stay safe – and silence was a big part of that. The things that remained unsaid were the key to their weaknesses.

They couldn't afford to let those things slip, not if they were to survive.

In fact, we didn't interact that much with one another. We were only really together in the communal areas at breakfast and dinner, and all under the watchful eye of Boss Man and The Bear.

When they were there a tense and ominous silence reigned supreme.

It didn't bother me though.

I wasn't scared of feeling uncomfortable. I could cope with the quiet and the dire 'chips-with-everything' food. After all, I'd spent the last few months tearing through the streets with the worst that the town had to offer; this place had nothing on that.

It was the routine I found hard. At 9pm, after dinner and a bit of time watching TV, it was time for bed. I hadn't gone to bed at 9pm since my dad was alive.

Dad's death had unsettled my routine from the moment the words fell from my uncle's mouth, travelling down the phone line and hammering at my eardrum.

Your dad's dead. Your dad's dead. Your dad's dead.

First, it was the disbelief, forcing my eyes awake when I should have been asleep. Then it was listening to my mum's guttural sobs throughout the night. Then it was the rebellion, roaming the streets and driving in stolen cars at 11pm and well into the early hours.

I don't know if I was just indignant at being forced to stay in, or if the throwback to a routine my dad used to impose took me by surprise, but for the first few nights in the home, I just couldn't sleep.

Lying in bed, I felt a gaping sense of emptiness in the pit of my stomach that refused to allow me to settle.

It didn't help that Callum snored like The Gruffalo.

I tried to block out the noise rattling around the room by doubling my cushion up and wrapping it round my head, but to no avail, so I leapt out of bed.

'Callum, pack it in,' I said, nudging him in the back.

Nothing. The snoring continued, so I stood on his bed and kicked him in the back. Still the snoring continued, so I positioned myself behind him and pushed sharply.

CLUNK!

Callum hit the cold, tiled floor and the incessant rumbling ceased.

'What the...?' Callum grunted, as he came round at the foot of the bed.

'You were snoring,' I said.

'Oh, sorry,' he said, crawling back into bed.

As the days and nights passed, exhaustion kicked in. And it wasn't just Callum that made it impossible to sleep. It was the light streaming in through the thick windows at the crack of dawn each day.

'Why don't we have curtains?' I'd asked The Bear one day, bleary-eyed.

'Cause you kids can't be trusted,' she said matter of factly. 'You end up trying to hang yourselves.'

I was taken aback. If kids were trying to kill themselves, there must be a reason? Surely it was their job to sort it out?

This was a *care* home, wasn't it?

I soon found out the answer to that.

* * *

On my third day in the home, I woke to the sweet smell of fresh baking tickling my nose. As I floated peacefully in that warm void between sleep and being awake, my great-grandma slipped into my mind. She was a strong woman, had spoken up against the IRA in her early twenties and as a result had been forced to leave Belfast quickly, without a pot to piss in.

In England, she never had a penny to buy bread and cakes, but she made her own and shared them with everyone. You could smell her house from the bottom of the street.

As I pulled on my dressing gown and padded along the cold corridor towards the kitchen, the smell of fresh baking conjured happy images in my mind and put a spring in my step. Turning up on Great-grandma's doorstep you'd be met by a beaming smile, a pot of thick tea, and a huge pile of freshly baked cakes and biscuits – 'They're all for you, my love, take as many as you want.'

Well, the smell escaping from the kitchen might have been the same, but the scene that greeted me in the breakfast area that morning was a world away.

Turns out the kitchen was off-bounds. Whatever smelt so good clearly wasn't meant for our consumption.

I don't know what I was expecting. Maybe some genuine human interaction, or at the very least some biscuits – but my heart sank when I stepped into the room.

It was dead. No staff, no children. It was almost ghostly.

The warm glow of the memory of my great-grandma was sucked away in an instant, as my clinical surroundings closed in on me and the feeling of emptiness overcame me once more.

Suddenly my ears pricked up: someone was whistling.

I stuck my head round the corner of the door and looked down the corridor. A cleaning lady in a neat blue tabard was throwing bleach onto the floor straight from the bottle as she whistled a cheery little ditty.

'Morning,' I said, boldly. 'How are you?'

Chatting to people regardless of who they were and where they came from was a skill I'd learned from my dad. Despite his small stature, his personality was enormous and he could strike up a conversation with anyone, anywhere.

She stopped whistling abruptly and her face seemed to change as she caught my gaze. The cheerful light dancing across it vanished and she stared at me with hard, cold eyes.

To be honest, it sent a chill down my spine.

Maybe I've just startled her?

'Nice morning, isn't it?' I ventured more cautiously, like I was approaching a growling dog.

Still nothing. Just the same dead stare, never taking her eyes off me.

The sound from the mop sweeping across the floor became deafening, especially because it was barely damp. As I walked closer to her, my eyes started to sting and water from the fumes.

By now the smell of bleach overpowered anything coming from the kitchen.

The interaction can't have lasted more than a couple of seconds before she turned on her heels and walked off, tossing bleach indiscriminately as she went.

'I said good morning,' I repeated indignantly, raising my voice slightly. I knew she'd heard me, but she didn't even flinch.

I knew what it was: I was one of those broken kids. If I wasn't a threat, I wasn't anything. I was invisible.

Angry and disheartened, I returned to the breakfast area to make myself some toast. I was pondering what had just happened in the corridor as I went through the motions, so as I started buttering my toast I didn't even notice the Boss Man had entered the room.

'What the hell are you doing?' a voice boomed, snapping me out of my thoughts in an instant.

'Sorry, what?' I retorted instinctively, before I realised who I was speaking to.

'You can't even butter toast properly, lad,' he shouted, inching closer to me.

I looked at him perplexed.

I'd only been there a few days and I didn't know how things worked there. I was used to doing what I liked and the fact that I knew I wasn't even doing anything wrong only boosted my confident swagger.

'Chill out, will you,' I said cockily, not even dignifying him with eye contact. 'It's not your toast.'

CRACK!

A big outstretched palm connected with the side of my head.

I didn't even have time to wince as my body tried to absorb the blow and comprehend what had just happened. My face was burning and my ear was throbbing so hard I thought it must be bleeding.

Did he really just do that?

I'd been in many a fight with kids my own age and even older lads, but an adult had never hit me like that before. Viv preferred to push me around or grab me by the neck, too much of a coward to hit me square on. I might have gotten a light slap from my mum from time to time, after which she'd end up crying with the guilt, and my dad, well, he had never laid a hand on me.

You see, as a kid, when an adult shouts at you or hits you, it scares you. Your brain tells you to respond with emotion.

Just like that time Dad was angry with me when I asked if we could move to the estate.

Sure enough, as I stood in the kitchen stunned, my ear ringing like a siren, the pain receptors in my body kicked into action, telling my brain that I was a child in pain.

You are scared, you should cry.

But then something else kicked in. A feeling I wasn't sure I'd ever experienced before.

Don't let him see you weak.

I felt my insides tighten and my eyes glaze over as I supressed my natural urge to cry.

He stared at me with stone-cold eyes and I glared right back.

There was no remorse there, not like when Mum slapped me.

There's more where that came from.

This was just the start.

I was a care-home kid now. And that feeling I experienced, that was survival.

We stalked around one another in the kitchen for a few minutes until the ringing in my ears receded and my hearing returned.

Sullenly, I watched as the Boss Man gave me a lesson in acceptable toast buttering.

'You start with the corners,' he barked, shattering the silence between us. 'Then you fill the centre with just enough butter to spread it out and make it even.'

Talk about regimental.

But compliantly, I followed each of his orders again and again until I got it right.

That's what life in the 'care' home was – strict regime, suppression of emotions, compliance and silence.

Most importantly, silence. That was how we all hid our pain.

I'd never have let it show, but he scared me so much that day that I never buttered toast any other way ever again.

* * *

Later that evening I was back in my room with Callum. I was seething over the 'butter attack', as I'd come to call it, and I was hatching a plan to escape.

'I'm getting out of here, Callum,' I confided. 'I'm not taking this shit. You shouldn't either.'

In the few days I'd been at the home I'd already lost count of the number of times I'd seen Callum take a beating from the Boss Man.

'Why isn't your shirt tucked in?'

SMACK!

'Did you brush your teeth yet, boy?'

'Not yet, sir.'

SMACK!

The worst thing was that Callum didn't react at all. His dead eyes showed no flicker of emotion. Not anger, nor fear. He was resigned.

I, on the other hand, was not.

'This place is a joke,' I continued. 'They're supposed to be looking after us, but they're just beating the shit out of us.'

Even The Bear was at it. She was the Boss Man's right-hand woman and she had an iron fist.

I knew having Callum with me would be useful and I knew that he'd come with me. I'd told him I had cigarettes after all.

He'd jump off a bridge for a fag if I asked him.

That night, we made a good job of playing at getting into bed at 9pm for lights out at 10pm. Little did they know that we were still fully dressed under the sheets.

Adrenalin coursed through me as I lay in wait for the right moment, the blood pumping in my ears.

When the time came, we gingerly sneaked out of our room and dashed soundlessly down the corridors. We had the lithe, wiry frames of teenage boys, so being nimble wasn't difficult. Plus, I'd had plenty of recent practice breaking in and out of things, hadn't I?

We made it to the girls' dorm area. Ordinarily, my hormones may have kicked in and urged me to peek in – what teenage lad wouldn't? But I was on a mission and we were about to face our trickiest challenge.

The Boss Man lived in the care home. He even had a little flat in the girls' dorm area.

It always struck me as strange. For a place cemented in rules and regime, it would have better fitted the script to have his flat in the boys' quarters, especially since we were usually more trouble than the girls.

Maybe that's why he seems to favour the girls?

He was nicer to them and even gave them treats, letting them watch TV late at night in his room.

As we hung back in the shadows a few steps away from the door to his flat, my mind pulled me back to a few days earlier, when I'd had to take some paperwork to the Boss Man's room.

It was early evening when I'd knocked on the door. I remembered being surprised when, instead of being confronted by the looming presence of the Boss Man, I was greeted by the sight of Claire leaning against the door frame, hips tilted provocatively in a pair of tiny hipster bottoms and a sexy little crop top.

'What do you want?' she asked haughtily.

'I have to give these to sir,' I gulped, my body not quite sure how to react to the goddess-like figure before me.

'Give them here,' she huffed.

As she snatched the papers from me, I suddenly became aware of the room behind her.

There was a chocolate cake on the sideboard and bags of crisps were strewn across the bed, among a glittering rainbow of Crunchies, Kit Kats and Turkish Delight.

I gasped in amazement and envy as I peered further into the room.

What was that? It couldn't be...

Among the confectionery haven of the crumpled bed sheets, there was also a pile of dog-eared magazines.

I was too far away to see any details, but my teenage hormones could recognise a pair of tits a mile off.

Girlie magazines!

'What are you looking at?' Claire snarled as she looked up from the counter where she'd placed the paperwork.

'What are you doing in here?' I asked.

'I stay here when the Boss Man is away,' she hissed. 'What's it to you?'

Liar. I know he's working today.

I didn't say anything though. I just shrugged and said: 'Give us a Crunchie.'

In that moment, something in the room must have distracted her and she cut our conversation short.

'Fuck off,' she said. Then she slammed the door shut in my face.

The echo of the door slamming in my brain snapped me back to the task at hand.

As we passed the door to the Boss Man's flat, I couldn't help but wonder if she was in there again, reading girlie mags in those little hipster pants…

Focus, Chris…

It hadn't taken me long to learn not to question things at the home. That only got you in trouble, put you on their radar. One thing you didn't want when you were trying to escape.

Confident that no one was around, Callum and I darted across the hall and out of the fire exit. The cold air hit our warm skin and made it tingle as we ran through the back roads down to the town centre. I knew that warren of streets like the back of my hand. We kept to the shadows, well away from any prying policemen.

The streets had a different life at night and that excited me. It was like being part of a secret club, one you had to be brave and hard enough to be part of.

It was well past midnight when we got to the town centre. We didn't have a plan, just cigarettes and a pocket full of pointless copper.

Free of the physical and emotional confines of the home, we just wanted to run, go crazy and let it all out. Before long, we found some scaffolding around the Halifax Building Society. Fearlessly, we scrambled up to the top and sat down for a smoke. We could see right over Halifax, all the houses and shops nestled in the shadow of the hills that dominated the skyline and hemmed the town in.

For the first time in ages, I felt free.

I could have stayed there chain smoking all night, but we both knew by now that the police would have been alerted when the nightly checks on us revealed we'd done a runner.

I could almost imagine Boss Man's face, purple as a beetroot when he heard, but I didn't care. We just had to keep moving.

'Let's head into town,' I said. 'Grab some food.'

God knows where we'd find some – we didn't have any money and everything was closed anyway – but Callum followed unquestioningly regardless, slowly dragging on yet another cigarette.

We were slinking down a backstreet when all of a sudden a figure emerged silently from the darkness with the stealth of a cat.

I squinted. The form barely looked human. It was big and bulky and covered in what looked like matted fur.

Like a Yeti.

The only thing I could really make out were a pair of really clear, wide eyes.

I turned and looked to see if Callum had seen it too, which I guess he must have, as he was already starting to scuttle away.

The shit bag.

I was on my own and my heart was pounding as my body prepared 'fight or flight' mode.

'Hello?' I said firmly. 'Who's there?'

The figure emerged from the shadows and I gasped, then immediately burst out laughing.

Stood before me was a lad who must've been in his early twenties. He had hair like a girl's down to his shoulders with a beard to match and – oddly – a broken guitar strapped tightly to his back.

This guy's no threat.

My confidence returned as quickly as my fear dissolved.

'Fucking hell, mate, what have you come dressed as?' I laughed as he came closer. 'Gonna give us a song?'

He flashed an awkward yet good-natured but toothless grin from below his matted and tangled beard.

'All right, lads. Can you spare a bit of change?' he said.

I'd seen enough to know that this guy was a druggie. I didn't really understand why at the time, I just knew that *real* junkies always had no teeth.

And they're always asking for money.

I looked him up and down again. His clothes were torn and filthy and they looked like they were covered in—

As soon as I thought it, a downwind confirmed it. I gagged audibly.

He was covered in his own shit!

He instantly recoiled.

'I'm sorry,' he apologised. 'I'm homeless, you see, don't have anywhere to go and wash…'

I put my hand up to stop him.

'It's all right, mate,' I said. 'Do you want a cigarette? I'm Chris, by the way. That's Callum.'

'Mark,' he returned, accepting the smoke without hesitation.

Callum had sheepishly returned after realising I'd struck up a conversation, but he still kept a distance, probably because of the smell.

Rich for someone with feet that honk as much as his!

I'd never met a homeless person before and I was fascinated.

I guess Mark felt the same about us. To him we were equally alien – a pair of kids roaming the streets in the small hours.

We sat down for a smoke and we told Mark triumphantly how we'd broken out of the children's home.

'Ah, that place,' said Mark, a shadow crossing his face.

'You went there?' Callum asked.

Mark nodded. 'They put me in there years ago when they were trying to find me a foster home. But I just kept running away.'

Mark explained how his parents were both drug addicts who used to beat the shit out of him. He turned to drugs himself, said he even started taking heroin.

I nodded along like I knew what he was talking about.

That care-home kid façade kicking in.

Truth was I didn't really know what heroin was, let alone what it did to people.

'Did they not come after you?' I asked.

'At first,' he said. 'But I was almost 16. I was practically an adult. Eventually, they just stopped looking.'

'And that was that?' I ventured.

Mark snorted. 'They didn't want kids like me in the home. I didn't fit the mould. I was too much trouble, and too old, I guess.'

I frowned. But he had a point. There was a type of kid that the home seemed to favour. Broken. Resigned. Defeated.

Even the way they looked was different. They were dead-eyed and emotionless.

I couldn't quite put my finger on it, but I knew I wasn't like that.

And even through the layers of shit and dirt, despite his situation, Mark wasn't either. There was still a light in his eyes.

* * *

MARK

'I don't miss having a home, cause I never really had one anyway.'

Given his appearance when we met him and the path of life he'd found himself on, you'd never imagine Mark to be eloquent, but he was.

Despite being consumed by drugs, he was lucid and educated, had manners too. The night I met him he'd asked for change and thinking I'd never see him again, I gave him all of the coppers in my pocket.

'Are you sure?' he'd gasped. 'There's almost a quid here.'

'Of course,' I said.

When Dad met someone in need, he'd always swing to the rescue and I guess I'd gotten that trait too. It was instinctive. He needed it more than me.

While Mark didn't have the foundation of love and respect that I had, we did share one trait: the refusal to conform and accept the road that was offered to us. It was just that I started on a much safer road than Mark ever knew.

He was 15 when he was forced into the children's home after someone had grassed him up for begging on the streets, desperate for drug money.

'I'd have preferred to stay there,' he told me. 'It was fucking cold but you got used to it.'

I imagine anything must have been better than living with parents who were more bothered about ploughing through a shit-load of booze and cocaine than looking after their kid. That was Mark's reality.

'Sometimes they were so high they didn't even realise I was missing,' he'd said, matter-of-factly. 'They only really noticed when I stole their gear.

'On the street, I was free to do whatever I wanted and the world seemed a lot more beautiful and exciting in the dark. I even saw a UFO once.'

I'd have believed him if he hadn't told me seconds earlier that he'd dropped two acid tabs that night.

Mark found beauty in everything. That was what made him different to other care-home kids that I met. Even when, one freezing winter, his dad had given him a proper good beating, turned his face black and blue and left him with blood dripping in his eye, he found a positive.

'It made all the lights blur, like I was tripping,' he'd explained to me. 'Dad kicked me out but I wasn't even cold. The adrenalin was still buzzing around my body. Not from the fight, but from escaping that shithole.'

From that first night on the street, once the adrenalin had worn off and the freezing air started to make his lungs burn, he learned on his feet. Used what he knew about the town to fight his way through each night.

'I remembered, back in the day, when Dad used to take all the old papers and magazines to the big recycling bins at the back of Tesco's car park,' he explained to me. 'They had big metal doors at the back and all that paper would act as insulation. So that was where I headed.'

I knew exactly where he meant from when Dad and I had gone to take all of our old papers when I was a little kid. I loved being allowed to slide them down the chute and listen to the satisfying thud as they landed. It never occurred to me that someone might be living in there.

Mark told me that he counted himself lucky that the bins hadn't been emptied. He tried to wrap the papers around him, but his hands were immobilised from the fight and the cold, so he just buried himself deep between the thousands of papers. He said it was like being in one of those ball pools you'd play in as a kid.

Once again, turning terrible things positive.

'It was a Tuesday, I think,' he'd pondered. 'They get emptied on a Friday. Might be worth remembering that, Chris.'

Of course I'd nodded politely, he was only trying to help. Mark was generous with his advice. Despite me thinking our meeting would be a one-off, I began to see him everywhere around Halifax.

As he regaled his story, Mark said the worst thing about that first night was that the bin stunk of human excrement.

'Some dirty bastard had shit on my bedding,' he exclaimed.

I guess then he hadn't fallen so deeply into the world of drugs. At that point maybe he still cared?

He must have done, as he told me how the smell of fresh bread from the Tesco bakery had stirred him the next morning and he'd nipped into the shop toilet to freshen up, before swiping some fresh croissants from the bread section by the entrance and bolting through the doors and back to his bin.

The Mark I met that night wouldn't have got through the doors in the first place. The smell alone would have alerted the guards. It's hard to see a cycle when you're in it, but it's clear to an outsider.

After three days in the bin, Mark found the person responsible for the shit-stench.

'He was an old boy called Frank,' he told me. 'He was all right. Knew I was a minor, so he sort of took me under his wing.'

Frank was sixty-seven. He'd been homeless for nearly six years after his wife had an affair with his boss. He'd hit the bottle hard and ended up alcoholic and on the street. He was a good person, he'd just had his heart broken and it destroyed him.

No doubt in his time, through the alcoholic haze, he'd seen what the streets did to kids like Mark. So Frank taught Mark how to survive.

'He's how I know that Greggs throw all of the leftover food away on Fridays,' Mark told me, smiling. 'We'd feast like kings. Steak bakes, Chicken bakes, pasties – the lot.'

I took a mental note of *that* story.

Maybe Mark saw something of him in me, felt the need to return the favour that Frank had done for him?

Mark told me he stayed with Frank a while, a few months, maybe more, but Mark's family circumstances had given him a taste for drugs. It wasn't long before he found the 'A-list' of homelessness, or maybe they found him.

The crackheads.

For Mark it was the beginning of the end.

'Life with Frank was quiet, we lived in the shadows. We could find what we needed,' he said. 'But I needed drugs and you didn't just "find" them.'

He was right. The only way a 15-year-old homeless boy could get his hands on money was by begging or sucking cock.

Mark chose the former.

'I heard Frank froze to death one night, the poor old bastard,' Mark told me. 'I was sad, but by then I'd found other priorities.'

Begging on the streets to feed his heroin addiction.

And that's when the authorities found him, out in broad daylight.

A stain on the image of public welfare: a child begging on the streets – in this day and age!

Of course, he tried hiding in the den with the other druggies, the first place the police would look. He tried going home, but when he stole his parents' stuff he'd get the shit kicked out of him again.

That wasn't even the reason the home dragged him in though.

A domestic issue. Not a matter for the authorities.

It was the daylight begging that needed sorting.

But quite often, kids like Mark weren't broken *enough* for those in charge of the home's purposes.

'It was all right at first,' he said. 'But it was full of fake Good Samaritans who didn't really give a shit. They just worried about getting paid.'

They'd say whatever to keep abuse under wraps and money coming in.

Under that façade, Mark was a child drug addict generously given treatment and therapy by the government. But only for as long as he was legally their responsibility – after that, who gave a shit?

'I had too much to say anyway,' he said. 'By the time I got there, I was past their conditioning. Drugs were my master, not some nonce in his ivory tower.'

Just like me, Mark was a liability.

He was too far gone for the home – for anything, really. In the eighties and nineties, there was no real system. No coordinators to tell people about external help and no social media to enable you to find it yourself. When the home stopped looking for him, Mark just slipped out of society, like he never existed.

'The streets are where I'm happy,' he said. 'I play my music and meet people. I don't miss having a home, cause I never really had one anyway.'

You'd probably assume that drugs would have been the end of Mark, but they weren't. After years of playing his music on his shabby broken guitar and offering kindly advice to runaways like me, he met the same end as Frank.

Froze to death.

It's hard to see a cycle when you're in it.

I don't know how old he was, but it was too soon.

Perhaps meeting him was a red flag that I should have heeded. The signs were there, but I was already spiralling through my own cycle and rapidly out of control.

CHAPTER FOUR

Adios, Boss Man

Callum and I didn't take up Mark's suggestion of sleeping in the bins that night. We were on an adventure.

We stalked round the streets like we owned them until the sun started to peek over the Halifax hills. We were wild and free – we didn't have *time* to sleep, for Christ's sake!

Within hours it wasn't enough for me just to have managed to escape the home and be roaming the streets. I wanted to do something *exciting*.

Walking past the Superdrug store in town, I spotted a broken window.

If I can lever that open, I can get in!

'You keep watch,' I said to Callum. 'I'll force it open then get you in.'

I was skinny as a rake, but strong, so it didn't take much for me to force the frame wide enough to slip in. There was even room to squeeze Callum through.

Getting in was the victory, really. Despite plenty of goodies being on offer, we weren't really that bothered about stealing stuff. It wasn't like there was cash in the tills or anything.

So what did we take?

Batteries.

I mean, even an armful of Lynx Africa would have made more sense, given the financial burden Callum's smelly feet were putting on me.

But we went for shitloads of batteries.

It was completely pointless, but as we squeezed out of the shop and started running back to the rooftop where we'd started our evening, I was buzzing. It was exactly what I wanted to feel, and in that moment at least, I was sated.

The exhilaration didn't last long though. The sight of two teenagers running through the streets of the town at 4am with armfuls of batteries caught the attention of a couple of patrol coppers in a squad car.

I saw the blue lights out of the corner of my eye as the car sped towards us, nearly mowing Callum down.

The lad was useless. Couldn't run cause he had one stinking foot bigger than the other.

I think the coppers could see who the real troublemaker was, cause they leapt out of the car and one made a beeline for me.

Batteries flew everywhere, like confetti at a wedding, as he wrestled me to the ground, cursing me as I squirmed.

'Stay still, you little shit,' he growled.

The other one had made easy work of pinning Callum down.

They already knew we were from the home. Turns out we'd been reported missing shortly after we'd bolted. The Boss Man had eyes and ears all over town.

'Let's get you back,' he tutted. 'The Boss isn't going to be happy with you. He's not going to be happy at all.'

I could have sworn he smirked. Like he knew what was about to happen, but just didn't give a crap.

Whatever. He was right either way.

The Boss Man opened the door in his dressing gown as the police car pulled up the winding drive. It didn't look like he'd been woken up. It looked more like we'd ruined some other fun he'd been having and he was majorly pissed off about it.

We stepped inside while the policemen locked up the car.

Before even saying a word, he walloped us both hard and fast across the head, before the officers rejoined us.

Shithouse, I thought. *Doing it when the pigs aren't looking.*

'Thank you, Peter. Tony,' he said, giving each officer an apologetic nod, as Callum and I stood there with our cheeks burning through pain, not shame.

'I'm sorry I had to disturb you tonight,' he continued. 'I hope you'll have a quieter shift now.'

'Not a problem, Malcolm,' said Tony. 'Always happy to help you out.'

I was taken aback. I'd never heard his real name before. To us he was just the Boss Man, occasionally Mr Phillips and always a towering demon. Having a name made him seem human and it just didn't fit.

My blood began to boil.

So, these are his mates, are they?

At this point, I didn't care. I was still cocky, fearless.

I remember Callum glancing at me in horror when I started laughing.

Well, he's not going to abuse his power in front of a copper, is he?

I soon had my answer.

No sooner had the snigger left my lips, the Boss Man's hand was in the air and heading straight for my face again. I didn't even have time to react. As his massive hand collided with my ear, I swear I felt my eardrum pop.

I brought my hand up to my face.

'Owwwww,' I wailed.

'That'll wipe the smile off your face,' he said sternly.

I glanced over at the officers.

Surely they'd have something to say about this?

Turns out not. They were too busy laughing at the shocked look on my face.

If the Boss Man had lit the fire of my hatred of authority with the first time he hit me, those two laughing policemen fanned the flames of my rage.

From that moment, I was determined to show the Boss Man that he couldn't rule everyone with an iron fist. After all, I was Dave Cockcroft's son. I was a scrapper, just like him.

I knew Dad would never have stood for it. If there was such a thing as the afterlife and he could see what was happening, I was sure he would have jumped from his coffin and started World War III.

When I was nine years old, he nearly got himself arrested when a schoolteacher prodded me in my chest with a long pointy finger. He'd gone mental and marched straight into the school the next day, picked the teacher up by his collar and launched him across the classroom.

At the time his actions didn't seem to fit the 'crime'. It seemed to be a bit of an overreaction, if anything. But a short time in the home suddenly made it all clear. He didn't like people abusing positions of power or authority, especially vulnerable people, and who was more vulnerable than a nine-year-old child?

Mum wasn't as strong as my dad. I guess his death had left her vulnerable too. She'd already seen her scumbag boyfriend push me around a few times and found herself powerless to protect me.

How would she be able to stand up for me against the Boss Man?

He was mates with policemen and councillors. Important people. People with authority and a say in how things were run.

What's more, despite his domineering stature, he didn't come across as a tyrant. With the people he liked, those powerful people that visited the home for whatever reason, he was charming, hospitable and charismatic.

He would have won my mum over with a few kind words and a smile.

I knew I was on my own.

* * *

Three weeks later, I still had the Boss Man's handprint across my face.

'I'm going to fuck him up,' I told Callum. 'I swear, I'm going to take a baseball bat to him then run away.'

Callum didn't respond.

'How can you not be mad?' I hissed, exasperated by his acceptance of the situation. But he just shrugged.

Callum was like the Boss Man's obedient dog, grovelling at the feet of his master, begging for scraps of approval. When I turned up, I led him astray and the Boss Man hated that.

'Go pick up the leaves from the driveway, they make the place look a mess,' the Boss Man ordered Callum one day. Callum was straight to his feet, but I grabbed his arm.

'Don't do it,' I said. 'You don't have to.'

Obedient as ever. Callum sat back down.

'Okay, Chris,' he said.

I nipped out to the garden for a smoke, spent some time wandering round outside, alone with my thoughts. When

I returned to the house an hour or so later, I bumped into Callum in the corridor. He was limping.

'What happened?' I asked.

'I fell down the stairs,' he mumbled.

Bullshit, I thought immediately. *He was pushed.*

My suspicions were proven the next time Callum was ordered to run an errand. He never listened to me again, just set off like a whippet.

I almost felt guilty. But in my mind, it was all part of the fight.

If you fought back, change would come.

Wouldn't it?

Weeks turned to months and my battle with the Boss Man continued. For a while, I had a probation officer who would pick me up and drive me out of town on to the moors. It was quite good fun. He used to tell me that if I looked hard enough, I'd find gems worth millions. He used to stand back and watch me as I scoured the grass, with this weird distant look in his eyes. I never understood why he was so nice to me. In the end, his beady eyes started to make me feel uncomfortable. I never found any of the bloody gems either. So one day I refused to go.

'You have to come,' he'd roared. 'Get in the car now.'

I stayed put and I could see his blood boiling. 'No,' I said.

'You ungrateful little shit,' he fumed, kicking the car like a child having a temper tantrum. I couldn't understand what the big deal was. He'd have some free time now.

Why did he look so angry and defeated?

The weirdo.

I shrugged it off, but I never went with him again. I'd found a more enjoyable pastime than hunting for invisible gems –

breaking out of the home to have the Boss Man's cronies chase me round town.

I remember running away one night with Lottie. I liked Lottie more than Claire, because she was more down to earth.

Claire swanned around like she owned the place.

Well, she was the Boss Man's favourite.

Lottie, on the other hand, got treated like Callum and me. She was a little bit better behaved, or maybe more street-savvy.

Toed the line to avoid a beating.

One night we sneaked out together. We'd managed to scrape some money together to buy a bottle of 20/20, which we swigged off before casually having sex on the seat back of a broken-down bus in the old bus station.

Back then it wasn't normal for young people – especially young girls – to be so blasé about sex. Even for older teenagers from nice homes with steady boyfriends, it was taboo.

I remembered that much from my old life.

Afterwards, we sat together smoking and she told me that she had an older boyfriend who was in jail – she'd been having sex with him for ages.

I guess I wasn't complaining, but beneath my 'care-home kid' façade, I was shocked. She was only 15.

We didn't talk about much while we were roaming the streets, just the people we both knew from around town. We preferred to fill the silence with mischief and mayhem. That night we found a Vauxhall Astra in a quiet street just outside the centre of town.

'Let's break in and drive it all the way to Timbuktu. London. Anywhere that's a million miles from the home,' Lottie said.

Neither of us could drive, but it seemed like a good plan at the time.

Of course, we had no idea what we were doing, despite Lottie having a decent training ground from hanging around her criminal family. Inevitably, we set a screaming alarm off, cutting short our fun.

'Shit – run,' Lottie gasped.

But it was futile. The Boss Man's henchmen were already out in force looking for us; we'd been clocked as missing earlier in the evening.

By that point I was used to the beatings, the withdrawn privileges where they didn't feed you or isolated you from everyone.

This particular night it wasn't the Boss Man but The Bear waiting for me. I felt every blow she dealt me, but I refused to wince.

Be defiant. Don't show weakness.

The reception was different for Lottie. She was sent to her room without supper. That didn't matter to me; I was glad she hadn't got a beating.

I'd grown a skin so thick nothing the Boss Man or The Bear could do would hurt me. I'd put up an impenetrable wall and even his explosions of anger didn't faze me.

Yes, he might had been able to break my skin. Make me bleed and bruise me. But I wasn't like Callum, I wasn't going to be beaten into submission like a dog.

I was Dave Cockcroft's son after all.

That fact might not have meant anything to those bastards in the home. Maybe that's why I never said it out loud. But it did to me.

It meant everything to me.

My rebellion continued until one night – and I'm still not sure why they did this – the police tore me from the streets, and instead of taking me back to the home, they took me to my grandma and grandad's house.

Grandma was a tough woman and a devout Irish Catholic. When my mum and dad first met, she hated him. She knew he'd grown up in care and she saw children's homes as a place where the devil worshipped.

'Nothing good comes out of those places,' she'd said.

But over time, Dad charmed her. Treated my mum like a goddess, protected his family like a lion, and proved to her that he was the exception to the rule. Before too long, she was like the mother he never had.

After all that, you can imagine her horror when Mum agreed for me to go into care.

'I'll never speak to that woman again,' she vowed one night when she visited me.

That woman.

Her own daughter.

By the time I was carted to her house by the police, she had kept that promise.

That night, she called the home and arranged to collect my things. My sister was already living with her.

I hunched in the hall, listening to their conversation on the phone.

'That lad needs to be disciplined properly,' I heard the Boss Man sneer, his voice tinny and distant down the line.

'That's what you call what *you* do?' Grandma snorted, knowingly. She knew the score.

'Chris will do better at home with his family,' she told the Boss Man sternly before hanging up.

I doubt he cared I was going. Good riddance, he probably thought. To him, I was nothing but an upstart, a hindrance and an inconvenience.

Well, the feeling was mutual.

Adios, Boss Man. I'm gone.

After that day, I only ever saw Callum and the girls if our paths crossed in town. Before too long, Lottie vanished completely. Whispers spread around the streets.

They drugged her and sent her to another home in Wales, the poor cow.

It wasn't the first time I'd heard about kids being ferried between two homes. But when I heard it this time, my stomach sank.

I hope it was nothing to do with our adventure.

It probably was, though. Either that or the fact that the Boss Man didn't like that she didn't suck up to him like Claire did.

The snotty cow.

CHAPTER FIVE

Rebel Without a Clue

I didn't make life easy for my grandad or grandma. *Especially* Grandma, bless her heart. It's a good job she was tough, otherwise God knows how she would've coped.

It wasn't like she didn't have enough to worry about.

It was 1994. The economy was going down the shitter – even as a kid I could see that. Not the best time for an ageing woman to be lumbered with two extra mouths to feed.

There was an air of instability. A sense that the whole country was teetering on the precipice of complete chaos. Not that it bothered me. I revelled in it. Without the regime of the care home to restrain me, I ran wild.

I was a free soul with no rules and no one telling me what to do. I was a rebel, but one without a clue.

Truth was, I was so consumed by my newfound freedom that I couldn't see the dangers around me. Not really.

The council estates my dad had warned me about became my playground.

His voice may have echoed in my ears, but I couldn't understand what he'd feared so much.

It's just not a good place, son.

What was he talking about? It was the *best* place.

I felt safer there than I ever did at the home.

Life was exciting too, a world away from the monotony of the home's Dickensian routines.

The system had given up on me, decided I didn't fit its rigid mould, so I slipped away. I became invisible, living from house to house and couch to couch, mixing with other people that polite society forgot. Drug dealers, burglars, prostitutes and addicts...

At 13 years old I was introduced to a world of dance music with ten beats to a bar. You needed acid to keep up with it. People seemed to need drugs to cope with a lot of things.

Technology pumped out of factories faster than we could steal it – shiny space-age-looking CD players, tiny Walkmans and mobile phones as big as my head.

Unfortunately for the shopkeepers of Halifax, security tactics weren't quite so cutting edge.

Lucky for us, though. Business on the streets was booming. Local drug dealers and burglars accepted me with open arms.

I thought it was because I was this cool young kid with the reputation for being a scrapper.

Dave Cockroft's kid.

Looking back, though, it was down to nothing more than my speed and stature. I was small for my age, just like Dad had been. I could squeeze into small windows and open doors, breaking and entering without leaving a trace. I could also sprint away from the police with ease.

All very useful traits to my new friends.

Grandma tried her best, but with Dad gone, Donna struggling to come to terms with his death, and Mum crushed and contained by Viv, I didn't have a family any more, let alone a home.

The gang of criminals I befriended showed me things I hadn't felt since before Dad died. Protection. Solidarity. A place I could call home.

That place was the streets.

The gang from the estate and the 'Bus Station Crew' – the name explains itself – became my family.

How ironic was it that roaming the streets with dangerous criminals felt safer than the institution the government had created to protect kids like me?

Running 'errands' for drug dealers and helping burglars into shops and homes earned me a pretty penny. I looked good too; always had the latest Nike Air Max trainers, new Levi's, even that grey Fruit of the Loom jumper that all the celebrities were wearing.

Yes, I had money in my pocket for all the wrong reasons, but that was how I survived.

People liked me and, what's more, they looked out for me. That's what you needed on the streets.

There was one guy in particular, a few years older than me, who really took me under his wing.

His name was Terry. No one messed with Terry.

Terry was a bodybuilder. Early on I remember thinking he looked just like Popeye, with cartoon-like bulging muscles and this larger-than-life presence when he walked into the room.

Terry's physique wasn't lost on me the very first time I met him either.

He was chasing me through the Square Park.

Turns out, a lad I'd punched in the face was his little brother.

The kid had actually asked me if I knew who his brother was. 'Sure,' I'd said, cockily. 'So what?'

I didn't know him. But I didn't care. I was tougher than anyone, and if I wasn't, I could run faster than them.

'You're dead meat,' the kid said menacingly after I'd punched him.

Minutes later, I caught a glimpse of his fearful older brother. He ran like a panther, both arms moving in sync with his athletic legs. He was terrifying.

He chased me round town for God knows how long. Soon I started to tire.

Shit! He's going to catch me.

It wasn't the first time I'd found myself in such a situation. Genuinely fearing for my life.

I might have to use my secret weapon…

During my time on the streets I'd found myself something of a 'get out of jail'– or at the very least an 'avoid a beating' – card. I didn't use it often. Reckoned it might wear off if I did, but it hadn't failed yet.

I shouted out my own name.

'I'm Cocky,' I wheezed, slowing down and raising my hands in a gesture of surrender. 'Chris Cockcroft.'

I held my breath. Everything seemed to move in slow motion as the words travelled along the airwaves.

Suddenly, the man slowed down, his pace decreasing as he absorbed each syllable. 'Dave Cockcroft's lad?' he shouted, gasping for air.

'Yes,' I replied, heart pounding.

And with that, he stopped. Inches from my face.

I exhaled in relief.

It worked. Thanks, Dad.

It was like he was there protecting me – or at least his reputation was.

But I wasn't quite out of the woods yet…

'Why did you hit my brother?' he snarled.

'He threw a huge stone at my head,' I said, shaking like a shitting dog.

He paused. I could tell he was sizing me up. Weighing up the situation.

I stayed glued to the spot until he spoke.

'Okay,' he said. 'Well, now you know who he is and I know who you are.'

I nodded.

'Don't do it again,' he said. 'I'm Terry, by the way.'

And just like that, we became friends.

Turned out Terry's old man, Mick, had been a good friend of my dad's.

Well, everyone knew Cocky.

Terry was part of a big family with a tough reputation around town. They really ran the show, so it helped to be on his good side.

God knows if you weren't you'd feel the wrath of his mass.

Terry and I had a good thing going.

With our dads' friendship, I guess he felt a little responsible for me. I'd stay in his family home and they'd make sure I was fed and safe. Made sure no seedy street inhabitants took advantage of me.

You see, although I'd spent the best part of two years being a complete tearaway, I still came from a good family and a good home.

You're not like us, Chris, my street friends would say.

To be honest, that would get my hackles up.

What did they mean?

I could fight like them. I wasn't scared to go on the rob with them. I was a 13-year-old lad who regularly smoked weed and dropped acid, for God's sake. How much more like them did they want me to be? But I'd not been born into that survive-or-die mentality.

I was learning it, sure. But my ability to sense danger wasn't as innate.

Through my time in the home and hanging round on the estates, I had started to realise that there were some grown-up men, or rather a certain type of grown-up man, who liked to spend time around much younger girls. And boys.

I knew those types were NOT part of my street family. But I didn't think much more of it. Just avoided them.

Terry was far more attuned to their threat. His eyes had seen more than mine ever would. He knew how those men perceived me, all dressed up in my fancy gear, with my lithe body and cocky attitude.

I thought I was hard, but Terry knew what I was to them. Prey. A challenge. Something to be broken.

And it wasn't just the nonces. It was the other dealers, the burglars and street kids who could also be a threat.

What I'd learned about fighting in the home wasn't enough to sustain me in the street. I learned that the hard way, when I took a beating from some older lad in town. I didn't know who he was, didn't even see it coming. All I knew was one minute I was walking down the street. The next I was on the deck and covered in my own blood.

When I got back to Terry's he took one look at me and leapt to his feet. 'What happened?' he growled. 'Who did this to you?'

I shrugged, then tried to describe my attacker.

'Let's find him,' Terry said.

Without a moment's hesitation, he dragged me out of the house to his van, picking up a baseball bat and hammer on his way out.

Terry was a good man. A criminal. Yes. But a good man who was driven by a sense of street justice. We might have been outside of the law, on the fringes of society. But there were still rules, codes of conduct.

We must've looked suspicious as hell driving round slowly, craning our necks as we checked people out.

Is that him?

Too tall.

Is that him?

Too short.

Is that him?

Yes.

It was as if Terry was set on a spring. He pounced on the lad as unexpectedly as he'd attacked me earlier that day. Except he was pummelled by Terry. It must've felt like a bus had hit him.

I was horrified inside, but excited too.

See. That was what happened if you messed with me, Chris Cockcroft!

Safe to say, no one messed with me like that again.

Terry and I were thick as thieves. He looked out for me, and I looked out for him. I stole on demand for the big man. Why wouldn't I? He took care of me *and* paid me a handsome fee.

Not only that, he taught me how to fight. I mean *really* fight. Not the scrambles I'd had in the schoolyard or even at

the home. Street fighting. He thought it was especially important after I'd been jumped.

Terry was brutal, but then, he had to be.

'Come on,' he goaded me one day. 'What are you going to
do if someone comes at you, eh?'

I started to put my fists up, but before I could...

THWACK!

A firm blow landed on the side of my face, burning
my skin.

'Not fast enough,' he scoffed.

THUD!

'Come on,' he said, as blood trickled out of my nose. 'If you
think you're so hard.'

SMACK!

He didn't stop. He rained blows down on me so fast and
hard that I could barely react. My vision became blurred and
tears started to roll down my cheeks.

'Crying like a little girl, are you?'

He was relentless.

His girlfriend, Leanne, had been watching in horror. Soon
she was crying too.

'Terry, stop it,' she pleaded. 'He's had enough.'

'He's got to learn, Leanne,' he said. 'Or they'll eat him alive.'

I really wasn't sure who 'they' were. All I knew was this
cycle of Terry goading me into a fight would happen over and
over, until one day, I snapped.

Terry started his usual, poking and prodding. Taking the
piss then knocking me around.

I balled up my fists and felt rage burning inside of me. Two
solid years of anger and pain came flooding out.

I was sick of people telling me what to do. Sick of being treated like a kid. Sick of people saying 'you're not like us'.

I fucking am!

I went off like a rocket.

I threw myself at Terry, punching relentlessly – round his head, his face and his stomach, any bit of flesh I could reach.

It wasn't Terry I was mad at. I knew he was just trying to toughen me up and I respected that. No, in my blind fury I was beating seven shades out of my own pain.

Dad's death.

Mum abandoning me.

Viv beating me up.

The Boss Man.

I was like a rabid dog, fighting as if my life depended on it. Terry took every single blow until I couldn't manage another punch.

I slumped on the floor, drained.

Terry smiled. 'Looks like we've got ourselves a fighter. Finally.'

Truth be told, I didn't do much damage to Terry. In fact, I didn't want to. But I felt great. For the first time since my dad died, I'd really let go.

I guess with Terry by my side I was safe.

I know Dad would have been furious that I was hanging round on the streets. He'd never wanted me to see this life.

But since fate had inducted me into this world, I was certain he'd be happy I'd ended up with Terry. You see, he brought order to my chaos. Treated me like a brother. And let me do what I wanted – in moderation, of course.

* * *

TERRY

'I don't regret the things I did. They made me who I am.'

There was something about me and Terry.

It's like we were kindred spirits or something. Like me, he wasn't the same as the other kids we hung around with on the estate.

He was a few years older than me. While I'd grown up in Boothtown – the 'nice' part of town, you could say – he'd been born on the local council estate. His dad was a spineless piece of shit like my dad's father was – left his mum when he was a baby.

Terry worshipped his mother, and rightly so. When his dad left, Carol just picked herself up and got on with it. She was small, but tough as boots.

'She always had a job,' Terry told me proudly. 'She worked hard at the local newsagents and we always had food to eat.'

Not like most of the kids on the estate.

Everyone on the estate was poor. Terry said his mum just made sure they were comfortable within their poverty.

'She did the best with what she had,' Terry told me. 'She couldn't shower me with gifts, but every night she'd bring me a little treat from her work. A Twix or a Sherbet Dip or something like that.'

Small things like that meant a lot.

That's how Terry and I were similar. We'd been brought up around people with values, who actually gave a damn about us.

It wasn't the case for lots of the kids we knew. If they got sweets, it was probably in return for something unspeakable.

Bribery. Dirty perverts buying their silence.

Just like the Boss Man.

The contrast between the relative affluence that I grew up with and Terry's family's poverty meant his brushes with the police started earlier than mine.

'Crime was something to pass the time when I was a kid,' he said. 'I was a naughty little shit.'

The estate bred opportunities of delinquency. It was the perfect recipe for Terry's disaster.

'Didn't your mum go mad when the police kept bringing you home?' I didn't dare to imagine how my dad would have reacted.

He smiled. 'She was my mum, she always had my back over theirs. I couldn't half spin a yarn, though,' he added.

Turns out he'd once been caught smuggling ladies' shoes out of a shop in his coat. He had a crush on the hottest girl on the estate. Everyone was after her.

'She said she'd go out with whoever got her these shoes she'd seen,' he said. 'They were these high-heeled, shiny, expensive things from a posh shop in town.'

Determined to win her over, he'd done it but got caught in the process, which meant he had to explain himself to his mum.

'I told her they were for her,' he chuckled. 'That I wanted to get them for her birthday but cause I couldn't afford them, I stole them.'

'Did you ever tell her the truth?' I asked.

'Only years later,' he laughed. 'I haven't got a death wish, you know!'

It was a rough existence but an oddly safe one.

Terry shook his head. 'It wasn't like nowadays.'

'What do you mean?' I asked.

'Kids going missing all the time, getting picked up by paedophiles. The dirty bastards make my skin crawl.'

As a teenager, Terry was the leader of a gang that used to fight with kids from other streets and estates. They were called the Hammer Boys.

'Because we carried hammers,' he explained.

No shit, Sherlock.

'We never used them,' he added. 'It was a scare tactic. Plus, if Mum had found out, she would have clocked me one with it.'

Terry looked back on those days fondly. 'Kids nowadays will stab you. We just played "shitty door run" where we'd put a dog turd through someone's letterbox and leg it.'

By the time Terry was 14, his petty theft habit had escalated into selling drugs, heavy drinking and stealing cars. It was natural progression on the estate. A sort of street school system, where you had to learn the basics before you did the *really* interesting stuff.

'I was up in youth court twice a week,' he said. 'They must've been sick of the sight of me.'

It seems so, because in the end they sent him to Skircoat Lodge. The same children's home that I'd been sent to.

'They said my mum couldn't cope,' he told me. 'But I knew that wasn't true. They were making an example of me.'

There were ten years between our residencies there, but the monotonous routine was the same. All ruled by the Boss Man's iron fist.

Breakfast at 7am. Education until 3pm. Bedtime at 9pm.

'I fucking hated the place,' he said. 'The smell of bleach and the schoolwork. Especially the schoolwork. I'd never been good at anything academic.'

Like a caged animal, Terry explained to me how he'd lash out, smashing windows and running away.

That was until Mr Jackson took him under his wing.

When Terry described Mr Jackson, it was clear he'd been an inspiration.

'God knows what he was doing in that place,' Terry shrugged. 'He was an ex-bodybuilder. Had these huge arms and looked like the wrestler Giant Haystacks.'

Now, who did that remind me of?

'He actually seemed to give a shit too,' Terry added.

Well, he must have seen something in Terry. The man barely spoke, but one day he went up to Terry.

'You're a strong lad,' he said. 'You could put that to better use than trashing this place.'

'What do you mean?' asked Terry.

Mr Jackson opened Terry's eyes to the world of weight training. How he could change his body through lifting weights and eating right.

'I was a skinny little shit like you once,' he teased. 'Weighed seven stone. My grandad called me a "Belsen atrocity" – one of those kids from the war camps.'

In just six months, under Mr Jackson's guidance, Terry gained a stone of pure muscle.

I'll bet at first Terry thought Mr Jackson was a pervert – all the talk of bulging biceps and time in the gym. Today, he'd be investigated left, right and centre.

But Mr Jackson *wasn't* one of them. Just like Terry and I didn't *quite* fit the care kid mould, he didn't fit into the world he'd ended up in.

I bet the Boss Man hated that. The Boss Man hated anything and anyone he couldn't control.

Terry didn't have it easy, though. Mr Jackson was no pushover. There was a trade-off: no school, no gym.

Terry wasn't happy, but it was a fair compromise. He was committed to getting big. Trained every day.

Sometimes he fell off the wagon, skipped a lesson and got banned from the gym. But when he did, he made sure he got right back on it.

'I loved the gym more than I hated school,' he told me. 'Training became my life and remained that way even after I left the home at 16. I know now that Mr Jackson saved me.'

'By giving you focus?' I asked.

'Yeah,' he said. 'But he saved me from the wolves too.'

Just like me, Terry only heard about the rape and the abuse going on at the home after he'd left.

'I was one of the lucky ones,' he said. 'I didn't experience any of that medieval shit.'

'Do you think that's cause Mr Jackson was looking out for you?' I asked.

'Maybe,' he said.

After the home, Terry made quite a success of himself.

He did have one blip. Remember, he'd been born into a world of crime on the estate. So he got a bit greedy and ended up doing a bit of time – I never found out what for. But Terry, typically, turned it around.

'I used the time to get myself in good shape,' he said. 'Mind and body.'

Once he was out, he was unstoppable. He competed in Mr Northeast UK, set up a building firm and even got a couple of properties under his belt. He even had a kid, a little boy who was doing really well.

'Not bad for a kid off the estate, eh?'

His mum had died of cancer a few years before.

'You know, I don't regret the things I did, Chris,' Terry told me. 'They made me who I am. But I sometimes worry if my behaviour triggered her cancer.'

He'd stayed with her for the last few months of her life. Nursed her on her sick bed.

'She was so proud of me, Chris,' he said as tears welled up in his eyes. 'Everything I know now I learned from her – and Mr Jackson. Two people who really gave a shit. They dedicated their lives to my well-being.'

Terry was a humble man. Accepted responsibility for his mistakes. Acknowledged the people who helped him

I don't think he ever considered the positive impact he had on other people. He'd made me streetwise and taught me all about survival. He'd saved me from the wolves. But Terry wouldn't have it.

I wish I could say Terry's story ended there.

Bad boy done good, one of the ones that got away.

But he was born on to the street. It was in him, in a way it wasn't in me.

Despite his mum's ethics and tenacity, despite Mr Jackson's guidance, the streets had a way of pulling you back in, no matter how hard you fought to escape.

I'll never know the reason why Terry decided to end his life, but it seemed to me that the big man stopped fighting, that it got too hard for him. And he found another escape route.

I couldn't breathe when I heard how his family discovered him hanging lifeless from a tree in some nondescript field in Halifax. They had to cut him down. It was too late to do anything else.

Two kids by that time. My heart broke for them, for the love that they lost.

It broke for me, because I thought my friend was strong.

But most of all it broke for Terry, because I never got the chance to save him, like he saved me.

CHAPTER SIX

Into the Gutter

However dangerous it was, I preferred my life on the street to life at the home or with my grandparents.

I was with my friends all day, every day. Protected. I wanted for nothing, took what I could and sold it for what I wanted.

Remember that massive mobile phone I mentioned? It was the first ever Nokia 2140. I stole it in the morning and sold it for a five spot of red seal-cannabis resin, twenty Regal cigarettes and a box of matches a few hours later.

We owned the town in our baseball caps and Nike Air Max.

Or at least we thought we did.

I rarely went back to my grandma's. Instead, I'd find a random bed or couch in the house of a friend of a friend, or someone's dealer, to sleep on.

Everyone was the same, crashing where they fell the night before.

We weren't lazy though. We'd get up early in the morning and meet in town by the bus station, where all the drunks, addicts and homeless people congregated.

They were easy targets, ripe for stealing cigs and money off, sometimes because they were so out of it and sometimes because they were so stupid.

'Give me a cig and I'll give you a quid,' I'd say.

As soon as I had that cig, I'd be off, laughing as I went.

Sometimes, we'd beat them up for fun, but not if we had bigger fish to fry.

During the day, once the town was awake and bustling, shoplifting was our main focus. Pocketing batteries, sweets and CDs – whatever we could get our hands on. The security guards and shopkeepers knew all of our faces, but they couldn't stop us, even when they gave chase.

There were too many of us and we were all kids. We were too fast for them. Usually, they gave up or counted on the police to get us. Sometimes they did, sometimes they didn't.

I'd never felt as free as when I was running through the streets, wind whistling by my ears, my pockets full of loot with an angry shopkeeper in hot pursuit. It was like one big game of cops and robbers.

When we'd taken what we liked we'd head to yet another random house to listen to music, drink beer, skin up and get stoned.

Sometimes we ate, sometimes we didn't. But later on, as people became more drunk and high, the pace would pick up. People would dance and fight and the older ones would sneak off to have sex.

Every second was like an adventure for me. Whether it was a new drink or drug, or a new member of the gang, there was always something to explore, someone new to talk to. But the routine was always the same.

Days blurred into weeks and weeks into months. I'd lose track of time, never sure if it was morning or evening.

Everything in my life was on my terms.

Occasionally I'd go to school – reform schools and places that taught 'bad' children. Sometimes I went at the behest of my education officer and sometimes just for somewhere to go. When I did, I'd cause havoc and end up getting kicked out. I didn't like the way they treated you in the reform schools. As punishment, they'd lock you in the smallest room and leave you there for days. They called it the LOP room – loss of privilege – it was supposed to calm you down and instil discipline, but I'd go stir-crazy.

There were so many bricks for such a small space, you couldn't even turn around once the door was closed – before long, the walls would feel like they were closing in and I'd find myself making tiny movements with my arms to try and 'stop' it. It was like the bricks were spinning round and laughing at you. I'd come out sweaty and disorientated and even angrier than before.

Like a wasp that had been trapped in a jar and released near its captors, I stung back immediately. They just couldn't control me. I was expelled from two schools in two years, hauled up in front of Calderdale Youth Court and ended up with an impressive roll call of convictions for a whippet-thin 13-year-old.

Assault Occasioning Actual Bodily Harm; Burglary with Intent to Steal; Theft from a Person; Criminal Damage; Going Equipped…

The list went on. But I didn't care.

Soon the only school that would have me was a special school for broken, fucked-up kids like me – Beaconsfield Reform School. But even that didn't help. The only good thing about that place was that I got to see Callum sometimes. We'd sneak off and have a cigarette behind the main building. He was still weird, but it was nice to have a familiar face in my life at a time when everyone around me was changing.

By the time I hit 14, every hint of my 'normal life' had been erased. Hanging out in junkies' flats smoking cannabis resin, slugging back cans of Crest lager, fucking girls and taking acid. *That* was my normal.

Funny thing is, for a long time I didn't think anything of it. I was so immersed in it that it just felt… *right*. Like I was always meant to be there.

Until one day something happened that changed everything.

We were hanging out at the house of a girl called Susanna.

Susanna had been in care most of her teenage life, had a pretty shitty upbringing and had ended up on the streets after being in and out of numerous care homes, including the one I'd been in, as well as doing some time in jail for prolific shop-lifting and other petty offences.

I only met her when she was 18 years old and out of the system. She was one of the Bus Station Crew, always there causing mayhem.

I'd hung around with her for as long as I'd been on the streets, along with her boyfriend Mike, who was constantly in and out of prison.

She was a child herself, but she already had two kids by two different blokes.

She was a nice girl. Tough, but at the same time bubbly and compassionate. She'd do anything for her mates and give her last cigarette to a stranger, if they seemed to need it more than she did.

Trouble was, she'd gotten heavily into drugs. You could tell that from the state of her house, not to mention her dead eyes.

It was a council house. Two up, two down. The type they built specifically to contain reprobates. Cheap and nasty. All paper-thin walls and Astroturf lawns. A thin veneer of social care, papering over a whole load of 'don't give a shit'.

Inside it was rundown. More of a squat than a home. Graffiti covered the walls – gang tags left as decoration.

Other than that there wasn't much there. A couch covered in blunts, a TV, an old ghettoblaster pumping out UB40 and unintelligible rave tracks, a small table and a solitary armchair next to the window.

Aside from the heavy aroma of skunk filling the air, the dominating smell was damp and pungent. Probably from the dirty clothes and nappies that were piled up behind the cupboard.

It was one of 30 or so houses built on the site of the Hawkins' old farm, where my dad used to live. Just far enough out of town to make us scumbags invisible to the nice 'normal' people.

You'd have thought as a kid that had known a *real* home – clean and tidy, with pictures on the walls – I'd have been uncomfortable.

I wasn't.

By that point, I was used to hanging out in less-than-savoury surroundings.

I think anything too clinical reminded me of the children's home and its overwhelming bleach stench.

That night, it was a good gathering. There were some kids from the estate, a few of the Bus Station Crew and a few new faces, but everyone was getting along.

It was what we called 'Giro Monday', when all the older ones got their benefits. The atmosphere was upbeat and there was lots of money around. Everyone was generous. The beer was flowing, joints were being passed freely around the room and people made sure I was well looked after. There were perks to being the youngest in the gang.

People were dancing and Susanna and some of the older girls were sat on the floor playing peek-a-boo with her two young kids.

I noticed that they were crawling around on the bare floor, but didn't think much of it. I assumed at one point there had been carpet, but from the thick layer of grime and cigarette butts, you could tell it was long gone.

She'd probably sold it.

Whatever. I was in good spirits. That's why I didn't think twice when an older lad from around the estate came over to me.

He was heading upstairs with Susanna.

'Can you come and watch the bedroom door for me?' he asked.

I nodded. Senses numbed by the weed in my system, I floated upstairs behind them.

I assumed they were going to fuck and didn't want someone bursting in, but when we got upstairs I noticed they'd left the door slightly ajar.

Oh, aye?

My teenage hormones kicked in. I peeked around the crack, holding my breath. But it wasn't the scene I expected.

The lad was holding a metal spoon over a flame, heating up the liquid in its shallow bowl.

Heroin.

I'd seen junkies glazing up spoons before, but never really stuck around for the rest. I was frightened, but I couldn't look away. My mouth was dry as I watched him collect the liquid in a needle then place it on the side of the bed.

It was like I was watching a film in soft focus, a methodical slow dance.

Susanna extended her arm and they smiled at one another. He wrapped a belt tightly around the top of her arm. Her arm drained of colour as the lad kissed her aggressively on the lips and started groping her breasts. Before too long her skin was almost translucent, just a faint blue-black network of veins visible, straining to the surface of the skin. He explored her arm for a few seconds, then selected a vein and pierced the surface of her china-like skin, before plunging the heroin deep into her.

The effects were instantaneous.

Susanna let out a sigh, long and low, like she was having an orgasm. Her eyes rolled backwards and she fell onto the bed, her boobs falling out of her loose blouse as she went.

All I noticed at first was a rush of blood to a certain part of *my* body. Susanna's boobs were massive. And I was at the peak of puberty. There was also something quite euphoric and hypnotic about it. The ritual, the glow of the flame…

Mind you, I was stoned.

But then I stepped back and took in the whole scene.

Zoomed out and refocused in HD. Saw the reality.

The needles. Blood on the bed covers.

There are kids in the house.

Truth be told, it snapped me right to attention. I gasped audibly.

Shit, he'll know I'd been watching.

In a panic, I pulled the door shut and bolted back downstairs to the party.

For an hour, the image played over and over in my mind.

Her face. Her veins straining against her skin. That noise…

I'd taken a lot of drugs and knew the effects they could have on the body. But that?

I'd never seen anything like it.

Eventually they emerged from upstairs. Everyone in the party cheered and wolf-whistled.

'Go 'ead, lad!'

The jubilant hand gestures made indicated clearly that they'd had sex.

No sooner had they returned when another couple made their way to the room. Once again I was called on as lookout. And I was time and again throughout the evening. By the tenth or eleventh couple, I wasn't sure what I was even meant to be watching for. Everyone knew what was happening.

Two by two, my friends and acquaintances came down those stairs lurching like zombies, bodies numb and dead behind the eyes. The party had gone from Class C to Class A in the bat of an eyelid. I felt uncomfortable.

'Do you want a hit?'

I looked over to see an older man I didn't recognise next to me.

'He can't fucking have one,' came another voice, almost immediately. This time it was one I did recognise. It was the drug dealer who'd been supplying us all day.

The last thing he wanted was a teenager OD-ing on him.

I wasn't tempted anyway. In fact, I was scared.

The way everyone's consciousness seemed to be sucked away from them, bodies collapsing on the floor where they stood, Susanna's kids screaming for their mum…

The skunk was making me paranoid.

As the light faded, the music became heavier. People came and went until I lost count of how many had passed through.

I felt panic tighten my chest. I started struggling to breathe.

Someone's going to die, I thought.

I wanted to leave but I was paralysed by fear.

The party had started at 11am. By now it was after 8pm.

I knew that because through all the noise someone had put the TV on and the *EastEnders* theme tune was playing.

DUM DUM, DUM DUM DA DA DUM…

It couldn't have been more perfectly timed as seconds later, I heard glass shattering before bodies dressed in black came piling in through the windows.

'POLICE!' someone shouted.

I couldn't make out if it was a shout of warning from a partygoer or an announcement from one of the cops, but either way, I knew there was only one reaction.

RUN!

It was easy for a skinny little teenager to slip away. I would have hardly hit their line of sight.

I bolted off down the back alley and ran for miles. Didn't stop until I got back to my gran's house.

That night I went to bed without saying a word to anyone, but I couldn't sleep.

I couldn't quite put my finger on it, but something bothered me.

Niggled me deep inside.

Terry's voice rang in my head: *Keep away from the smack-heads, Cocky. There's no way out of that world.*

Terry may have been involved in some less-than-savoury activities, but he'd always wisely steered clear of heroin and anything to do with it.

And now I could see why.

I shuddered as I realised that I was slipping deeper into the seedy world of narcotics and I knew that wasn't me.

Suddenly, the penny dropped. I knew what was bothering me: I'd degraded myself. I was like a rat scurrying around a sewer. It didn't get any lower than this and I knew my dad would have been horrified.

What next? I thought. *Begging?*

I sat bolt upright in bed and slapped myself across the face.

Remember who you are, Chris, I told myself.

Yes, I'd had a hard few years. Yes, I certainly wasn't the same as I'd been before Dad died. I *was* broken. But there's broken and then there's shattered.

I slapped myself again, this time harder.

You're 14 years old, Chris.

Normal teenagers didn't hang around smackheads acting as lookout while they shot up. They were playing in the park, or at home doing schoolwork.

Remember who you are, Chris. You're Dave and Diane Cock-croft's son. You had a nice home and a normal life.

That was still who I was. I still had a faint glimpse of a halo drifting around my head. I'd just lost my way.

Just as quickly as the adrenalin from hitting myself coursed through my body, I crashed as the skunk started to wear off. Sinking into my bed, weak with exhaustion, my heavy eyelids slowly came together.

As I drifted off, I hoped to escape the scenes I'd witnessed, but there was no respite. The darkness crept into my dreams and pulled on the thread of my fear, unravelling the night's events in my brain.

Scene after scene from a horror movie I'd just lived.

The dark blood on the bed sheets.

The stricken faces of Susanna's kids, wide-eyed and screaming with tear-soaked cheeks.

'I'm hungry, Mummy,' they wailed.

In my dream I ran up the stairs to get her.

'Susanna!' I shouted.

They needed their mum.

I burst into the room, grabbed Susanna, shook her, but she just lay there.

Was she…?

I couldn't tell if she was dead or alive. She was corpse-like and motionless, but her eyes were open and looking right through me.

The kids' screams echoed up the stairs as the heavy dance beat intensified, the two sounds becoming intertwined and pulsating in my ears until it felt like my brain would explode.

I bolted awake, soaking and gasping for air, my heart pounding and my whole body shaking.

I knew I'd witnessed something that night that could only get worse.

Heroin wasn't like weed, or acid. That drug had no master.

What if next time Susanna didn't wake up?

What if someone made me try it?

What if the kids got hold of it?

Those poor kids.

They'd probably end up in a children's home somewhere, broken and alone.

In that moment I made a decision.

Never again.

I didn't want to be there next time. I didn't want to be part of it. It was time for me to make a change.

In the days that passed, I learned that a few people had been arrested, but most people got away. The police knew exactly who they were going in for.

Social services took the kids away, of course. I wasn't one to side with the authorities, but what I'd seen that night had scarred me.

'Best place for them,' I'd said to one friend.

It must have been bad for me to say that.

As for Susanna, she seemed to drop off the face of the earth. To be honest, I tried not to think about her, it just made me feel guilty.

Maybe I shouldn't have watched the door?

I had no idea at the time how Susanna's life had come to that point.

* * *

SUSANNA

'All I ever wanted was to be loved. Now all I want is to die.'

Some years after that night at her house I bumped into Susanna in town. She looked far better than I could have expected from the last time our paths had crossed.

Perhaps we should have stuck to small talk, some jokes about the old Bus Station Crew and the few nights out we'd shared, then gone our separate ways. But that night had such a profound effect on me that there were things I just had to know.

'How did things get to be so bad?' I asked.

'I was doomed from the start,' she replied, candidly.

Susanna was six years old when she ended up in the children's home. She'd never known her dad and her mum was an alcoholic and drug addict.

You can see the cycle already, can't you?

Tiny and fragile, Susanna was left to fend for herself while her mum vanished for days on end, feeding her habit – or finding ways to fund it.

The cupboards were always empty and when Susanna cried because she was hungry, or cold, or just because she was a child that wanted a hug from her mum, no one came.

'All I ever wanted was love,' she said, with no hint of light in her heavy eyes. 'The children's home felt clean and safe at first.'

Well, anything was better than the neglect she'd been living in.

There was food on the table at breakfast, lunch and dinner. She could watch TV.

'And my key worker, Tariq, would always come and say goodnight,' she said.

It was more than her mum had ever done.

'He was nice to me,' she said. 'They all are at first.'

Susanna was lulled into a false sense of security. Not that she realised it at the time. But she soon would.

'I'd been living at the home for two years,' Susanna said. 'I was eight years old by this time. One night Tariq came into my room when I was alone and in my pyjamas getting ready for bed.'

Tariq was in his late thirties, short, overweight and with a habit of dousing himself in pungent, cheap aftershave.

It was normal for the key worker on shift to make sure everyone was in bed at 10pm. Everyone at that time being Susanna and the only other female resident, a 14-year-old called Carla.

But that night was anything but normal for Susanna.

'Tariq came in and shut the door behind him,' she said.

'You should be getting ready for bed,' he'd told her sternly. 'I'll help you.'

'I'm okay, I can do it myself,' she'd replied nervously.

That was when the mood changed. Tariq grabbed Susanna's shoulders and forced her down onto the floor.

'I remember the cold tiles hurting my knees,' she said. 'I remember him saying we could do it the hard way or the easy way. I didn't know what "it" was, but I knew I didn't want it either way.'

But she had no choice.

Tariq took out his penis and forced it in her mouth.

'I was so small and he was just forcing himself down my throat. He kept calling me a good girl and telling me I was his "favourite".

'I was crying, trying to catch my breath. I thought I was going to die. To be honest, I wish I had.'

Tariq didn't stop there. He grabbed Susanna by her long dark hair and dragged her to her bed, where he pulled off her pyjama bottoms and bent her over the frame.

Then he raped her.

'I didn't understand what was happening,' she said. 'How could I? I was eight years old. All I knew was that I was in pain. Agonising pain.

'I sobbed and sobbed. Asked him to stop. I couldn't fight, I was too young, too small and too scared. All he kept saying was how fucking good I was and telling me to stop crying.'

As suddenly as it started, it was over. For that night, at least.

'He just stopped and slumped over me. I could feel his weight and smell his aftershave all over me,' Susanna said. 'I understand now what that meant. But then I was just scared and confused.'

'See, that wasn't too bad, was it?' Tariq had said cheerfully, pulling his pants up.

No fear, no remorse. Just back to business as usual.

'I was stood there crying and shaking. Blood dripping down my legs,' Susanna said. 'I just kept saying that I wouldn't say anything if he left me alone.'

'If you tell anyone I'll have you locked up with the crazy people,' he'd growled at her, before adding, 'Who'd believe you anyway, you little slut?'

I gasped. *Slut?* She was eight years old.

'I remember my mum being called a slut,' Susanna said. 'And even then I knew I was nothing like *her*.'

Susanna had shouted, hoping that Carla would come and help her. But the older girl already knew the score and steered well clear.

You see, Tariq had first paid a visit to Carla's bedroom when she was 11.

'Shut the fuck up! Don't want to wake the other little girl now, do we?' Tariq had shouted, before forcing a sweaty, pungent kiss on Susanna's lips. 'She'll get jealous.'

Then he left.

'I didn't know what to do, so I just grabbed my doll Daisy and curled into the corner of the room,' Susanna told me. 'There was this red river of blood flowing out of me and I couldn't stop it. I remember sticking my socks between my legs to soak it all up.'

Tariq returned, night after night.

'I stopped caring about myself the third time I was raped,' Susanna told me. 'When it happens once you have a chance of getting over it. But 20 times in a week? It just becomes dormant in your brain. You stop feeling – or at least find ways to.'

It wasn't just Tariq. He'd bring his friends round too.

'Fridays were the worst. They'd have been drinking and be really aggressive,' she said. 'I lost count of the number of times they choked me unconscious as they raped me.'

'Why didn't you tell anyone?' I asked.

Susanna shrugged. 'I think people knew. They just didn't care.'

She told me how her social worker, Paula, would visit the home regularly.

'She'd ask question after question,' Susanna said. 'They're trained to read everything – your body language, your physical state, your reactions to silly questions, your silence. Anything to condemn you as crazy so they can close the file on you. I'd just shrug and stare at her. I was too scared to speak up about Tariq, I just hoped that she'd see it in my eyes.'

'Did she?' I ventured, gently.

'I think she did,' Susanna nodded.

'So why didn't she do anything?' I asked.

'Too much paperwork,' Susanna replied with a twisted smile. 'She always just reminded me to be grateful I wasn't on the streets. At the end of one meeting I burst into tears. I remember Paula hugging me. She had this big floppy scarf wrapped around me and I felt so safe. I hadn't been hugged like that in a long time.'

It was a brief moment of comfort for Susanna. Those moments were few and far between.

Tariq's abuse continued for many years. Night after night it happened. Until one time, Susanna snapped.

'I was making a sandwich in my dressing gown in the kitchen,' she said. 'He came in and pushed his knees into the backs of my legs so I fell down. He ripped open my gown and put his hand between my legs, forcing his fingers inside me.

'I called him a cunt, so he squeezed washing up liquid in my mouth. I didn't care, tasted better than his fake aftershave,' Susanna said, her eyes emotionless. 'Then he dragged me down the corridor by my hair.'

Susanna knew what was coming, so she kicked and screamed, grabbed on to doorframes to try and delay the inevitable.

What Tariq didn't realise, as he dragged her away to rape and abuse her, was that Susanna still had the butter knife in her hand.

'I was screaming for help but I knew no one would come, so I took matters into my own hands. I didn't even think, I just swung my arm and thrust the knife deep into his neck.'

Survive or die.

That was the life of a care-home kid.

'I remember the silence, then him screaming out in pain. He was crying out in pain, like a fucking scared baby.'

At the time, the home was at full capacity. On hearing Tariq scream, its residents poured out onto the corridors. Susanna was kicking Tariq in the face over and over.

'Die, die, die!' she screamed. No one stopped her. They were all too relieved. Especially when he made a noise like an animal being slaughtered by a butcher.

'I never felt so good in my life,' Susanna told me. 'I thought it was over.'

Unfortunately for Susanna, Tariq survived.

And just like that, *her* life ended.

Condemned as crazy, Susanna was shut away in a secure unit.

File closed. Forgotten.

The authorities there could smell a broken spirit a mile off. Susanna was right: she was doomed from the start.

'They were ready and waiting for me when I got there,' she said. 'They knew there was absolutely no one who cared for me, so I was easy prey.'

And so the abuse continued.

Not just sexual. There were medical experiments and drug tests.

With no home and no roots, broken children like Susanna weren't treated as human. Just slabs of flesh, perfect little guinea pigs, or an outlet for perverts' vile sexual predilections.

When Susanna was released into the world, she was even more broken than before. Shattered by the treatment she received in the guise of care and abused by the very people charged with protecting her.

'All I wanted from the start was love and care,' she said. 'But that was never going to happen to me. The streets are the only place I feel safe now. I haven't been raped for years now. Well, you don't need to be if you're getting paid for it, do you?'

We never talked about that night at her home. Her story had told me all I needed to know.

She was another victim of a broken system, one that hid abuse beneath a thin veneer of respectability. One that saw the most damaged people in society and swooped on them like vultures.

I knew then that I wasn't like her. I never had been. I was surrounded by the remnants of my old life, the love of my family like a protective force field that couldn't be broken down, not in the same way.

You see, unlike me, Susanna had been born into a world without hope, a field of weeds strangling the beauty out of life at every unfortunate turn.

She was alone from the start and never knew love.

Tragically, she left the world in the same way a few months after our meeting. Alone in a dirty squat with a needle hanging out of her arm, trying to medicate a way out of her pain.

Finally, she'd escaped.

CHAPTER SEVEN

Fighting Free

In the weeks and months that followed the police raid at Susanna's a saying that I'd heard – God knows where – kept drifting to the forefront of my mind.

We're all given the same opportunity – to live a life. What we do with it, that's up to us.

After seeing the hands that friends and acquaintances had been dealt – Callum, Susanna, Mark – I wasn't sure the opportunity was all equal, but there was one thing I was sure of: I was one of the lucky ones. I had a choice.

I could continue my descent into a life of crime and addiction or find a way out.

Live or die

Yes, my life was far from perfect. My home was still broken. I was still broken.

My mum was living with an abusive and controlling man, so I couldn't go home. My grandma and grandad were getting on and I knew my wayward activities were putting a strain on them and Donna too.

'We're all so worried about you,' Gran would say. 'You need to sort yourself out.'

It was like the scales had fallen from my eyes. Suddenly I realised I'd been lashing out, rebelling at the pain inside me after Dad's death.

But everything I'd done had got me nowhere.

Dad was still gone, but I still had a life to live. Was I going to quit or keep fighting?

I'm a Cockcroft; I'm a scrapper; I'm going to keep fighting. I'm going to survive.

One day, the phone rang. It was a friend of my gran's called Alan, who trained boxers in a local gym. He'd known my dad growing up, so when I answered I assumed he was calling to check in on Gran.

'I'll just get—' I said, but Alan interrupted me.

'It's you I'm calling for, Chris,' he said.

What had I done?

Gran was pretty forthright; if I was in trouble she usually had no problem telling me herself.

Had I worn her down so much?

'Oh,' I replied. 'Okay...'

'I've heard you're interested in boxing. I might be able to help you. Meet me at North Bridge tomorrow night at six o'clock.' Before I could respond, he carried on. 'If you're there, good. If you're not, you're not. It's your choice.'

The line went dead.

I stood with the receiver still against my ear as I absorbed his words.

It's your choice.

The cogs started turning. Gran must've seen a change in me. I'd been staying in more, avoiding some of the old crowd, and I'd mentioned that I wanted to try boxing. She'd seen a bit of the old Chris. This was no coincidence. This was her doing.

What I did with the opportunity, well, that was up to me.

Gran and Grandad were struggling to cope with me. I was 14 years old and the way I was going, I was heading for a stretch in a young offenders' institute at best, a return to a children's home at worst.

I loved the freedom of the streets, but my eyes had been opened and revealed it as a place I didn't really belong, or want to be.

Those days in Halifax, if you were from the wrong side of the tracks or a broken family like mine, it seemed there were two routes you could take – crime or sport. Crime really hadn't done me any favours, so maybe it was time to give sport a try?

I don't know why, but as I was pulling on my tracksuit and trainers, my stomach was in knots. Even as I walked the winding backstreets to North Bridge, the butterflies in my tummy were dancing around.

I had no idea what to expect. I was tempted to turn back, but I knew I had to fight. That's what Dad would have done. I was sure of it.

So at six o'clock, as the bell from the town hall chimed the hour, I was there. So was Alan.

'Good lad,' he said. 'Come with me, I'll show you the gym.'

The knots in my stomach loosened slightly. That was it. No lectures or stern talk. It felt like a clean slate.

From the outside the gym looked like any other dishevelled building around the town, with windows thick with layers of dust so black you could hardly see through them and paint peeling off every wall. But inside it was different. It was alive.

We climbed the steep stairs to the top floor of the old building. When we reached the top, I craned my neck to peer through the door, taking in the scene in the boxing gym. There were ten, maybe 20 men in the room, training, sparring or even just watching.

The smell of sweat hit my nostrils and ignited my senses.

Hard work. Graft. Life.

There was something else too, something I could taste on the tip of my tongue.

Fear.

I was streetwise beyond my years. I knew what it was like to be scared. But this was different. This fear was a call to action.

The dull thud of people hitting punch bags combined with the sound of feet gliding across the floor of the ring created a beat in my brain.

A room of fighters breathed heavily in sync with one another, punctuated by shouts from the ringside and grunts of pain.

It was musical, like a war song, and I was intoxicated by it.

My heart pumped in unison with every beat as adrenalin flooded my body.

Then I caught a glimpse of the words painted above the door of the gym.

We are all equal as one. Train hard or go home.

I'd already decided what I was going to do.

That evening, Alan took me through the basics, laid out the rules.

Meet at 6pm every night. Go to school. No drink, no drugs.

I nodded in agreement to every caveat.

I was excited, and not just for the new opportunity. I also knew that Danny King, the local boxing champion, trained with Alan in the gym too.

After I'd been read the rulebook, I hung around to absorb the atmosphere, and see if I could spot the local celebrity.

I scanned the room. There he was, tucked away in a corner of the gym, skipping at the speed of light, jumping from left to right and spinning the rope expertly over his head. Through the windows behind him, the towering hills of Halifax provided an ominous, gritty backdrop.

My heart raced with excitement.

He had this aura around him. Like he was Rocky Balboa or something.

I couldn't take my eyes off him, not even when he dropped the rope and started walking in my direction.

My jaw dropped wide as he got closer. He had a body like Peter Andre in the video for 'Mysterious Girl', with muscles rippling through his vest.

I wanted to look like that. I wanted that strength and presence.

I tried to say something to him as he brushed past me, but my mouth had gone dry and all that came out was a barely audible croak.

Was I star-struck?

Whatever it was, it lasted three months. In that time Gran found a school that would have me, Sowerby Bridge. I still hated it, but it was part of Alan's rules.

Up at 6am for a run. Go to school. Eat well. Stay off the drink and drugs.

If I fulfilled all that, every night at 6pm, I was permitted to train at the gym.

The compromise was worth it.

Turns out Alan had known my dad quite well, knew he was good with his fists. Well, I had to get it from somewhere.

He could see a mile off that I'd been rebelling against my pain over Dad's death. He wanted me to channel my anger and pain through boxing, keep me on the straight and narrow.

Training became my religion. I was committed, obsessed even, and my street fighting training by Terry made me a force to be reckoned with.

But it wasn't just the training that had me hooked, it was the atmosphere in the gym too. It was full of what Gran called 'real men' – tough but courteous, born survivors and protectors.

Just like my dad.

No one there had it easy. Everyone was fighting something: poverty, pain, the past. But they were choosing to fight. That was the difference.

They became father figures to me, filling some of the void left by Dad's death, and replacing the false camaraderie I'd experienced on the street with real guidance and care.

God knows I needed it, with Viv still slithering round. making Mum's life a misery – not that she'd admit it.

For the first time in years I felt focused and clear-headed.

Between Dad's death, the children's home and living on the streets, I'd witnessed some terrible things.

Even though I knew Skircoat Lodge had been closed down – for what reasons I had no interest in finding out – my time there and what followed still clung to me like a leech. The Boss Man dragging other residents around the home, Susanna cold as death and drug-addled on her bed. My mum at the mercy of Viv's fists.

The images clouded my mind constantly. Dancing menacingly in my head at night, they brought nightmares that gripped my chest and jolted me from sleep, panting with fear and drenched in a cold sweat.

But now, that fog of fear was lifting. The dreams became less and less frequent. I became mentally stronger.

I felt physically powerful too.

The stronger I got, the more I could stand up to Viv.

I wasn't a scared little boy any more, and he could see that. If he threatened my mum or me when I was there, I'd brace up to him, flexing my newly formed muscles.

'What are you going to do?' I'd say. 'If you do anything, I'll kill you.'

Rather than going for me like he had done in the past, Viv would slither away like the reptile he was. He knew he couldn't control me now, even if Mum was still under his spell.

Of course, I never intended to kill him. No matter how much I wanted to when I saw the bruises on my mum's face and body.

I used the only language a man like Viv understood: violence, or at least the threat of it. But I was my father's son. He was protective, but peaceful. Strong, yes. Wouldn't take shit. But he'd never stoop so low as to take a life, no matter what anger he was harbouring.

I revelled in my newfound strength.

Eventually, the memories from the children's home, from tearing through the streets and that terrible night at Susanna's began to fade away.

It felt like a turning point, like I was finally fighting my way out of my grief, instead of collapsing into it.

Life felt like it couldn't get better, until one night when I was sparring with a new kid in the gym.

As I slid around the ring, I suddenly became aware of a pair of eyes on me. It felt like someone was boring holes into the back of my head, but I couldn't turn to look. Didn't want to get knocked out, did I now?

Then I heard a voice.

'Duck, slip… now move,' instructed a broad Yorkshire accent. Distinctive, slightly nasal – presumably a fighter who'd had his nose battered in more than once.

Then I realised. It could only be one person.

Oh. My. God. It was Danny! The local champion was guiding ME!

I followed every order exactly on cue. Danced that kid round the ring, swinging left and right until the bout was over.

'Nice one, kid,' said Danny, shaking my hand. 'You've got some skill there.'

I was so in awe I could barely speak, but somehow I managed to reply.

'Thanks,' I said. 'My dad used to box.'

From then on, I was Danny's shadow.

Every morning we jogged three miles together. We trained together every night and I absorbed his every move and tactic, like an observant sponge.

Danny was a god to me. Not that I believed in all that shit, but it was the closest thing to it I could imagine.

Boxing and fitness became my religion. The gym was my church and Danny was my saviour. He was strong, focused and successful – everything I wanted to be. He didn't have weaknesses. He was always in control.

Sometimes it made me angry that I hadn't had that control when I was fighting the grief of losing Dad. That I'd been weak and became something I disliked.

I hated that people were still sceptical, waiting for me to put a foot wrong and fall back in with the old crowd.

I guess sometimes I lost sight of how far I had come. Inside I still felt like that angry 12-year-old, tearing thoughtlessly and recklessly through the streets.

It took others to remind me that I wasn't.

One day, as I made my way through the weights room to get to the boxing gym, I felt a hand grab me. When I turned round, my heart sank.

It was a familiar face and one that had arrested me on more than one occasion.

Immediately I went on the defensive.

'I've not done nothing, PC Dixon,' I snapped, springing backwards. 'I'm just going to train.'

PC Dixon raised his hands in mock surrender. A smile crossed his lips and I realised this wasn't going to be one of our regular encounters.

'I know, lad,' he said. 'I've been watching you train with Danny. You're doing well.'

'Thanks,' I muttered, shuffling awkwardly from foot to foot.

'I always knew you weren't like the other kids,' he continued. 'And I was right. Look at you now. They're going to die or end up in jail. You won't.'

My chest swelled with pride.

'Keep it up, kid,' he said, gently bumping my shoulder with his fist.

'I will,' I said. And I meant it.

I mean, if Danny could do it, why couldn't I?

Danny hadn't had a good upbringing. I knew his mum had struggled with drugs. Still did, according to rumours. But he didn't let it show. He just dealt with it like a man. No acting up. No arrests. Just got on with it.

So I did what Danny taught me. Channelled my anger into getting stronger and better.

As I improved, so did Danny.

Fight after fight he flourished. Soon he was even offered a shot at the area title.

This man had no flaws. No weakness. He was invincible.

Or so I thought.

Then one night, after about ten months of training together, I went round to Danny's mum's house with him to drop off some shopping he'd picked up for her. She only lived two blocks down from Danny's flat in the outskirts of Bradford so I offered to help.

Danny asked me to wait at the door when we arrived.

I nodded. He was private about his family and I understood that, so I just waited, watching the nightlife emerging on stolen bikes, all under the beaming, incandescent light of the police helicopter overhead. That had been my world not so long ago, but now it felt so far away.

My thoughts were suddenly interrupted by shouts from inside Danny's mum's house.

Was he calling for help?

There was fear in his voice, but I couldn't make out the words.

I'd never heard Danny scared before. Instinctively, I snapped into fight mode, bolting in and grabbing a knife from the kitchen worktop.

For some reason, I paused and wiped it clean of the chocolate cake it was covered in.

What the hell, you idiot! What difference will it make?

The shouting had stopped, so I slowed my pace, holding my breath as I walked through the hall and crept up the stairs. I was worried.

Where was he? Why had he fallen silent?

The house was a mess, empty vodka bottles everywhere and a musty odour hanging in the air.

When I reached the landing, I could see one door ajar, so I crept gingerly over and peered round the frame.

I took a sharp intake of breath, like I'd been sucker punched in the stomach.

The room was covered in a film of filth with used needles decorating the barely visible floor.

And there in the middle of the room was Danny, sobbing.

He was cradling his mother as she lay unconscious and naked but for the blanket he'd pulled across her, with a needle hanging out of a vein in her right arm.

'Is she okay?' I asked.

'Go home, Chris,' he said, stroking her face. 'I don't want you to see me like this.'

'I can help,' I said.

'Just go!' he snapped, his voice cracking as tears rolled down his cheeks.

What else could I do?

My heart felt heavy as I walked home. I'd never seen a man so vulnerable. I thought Danny was made of stone but it turns out everyone has a weakness, a personal Achilles heel.

Dad was mine; Danny's was his mum.

That night I couldn't shake the image of him, sat like a scared boy with a tear-soaked face. But experience had taught me not to ask questions, so the next day at the gym I acted like nothing had happened.

Danny didn't speak to anyone that night, not even me. Took him a few weeks to get back to normal, but I guess that was how he coped.

The gym was his escape.

Maybe his coach, Alan, was his saviour, like he was mine? Alan had coached Danny from childhood. He never went to school, the only education Danny had was in a children's home, and even that was minimal.

Alan worked hard to develop a work ethic in Danny, kept him out of jail and nurtured him to become a champion. In many ways he was like a father to Danny.

* * *

With the area title coming up, it was like the old Danny was back. I'd never seen him train so hard in his life. He was in the best form of his life, seeming unstoppable.

That was until Curtis rolled into town.

Curtis was Danny's half-brother.

He reminded me of Fagin from *Oliver Twist*; a vile creature with no morals and an aptitude for causing mayhem.

His reputation must have preceded him, because Alan wasn't happy.

'You don't need him around you right now,' he said to Danny. 'He'll drag you down.'

Danny would nod obediently, but he couldn't resist the pull of his wayward brother. You see, Curtis was emotionally manipulative. He knew Danny was a good man and believed family was family, regardless.

I think Danny felt responsible for Curtis' misfortune in some way. Not that it made any sense. They'd been born into the same life, Danny just chose to fight.

I felt sorry for Danny. He was doing what most good people do. Putting his family first. It wasn't his fault he'd been born into a brood of scavengers and crooks.

He and Alan started arguing a lot, but I stayed out of it and focused on being a mate to Danny.

One night I went back to Danny's flat after training. For someone so precious about his appearance – he was Tango orange from practically sleeping under a sunbed – his flat was a tip. It had no carpets and two old car seats as furniture and it was absolutely freezing. It reminded me of the squats I used to party in, and I tried to supress bad memories.

This is Danny's flat. Nothing bad will happen here, I told myself.

I was just starting to relax when Curtis turned up unannounced with a skinny, bedraggled-looking girl who couldn't have been older than 17.

'This is Rosie,' he said as he barged in like it was his place.

I gave a nod of acknowledgement and the girl flashed a luminous yellow smile at me. I immediately noticed brown stains mottling her gums. My stomach lurched as realisation set in. She was a crackhead, probably a prostitute too.

I'd seen it all before. Curtis was using Danny's place to do his dirty work. This poor girl was about to be used as a sex toy. I sat silently as events unfolded before my eyes.

Bizarrely, Curtis licked her face as he chuckled to himself, before forcing her mouth open and blowing smoke between her lips. Rosie lay there, eyes glazed over like she'd gone to some other place – there was no hint of care or respect from Curtis, she was just his plaything.

Inside I was screaming, *Stop it. This is wrong. She's someone's daughter, maybe even mother.*

Suddenly Danny stepped over towards the makeshift couch.

'Come on, then,' he said, laughing as he started removing his trousers.

Please, no... I thought.

But I said nothing. Despite everything I'd experienced, I was still a kid. Danny and Curtis were older than me and given the situation, I was scared.

The two brothers devoured Rosie before my eyes, like a pair of wolves feeding on an animal carcass.

Danny kept slapping Rosie's face and spitting on her to get a laugh out of Curtis, but I don't think she was conscious enough to be in on the joke as heroin had clearly taken hold.

I wanted to cover my face with my hands, run away and scream at him: *You're better than this, Danny!*

But I was frozen. Just laughed along on autopilot, while I willed it to end.

I'd never seen Danny behave like this before, but it didn't take an expert to know this wasn't his first time.

I'd always thought Danny and I were alike, but now my illusions had been shattered.

I left without saying a word. I had no idea what I was going to say to him the next time I saw him. How could I ignore what had happened?

Couldn't he see the irony of treating a smackhead like that, when his beloved mother was a victim of the same affliction?

It seems I didn't need to worry though, as shortly after that Danny went missing. Then, a man who had taken a fancy to his mum had been found beaten half to death in the street. The whole town was out looking for Danny and as one of his closest friends, everyone had questions for me.

'Is there anywhere he goes for privacy?'
'Does he know anyone out of town?'
'Did he say anything to you?'
Truth is, I knew exactly where he'd be.

When things got tough, Danny sprinted up into the magical, mystical hills that surrounded Halifax to consume the peace and silence. He found solace there.

I must have been the only person who knew, but I kept my mouth shut.

I was mad at Danny for letting me down, for being less than the man I thought he was. But he wasn't wholly to blame. He wasn't much different from the Bus Station Crew or the kids at the home.

He'd been born into chaos and drug addiction, had to drag himself up, and had done a pretty good job of it too. But like Susanna he was doomed from the start. He fought like a Pit Bull, but could never quite escape his life. It was in his blood.

I'd expected too much of him.

I really didn't want to believe he'd attack this guy, even though his injuries suggested otherwise.

'That's not like Danny,' I said to people. 'He's too controlled. I'm sure I saw him that night anyway.'

I gave him an alibi, fought his corner while he wasn't there to do so.

But the next time I saw him, his knuckles were a mess, all blistered and bloody, with bits of flesh hanging off.

I honestly felt my heart break into a million pieces. *I thought you were different.*

Danny started training again, but nothing was the same. His family's poison had seeped into his life. Curtis was on the radar of every drug dealer in town and he owed money to everyone at the gym too.

It wasn't just Danny that had the burden of Curtis, it was bringing the gym – my safe haven and new family – crashing down too.

Danny's talent was undeniable. Even while all this was going on he beat his number one contender and had the biggest payday of his life. It should have been the making of him, but instead he handed every penny to Curtis to pay off his drug debts.

Family first.

Not long after Danny beat the number one featherweight contender. Overnight he became a well-known sports person-ality, with his picture in the paper and on local TV.

'They want you to fight for a world title, Danny,' Alan said excitedly one day. 'A *world* title.'

It was a one-way ticket out of Halifax. It would help him get away from Curtis and get his mum the help she needed.

'Tell them no,' he said, without a hint of emotion. 'I'm quitting.'

'B-but…' Alan stuttered.

'I said *no!*' Danny shouted, storming out.

Every single one of us in the room stood slack-jawed. You could have heard a pin drop.

For weeks after the gym was broken, stale with disappoint-ment. Alan was devastated and I was shattered. I'd put Danny on a pedestal and treated him as an idol. I'd put all my faith in him, like I used to with Dad. The foundation of my strength felt like it was built on his success and his quitting rocked me to the core.

In a way, it was like when Dad died all over again.

The anger built up inside and all I wanted to do was lash out. Good job I had the gym this time. Without that outlet, who knows where I might have ended up?

Danny's life spiralled out of control from that point. He'd quit to try to keep his fragile family together, but he couldn't beat his mum's addiction for her. In fact, it killed her. I heard that Danny had been the one to find her. She'd been dead for six weeks, rotting in her own faeces.

In six weeks no one noticed, no one came. No one cared.

After that Danny hit the bottle hard and before long, he was all over the local papers. He went from local hero to alcoholic zero in a matter of months.

FORMER BOXER ARRESTED FOR DRUGS

FORMER BOXER BEATS HIS GIRLFRIEND IN DRUNKEN RAGE

FORMER BOXER SLEEPS WITH UNDERAGE GIRL

I couldn't bring myself to acknowledge him if I did see him around. I don't know if I was sad or angry or both. Truth is, when Danny quit boxing, it felt like he quit on me too. What I didn't realise was that he'd actually quit on himself.

He became another victim of the broken system that abandoned him from the day he was born.

* * *

DANNY

'The fight for life begins at first light.'

Danny was born into a world that had no doors, no exits; no way out – no matter how hard he fought to find one.

The only sustenance that flowed to Danny through the umbilical cord was a concoction of vodka and crack. His fight for life began at his first glimpse of light, with doctors rushing him to an incubator when he was born two months premature.

'The doctors said Mum's prolific drug use caused my early arrival,' Danny told me. 'I needed more of the same shit she was taking, so I pushed hard to get out.'

Danny was a fighter from the get-go. Most kids born premature and addicted to drugs and alcohol don't make it.

But Danny did.

Doctors and nurses weaned Danny off the drugs in an incubator, giving him baby doses of morphine mixed with special protein milk. That's how he got the vitamins and vital fluids he needed to stay alive.

'My mum always told me that I was a fighter from birth,' Danny said. 'A natural born survivor.'

What other choice did he have?

Nothing about Danny's start in life was normal. Apart from the few days after his birth, his mother had no contact with him until he was six years old. He was in and out of hospital for years and in the hands of the authorities from day one.

By the age of eight, Danny had been passed around six different foster families. His mum rinsed each one for whatever she could get.

'I need food,' she'd plead.

'I just want to buy Danny a present,' she'd say.

It was always for drugs.

'Whenever I saw Mum it was under the supervision of the social workers,' Danny recalled one day. 'She was always covered in bruises from head to toe. I don't ever remember seeing my mum without a black eye.'

Danny was 12 years old when he was sent to a children's home.

The onset of teenage hormones had put an end to his last foster placement, when he'd taken a liking to his foster parents' daughter.

'I crept into her room one night and tried to kiss her,' he told me. 'She freaked out and started screaming and before I know it, the police are there and I'm being accused of rape. I didn't even know what that meant at the time.'

The home was nothing like what Danny had grown up in. In many ways, he'd been lucky, living in nice houses with good families, food in his belly and clothes on his back.

'Just because a dog is born in a stable, it doesn't make it a horse,' Danny said. 'I was a Pit Bull Terrier, regardless of where I'd been brought up.'

Danny showed his aptitude for boxing at the home in spectacular style.

'The Boss Man was this big, tall African guy, a devout Catholic who looked like the Grim Reaper. He ran the home with a fat woman who looked like Sloth from *The Goonies*. She had facial hair and a dodgy eye, so I called her pirate.'

Every time she called his name the response from Danny was the same.

Arrrgh, Captain!

'She'd chase me around the winding corridors with a cricket bat, taking swings at my head,' Danny laughed. 'I got really good at ducking and diving. She never caught me because I was too fast. That's how I knew I'd be a good boxer.'

It wasn't just skill that kept Danny moving, he had a condition called akathisia as a result of all the medication they pumped into him as a baby to keep him alive.

'I was wired as a child and the Grim Reaper hated it,' he said. 'He liked his home still, calm and quiet – everything I couldn't be.'

Danny was never in favour at the home.

'One night the Pirate caught me off guard while I was in the bath. Laid into me with her cricket bat like I was a piñata,' he said. 'I jumped out of the bath butt-naked and had a choice

– save my knees or my dignity, so my knees took the brunt of the attack.'

All that over being called 'Pirate'? Hardly befitting of an adult charged with the care of vulnerable young children. Danny's legs were black and blue for months and it took him weeks to get the rhythm back in his legs.

'I never fitted in,' Danny said. 'Anyway, the Grim Reaper had an eye for the ladies, if you know what I mean?'

Just before he turned 13, it was decided that Danny's mum was no longer a risk to him – according to social services. And just like that, with a click of the Grim Reaper's fingers, Danny was sent home to his drug addict mum.

By this time Danny had a brother, named Curtis Brown.

She'd named him after her dealer boyfriend – Curtis – and what they called heroin on the streets – Brown. What a way to name your kid.

Danny knew the dealer was Curtis' dad, because he knew his mum gave him 'special favours' in return for drugs when she was short on cash.

She'd call him from the payphone across the street, using their 'code' – not that it was rocket science.

'Hi, it's me, I'm looking for Mr Curtis Brown.'

'He's not in, but I'll tell him you called.'

That was how they communicated a drug deal. The police had clocked the old way of setting fireworks off in the backyard, when it seemed like a certain side of Halifax was in a constant mode of celebration, not just on Bonfire Night or New Year's Eve.

'I think Mum was happy I was home. She needed the extra child support money.'

'For looking after you both?' I asked.

Curtis was six years younger than Danny.

'Nah, for more drugs,' he replied. 'It was me that ended up looking after Curtis. He was so little and helpless.'

Danny went from the relative comfort of foster homes and the care home to living on a council estate in the home of a crackhead. He started stealing and fighting. But it wasn't to rebel – it was to survive.

'I had to steal food most days for me and my brother,' he explained. 'Otherwise we would have starved to death.'

'Surely the police knew, the authorities – couldn't they help?' I asked.

'Mum was an addict, always begging for money and causing problems. She was a pile of paperwork waiting to happen,' Danny said. 'Social services avoided us like the plague.'

They were wiped clean off the list of high-risk priorities by the authorities.

Danny never went to school. Well, how could he? There was no one to take him. His mum was only conscious for one hour of each day, an hour she'd use to score more 'Curtis Brown'.

When he was older, he tried. Got himself to a school, but it didn't work out. By that time he was a feral animal, fighting and stealing things from the staffroom.

'The teachers didn't want me in their classrooms,' said Danny. 'So I just stopped going.'

Turns out, Danny's education inspector was too scared to come to the estate. The last time he came looking for him, he got mugged. He wasn't coming back after that.

Once again the system failed – those people and bodies that were supposed to stand in Danny's corner left him to the wolves.

'Curtis was in trouble with the wrong crowd from the moment he was big enough to leave the house alone,' Danny said. 'I always felt guilty because he'd not had the same start as me – the nice foster homes and M&S baked beans. He'd been stuck in that shithole house from day one.'

So we weren't really all given the same opportunity, were we?

Fortunately, Danny was a fighter. He chose how to live his life. He found ways for him and Curtis to survive.

He tried the legitimate route, knocking on doors offering to clean gardens and wash cars. In return, he got money for food. But it wasn't a lucrative enterprise, and most days he'd have to rely on stealing to fill his and Curtis' bellies.

'The first time I stumbled upon the boxing club my plan was to pretend to do a boxing session, and when everyone was training to sneak into the changing rooms and take everyone's belongings to sell.'

Danny crept into the changing room after a cursory circuit and was rifling through some bags when he noticed a figure looming over him: it was the boxing trainer. A veritable giant in comparison to Danny's wiry eight-stone frame.

Caught red-handed, Danny feared he was in for quite the pasting that night. But instead of kicking off or calling the police, the man looked at Danny, took a crisp £5 note out of his wallet and handed it to him.

Danny's jaw swung wide: he was rich.

The man didn't ask Danny much; he didn't need to. He said his name was Alan. He'd been brought up on the estate too, knew Danny's mum because he went to school with her. He knew exactly how tough it was for kids like him growing up there. He'd lived it.

That £5, for a kid in Danny's situation on that estate, was like being handed the winning lottery ticket.

But the man didn't stop there, he offered him a lifeline too.

'Come to the gym every night. I will give you a week's worth of spending money and I will feed you,' he said.

'He was the kindest man I'd ever met,' said Danny. 'I was starving and I had to look after my little brother.'

Dutifully, Danny went to the gym the next day, and the day after that, and the day after that. He fed his little brother and himself. Built himself a skill and a reputation as a fighter and a champion. In and out of the ring, Danny was a survivor. He started his fight every morning – 6am at first light – and didn't stop until sundown.

'It started as a way to feed my family,' he said. 'But boxing became my life, my escape.'

Alan and the guys at the gym became his family, like they would to me.

For many years, Danny fought to survive. Fought to support his mum and brother.

Danny was almost a world champion.

Almost a crack addict's kid gone good.

Almost the one that fought his way out of the broken system.

Almost.

CHAPTER EIGHT

One-hit Wonder

Danny quitting boxing hit me hard, but I managed to channel my anger. That was at least one thing his abandonment couldn't take away from me – the determination to succeed and make something of myself.

I continued to train: a 6am run every day; clean living; daily sessions in the gym. The ritual had become a part of me – my life and purpose.

My family were happy enough.

The camaraderie of training and the friends I made at the gym kept me out of trouble, so there were no late-night police visits any more.

That said, life was still pretty shit in Halifax.

In the shadow of the town's green hills, thousands were struggling to put food on the table. So many kids roam the streets while the wolves watched from the side-lines, waiting to claim their next victim. Drug dealers, paedophiles, rapists and abusers were out in force, feeding off desperation and poverty.

The gym was my protection. A place of hope in a town that seemed devoid of any. And not only was I safe, I was happy. Having fun like a normal teenage lad.

Normal.

It was a word I hadn't connected with myself for a long time, but for the first time in years I actually felt it.

As the weeks turned to months and the months into years, it began to feel like I'd found what I'd been looking for. A safe space, a purpose and a family to replace the one that had been shattered around me – I was home.

Compared to what I'd experienced in Skircoat Lodge with Callum and on the streets with Terry, life was pretty mundane. But it suited me fine.

When I was training it was like being enveloped by a giant protective bubble. The world went on around me, but couldn't reach me. My anger about Dad's death, about the way Boss Man had treated me, about Susanna and Callum and Mark and Danny, it all just slid away. It was just me and the steady slap of my boxing gloves, punctuated by my own breath.

I wasn't even that bothered about fighting any more. It was in sparring and training that I found my energy.

That said, I still got pretty good on the amateur circuit. Took on loads of good lads who were fighting to keep fit, or out of trouble.

It was harmless fun. Rough and ready, yes. But when you were done you shook hands with your opponent and sat down for pie and peas together, win or lose, like good sportsmen did.

With my newfound focus, I was finally starting to feel like myself. To feel fixed. I'd found something I was good at and was gaining recognition for the right reasons, not just for being the local tearaway.

It wasn't just in the ring, either. One of the caveats of me being allowed to go to the gym was that I had to go to school too. Being there and actually staying there meant I got involved in other sports. I even made it to the Calderdale School Athletic Championships in the 800 metres.

Typically, I was pretty cocky about the whole thing.

Cocky by name, cocky by nature.

I'd been told about one lad who was the favourite to win. His name was Jonny Stewart, the 15-year-old son of a working-class Glaswegian family from Ovenden in Halifax, near where I grew up.

'I'll kick his arse,' I boasted, chest puffed up as I paraded in front of a couple of girls sat by the long jump.

I'd been prepping for this, so I felt unbeatable.

Then I saw him. Or, more accurately, I saw his shoes.

They were the best running shoes I'd ever seen, probably because they were the *only* real running shoes I'd ever seen. They looked light as a feather and sleek as hell.

As we lined up at the starting blocks, my second-hand Gola Sprints looked a joke. But there was no time to ponder on it.

Marks… set…

The gun popped.

I pushed hard but I couldn't keep up. Jonny smashed over the finish line in record time.

I came a distant second.

'Great race,' I said to Jonny after I crossed the line.

'Thanks,' he said.

We got chatting and turns out we had loads of interests in common. We started running together and I took him to the gym to train.

He was different to my street friends, and also to the guys in the gym. He still had his mum and dad. Walter and Sandra were together and still madly in love.

His home life was exactly what I imagined mine would have been like if Dad was still alive. At first I was envious, especially of the close relationship he had with Walter. But his family was so welcoming that when I was with them, they made me part of it. There was no need to be jealous.

Going round to his house to have a brew and a scone with his family was just another glimmer of normality returning to my life.

As time passed, Jonny and I became inseparable. I transformed from a skinny little teenager into a strong, muscular man.

I might not have been much cop on the track, but girls flocked around me as my reputation in the ring grew. They started hanging round outside the gym, or going to pubs they knew my friends went to, but I wasn't in the least bit interested. I didn't have time for a girlfriend, or even a fling.

I was dedicated to my sport and had grabbed another kind of attention.

The professional boxing world had its eyes on me. I knew there were pro scouts watching me and I'd told Alan I wanted to give it a try. I really believed I had it in me to be a champion – how could I not with my focus and drive?

I wanted him to train me, but Alan was planning to retire.

'I can't take you on,' he said. 'But I'll make an introduction.'

True to his word, Al introduced me to Kevin Spratt, a trainer at a pro gym over in Bradford. I arranged to go and meet him and the renowned promoter John Celebanski for a training and sparring session. That was how it was. The pro gyms wanted to see what they were investing in.

When I arrived, I swear I could smell blood from the front door of the gym, sweet and pungent. Maybe I should have been scared, but I wasn't.

I was excited.

That is, until I spoke to Kevin.

'Mr Celebanski won't be joining us today,' he said. 'He couldn't make it.'

I was deflated. He was the decision maker.

I'd come all the way to Bradford for a glorified training session. I knew I'd have to impress Kevin enough for him to insist that John took a look at me. So I got stuck in and after the session I waited eagerly for the verdict.

Kevin barely looked at me. 'We'll be in touch,' he said.

No questions, nothing – just thanks and goodbye.

I told myself to give it time. But patience isn't the virtue of a jacked-up 18-year-old.

During my time in the home and on the street, I'd done things I knew Dad wouldn't have been proud of. Mum had fallen apart, thanks to Viv, and Donna had issues. I felt like we'd all let him down, so I wanted to do something to give the Cockcroft name its shine back.

I also wanted the recognition Dad used to get, the nod of acknowledgement and respect. Being a pro boxer was like being a god in Halifax. I'd gain that respect in a heartbeat.

But weeks passed and I still heard nothing more from Kevin at the Bradford gym. I trained harder to channel my frustration and anger.

One day, after my usual six-mile run and a few hours sparring in the gym with the lads, I was finishing up when a strange man approached me from across the room.

He was the image of an old-school Hollywood actor from a mob film, with a rugged, weather-beaten face and a bent nose. He had a distinct ex-gangster look about him, looking sharply dressed from a distance, but rocking a cheap Asda suit up close.

'You all right?' I asked, eyeing him suspiciously.

'You're in good form, lad,' he said. 'I think we could use a young fighter like you.'

My stomach lurched. *Use me for what?* The guy looked like a hitman, so I wasn't sure I wanted to hear what was coming next. It wouldn't be the first time that I'd seen a vulnerable kid's aptitudes or assets used for dark purposes.

I wanted to leave, but he looked like the kind of man that wouldn't take kindly to being walked away from.

'What do you mean?' I ventured.

'I'm talking about taking your boxing career to the next level,' he said. 'Going professional. John ... John Celebanski.'

He extended his hand as he introduced himself.

I heaved a sigh. *Thank God.*

John explained how after my session with Kevin, he'd watched me at a few sessions, unbeknown to me. Apparently, he'd been impressed. He felt I was ready for the big time.

I was excited about the boxing, but I did have some reservations. I'd heard stories about the underworld of the pro-boxing circuit, crooked and violent outside of the ring too. Just what I'd been trying to steer clear of.

But John had me sold.

'You'll be famous,' he said. 'And the money is really good.'

It was a seductive offer. After seeing Dad slog for pennies, seeing what being destitute led to and knowing what it felt like to have cold hard cash in your pocket, I was sold.

I spoke to Alan about the offer.

'It's a chance to make a bit of cash,' I said. 'I can't have you feeding me forever.'

'It's a different world going pro,' Alan said. 'Keep your wits about you. Remember who you are.'

I nodded solemnly. I knew exactly what he meant. *Don't get sucked back into that world.*

His concern was understandable; he had rescued me, after all, like he had Danny and countless lads before me.

But I was decided. I'd trained solidly and unwaveringly for four years. I'd be mad not to give it a go. I wasn't a quitter like Danny, I was going to make something of myself.

A few weeks later I signed on the dotted line and became a professional boxer with John Celebanski.

The change in pace from my old gym was marked, as was the atmosphere. They looked after me relatively well. Gave me access to good training equipment and space, coached me and made sure I was well-fed.

But there was no camaraderie. This wasn't a family, it was a business.

To the men in charge I wasn't a team member or a mate – I was an asset.

Sparring got more serious and I noticed a sting in the tails of the other boxers I trained with. I wasn't quite as sure that they didn't want to hurt me, despite being on the same team. But I just put it down to taking things up a notch. Cranking it up from hobby to potential career. Things were always going to be harder.

After six months of training, my first fight was announced. It was to take place in Glasgow in November.

'Who am I fighting?' I asked with nervous excitement.

'It doesn't matter,' said John. 'Just make sure you win.'

His face was unmoving, stone cold. I knew he meant it. The pressure came crashing down on me like a tonne of bricks. If I lost, there'd be hell to pay.

I was racked with nerves as the date drew closer.

The closest I'd come to this was fighting local amateur champion Terry Lowther in a sparring session. I'd crumbled under the pressure like a digestive biscuit dunked in hot tea.

I knew I was stronger and more skilled now, but one question kept spinning round my head: *What If I didn't win?*

Before I knew it, it was time and I was packed into a freezing-cold van with John and a few other guys for the six-hour journey to Glasgow – but I still had no idea who I was fighting.

Really?

To take my mind off things, I picked up a copy of *Boxing Weekly* and started reading.

TONY SYKES IN HOMECOMING FIGHT

I scanned the article. It was about an amateur champion who'd gone pro but then ended up in a bit of trouble with the police. The article didn't elaborate, but he'd been put in jail for five years. Now he was out and back in the ring.

I shook my head. Imagine all that pent-up anger, frustration. The article explained that he had a family – a struggling wife and starving kids – one that he hadn't been able to support when he was in prison. The fight was scheduled at £600 for six rounds, three minutes each way, win or lose.

He'd have his eye on that prize money, I thought.

I didn't envy the poor sod that was getting into a ring with a man like that.

There was so much at stake: his reputation, his family. I was about to turn to the next story, but a few words suddenly leapt off the page at me.

Scotland's Sykes…

Halifax…

Chris Cockcroft…

My heart started to race as the words floated around in my brain and slowly came together to make a sentence.

Scotland's Tony Sykes will take on Chris Cockcroft from Halifax.

I gulped audibly.

It was me!

I was the poor sod that was about to take on straight-out-of-prison Tony Sykes on home turf in Glasgow.

I sat in silence, palms sweating and fists clenched, fighting the urge to vomit with fear.

How the hell could I get out of this?

I'd read and reread Tony's stats, his fighting history and his colourful personal background. All signs pointed to one outcome: I was going to get the shit beaten out of me.

Of course it wasn't as simple as just changing my mind. The pro world didn't work like that. Money had changed hands and there were bets riding on my victory.

Just make sure you win.

Maybe I could ask them to stop at the services and then just do one? I had no money though, how the hell would I get home? And I'd go back to Halifax anyway, so they'd find me sooner or later.

By the time the towering grey tenements of Glasgow came into view, I was numb with fear. As the time approached, all my usual pre-fight rituals passed in a blur. I don't think my manager even noticed how terrified I was. If he did, he didn't give a toss.

Before I knew it, I was standing at my entrance to the arena. The walkway must have been only a few hundred yards but was stretched out in front of me like the Green Mile.

Dead man walking.

I took a deep breath and did my very best to put my game face on, swaggering out into the arena and trying not to let the façade slip and reveal the fact that I was terrified.

The arena was packed with about 300 people, but as I made my way to the ring it was silent. Not a single clap or cheer.

I swallowed over and over, fighting the urge to puke as I awaited Tony Sykes' arrival. Suddenly the arena exploded. A mob of 300 Scots leapt to their feet and burst into a patriotic rendition of 'Flower of Scotland'.

Bloody hell! I almost passed out.

They were singing a song paying homage to destroying the English in some bloody battle way back when. They might as well have been baying for *my* blood.

Tony hopped into the ring, arms aloft, absorbing the adulation.

Physically, we were evenly matched. But I could see his true power.

Desperation.

As we strutted into the centre of the ring, his eyes told me he was a rabid dog, foaming at the mouth and pulling to be let off his leash.

Strange thing was, I felt sorry for him. I sympathised with his urge to rip me apart, because I knew that this night meant more to him that it ever could to me.

I didn't stand a chance.

Moments later it was time.

DING, DING!

I pulled up my guard and circled Tony, searching for an opportunity to make contact. Almost immediately he threw a punch, but I ducked out of the way.

Weaving up and down and side-to-side to avoid his blows, I knew it was only a matter of time before—

SMACK!

There it was.

A right hook carrying five years' worth of frustration landed directly on my nose and I felt every bit of its force.

A bright light flashed and suddenly it all went black.

When I open my eyes the arena is gone.

I'm at home in Halifax and it's Christmas time.

Dad is sat facing me at the dining table, trying to say something, waving his arms in an upward motion.

'Dad?' I croak.

But it's like everything is underwater; I can't see or hear.

What's he saying?

I didn't have time to find out.

A light flashed again, bringing me back to reality and the sight of Tony Sykes' fist flying towards me again.

Shit – move, Chris…

But he was too quick. His fist landed directly in the centre of my forehead and I spun round. Then everything went black.

I was a total knockout in the first round. I barely even threw a punch.

Afterwards in the changing room it was frostier than the November air outside. I sat in silence as I nursed my wounds. Eventually, John looked at me.

'You made a big mistake tonight,' he said, chucking me an envelope.

'What's this?' I asked.

'Your pay,' he said. 'Not that you deserve it.'

I opened the envelope and ran my fingers over the crisp notes. There must have been about £300 there.

Not bad for a loser.

Kevin, my trainer, chipped in: 'We'll put this down to first-night nerves. But if you lose again…'

He trailed off.

'What?' I asked.

'There'll be big trouble,' he growled.

I looked at him, then down at the money in the envelope and then at my bloodied and battered reflection in the mirror.

Was this really worth it?

I didn't want to think what 'big trouble' in this world looked like, if just doing your job left you looking like this.

Without saying a word, I headed to the showers and turned the tap right up to drown out the gym noise and let the hot water soothe my stiff, aching body. I closed my eyes as water beat down on my head and replayed every moment of the fight. Every hook, every jab, every blow.

Dad's face popped into my mind, staring across at me from the table. Just like he had when I took Tony's first blow. For the first time in years a wave of sadness washed over me.

The memory was fuzzy and brief – I probably only blacked out for a moment, but it brought everything flooding back to me.

What had he been trying to tell me?

I needed him right now.

I'd failed spectacularly at the one thing I'd dedicated the last four years of my life to. The gym was the only place I felt happy.

I squeezed my eyes shut tighter as I felt tears forming. I was desperate to focus the image in my mind, to see what he was saying to me.

Suddenly the veil lifted.

Get up, Chris...

He was telling me to get up.

I leant my bruised forehead against the cold tiles as tears trickled silently down my face.

I couldn't hear you, Dad.

Would it have made a difference if I had?

What about if Dad had still been alive, if he'd been there to see me fight in person?

Would I be stronger?

What did it matter? I was a failure.

I dried and got dressed. Once I was packed up, I looked around the changing room and breathed in the musty smell of sweat.

Suddenly, the gym didn't feel like home any more. I looked down at the gloves in my hand and I knew.

This was my last fight.

I carried them gently to the counter by the lockers and laid them down, like a body being placed respectfully into a grave.

'I'm sorry, Dad,' I muttered under my breath.

* * *

For the entire journey home, I was left to sit in silence, like a naughty child who'd had a bad school report.

I didn't care what they thought, though. All I could focus on was the vision I had in the fight. The pain of losing Dad was back and it felt as fresh and open as the bleeding wound on my nose.

I didn't cry, obviously.

Turned out I'd been a master of hiding my pain for a good few years now. A master actor. I just didn't realise quite how thin the façade was.

As I sat staring out of the window at the hypnotic motorway markings, I realised what I'd done. I'd stepped out of my safe gym bubble and exposed myself to the wolves. They had won again, and all it took to shatter me was a slug in the face from a Scottish ex-con.

By the time we got back to Halifax, night was falling and the pouring rain made the hills appear as towering and ominous as I'd ever seen them.

As I slunk out of the van, I turned to Kevin. 'I'm done,' I said. 'I won't be fighting again.'

'Fucking pussy,' he hissed, before slamming the door and indicating for the driver to go.

Rain soaked through my jacket as I watched the van screech off into the distance. A familiar and unwelcome weight returned to my shoulders. Without boxing, what did I have?

I couldn't go back to the gym. Couldn't lose face. I'd ditched them in a heartbeat for cash, completely sold out. And look how that turned out for me.

I had nowhere to turn to for solace. The gym was no longer my home and I couldn't bear the thought of going to my grandma's.

There was only one place left.

* * *

I trudged through the streets towards Stoney Royd Cemetery. The rain had made the painfully steep hill sticky with mud, each step requiring monumental effort. Baking heat at Dad's funeral; relentless rain tonight.

Why is it always a struggle when I try to climb this hill?

Eventually, I made it.

I took a few steps and then collapsed next to Dad's grave.

Finally sure that I was alone, I let go. A guttural sound from deep within me escaped. I needed guidance. I needed someone to tell me it was okay. I needed my dad.

'I miss you so much, Dad,' I howled into the night.

Soon there was nothing left in me. The tears I'd held back year after year were gone, so I just sat in silence and stared into the darkness.

What do I do now? What's the point of my life?

I searched the sky for a sign, a star, a glimmer of hope.

Nothing.

I'd been hoping to find an answer. To have an epiphany, but instead I found myself empty.

Where could I go to find solace and drown out any screaming feelings of hopelessness?

The answer was simple.

At the bottom of a pint.

I made my way towards the Crown and Anchor pub. As I passed over North Bridge, by the gym, I remembered how Dad and I would lean and spit over the side to see whose spit hit the ground first.

Dad always won. He was a winner in every way, unlike me.

The pub was busy when I arrived. I needed the money from the fight for rent and food so I could only afford a few pints. Even so, I sank them rapidly.

'You okay, Chris?' a friendly voice said.

The jungle drums beat loud in the boxing world, so I had no doubt that everyone in town had heard of my defeat.

Immediately on the defensive, I spun round to see Dad's old friends Gary Tidswell and Ray Mason standing behind me. I sighed with relief. They were good guys.

'Yeah, I'm fine,' I said with a half-hearted smile, weakly shaking their hands.

I grabbed the remains of my third pint and went to sit at their table. Almost immediately, our conversation turned to Dad and memories of the good old days. I could tell they were both just too kind to probe me on the fight.

They obviously felt sorry for me, and I must have looked like shit, because they bought me pint after pint. I glugged them down like I was expecting to find an answer at the end of each one.

But I didn't. I just became more inebriated.

I hadn't touched a drop for months because of training. In fact, I probably drank as much that night as I had in the previous year.

One by one, I lost all my faculties. My speech slurred, I kept dropping glasses and when I stood up to try and go to the bar, my legs gave way.

'Right, you've had enough,' said the landlord.

He was right, of course. But I was having none of it.

'I'm fine,' I slurred, missing the back of the chair I was trying to pull myself up on.

'I'm not serving you any more,' he said sternly. 'You should head home.'

'I'm not going anywhere,' I swayed.

The landlord rolled his eyes and went to push me towards the door.

'Fuck off,' I said and drunkenly swung my fist towards him, missing him by miles.

I pirouetted dramatically and then crashed to the floor, landing on my face.

And you call yourself a boxer? Ha!

'Come on, mate, let's get you home,' said Gary.

He and Ray took a shoulder each and propped me up between them.

I followed compliantly as they took me outside and put me in a taxi with directions to my grandma's and some money.

I sat mute as the taxi drove me through the familiar streets, the hills towering above the houses casting their long, dark shadows.

I don't remember getting in, just waking up fully clothed on the bed at ten the next morning, with my first proper hangover in four years.

It wasn't going to be my last, either.

Slowly, the previous day's events trickled back into my mind, despite me temporarily managing to flood them out with booze.

Tony Sykes' fists pounding my head.

The blurry vision of Dad urging me to get up.

Sobbing beside his grave.

I curled into the foetal position and pushed my head under the covers.

What am I going to do now?

I couldn't move. I felt like I had rocks tied to every part of my body, dragging me down with the weight of my failure and insignificance.

How could this have happened?

I thought I'd found my way, somewhere to belong. But it wasn't to be.

Now I was lost again, but this time I had nowhere to go.

CHAPTER NINE

The Thespian

When you find yourself with no purpose, sometimes it's easier to stay lost than accept you have no place in the world.

After my defeat at the hands of Tony Sykes, I made getting lost my purpose.

I rapidly rediscovered drink and drugs. As an 18-year-old it didn't look as out of place as it did on a 12-year-old. I could do so much more, but got away with less.

You see, to the world, I was now a man. No one could see the broken, lost kid without a dad, trying to make sense of it all.

I moved out of Grandma's into a little bedsit in town that Mum had rented for me when I couldn't afford my own place any more. My relationship with her was still rocky. Viv still had his claws in her, and I was spiralling out of control. Neither of them wanted me under their feet.

We barely saw one another.

My late teens and early twenties were a blur of hangovers, highs and drunken sex.

I had friends from the streets, friends from the gym and friends like Jonny, so I was never short of a place to go.

As well as weed and acid, cocaine had become a thing on the scene in Halifax and I was well into it. I inhabited the night.

Drink after drink and line after line, I made it my business to be the life and soul of every party. My wild ways with women and substances were starting to gain legendary status in certain circles, but not everyone was impressed.

I didn't have a job to fund my habits and owed money to friends and dealers across town.

'You need to get yourself a job,' my grandma scolded when I visited her one day. 'You can't go on like this.'

She was as worried as she was cross. And she didn't even know about the drugs.

A lot of my friends from the street and the home didn't see the harm in it, but then it was all they knew.

'You're only young once,' they'd say. 'It's just a laugh.'

Other friends started to question my behaviour.

'I can't work out what you're trying to get out of this, Chris,' said Jonny one night in the pub. 'What is it you're looking for?'

Jonny liked a drink as much as the next lad, but he had no time for drugs. I could tell he was worried about me too, even if he didn't say it.

His question struck a nerve. Deep down I knew I was lost, but I was trying not to appear that way. I wanted people to think that it was my choice to be 'wild Chris' and 'party animal Cocky'.

But I wasn't convincing anyone, least of all myself.

If the night was my playground, daytime was my prison.

Fighting off hellish hangovers from the chemicals pumping through my body, I'd lock myself in my bedsit away from the world, sinking into a deep depression that only substances seemed to pull me out of – temporarily, at least. I'd lost all the mental strength and pride that boxing had given me; my squalid apartment was evidence of that.

It became clear that boxing had been a distraction from my problems.

The nightmares that had subsided while I was clean and focused returned in force.

Violent brawls.

Friends wandering round like zombies, high on smack.

The cold walls of the children's home.

Mum sobbing by Dad's grave.

Each painful memory seeped out from the corners of my mind where I had pushed them. Once again I would wake up sweating and panting, gripped by terror.

I self-medicated with drugs and booze. It was all I knew. But after a couple of years, the 24-hour party lifestyle began to wear thin.

I was living like an animal, but was certain I was destined for more.

Dad had been a dreamer. He'd only ever done the daily graft, but he always talked about how my life was going to be different. By persisting with the mundane, he pursued *his* dream of giving me and Donna a better life.

I'd thought finding fame through boxing was the way to this 'something more'. But now that dream was shattered.

What now?

As time went on, I went out less and less. Instead, I holed myself up in my hovel, watching the old movies that Dad used to love when I was a kid. I found solace in the memories of coming downstairs on a Saturday morning to the sound of his distinctive laugh filling the house. He sounded like a wheezing chimpanzee.

One time, when I was five years old, I remembered cuddling up next to him on the couch as tears of mirth rolled down his cheeks while he watched a black-and-white movie on the TV.

'Who's that, Dad?' I enquired, wondering what was so funny.

He pointed to the black-and-white character on the screen, hanging from a clock tower without a harness.

'That's Harry Lloyd,' he guffawed.

I was sure Dad had seen it a thousand times before, but his face lit up like he was seeing it for the first time.

From that moment, I was hooked. Buster Keaton, Laurel and Hardy, those programmes were such a spectacle, so outrageously over the top.

How did they do it?

As I grew older, I learned that those programmes were the way Dad escaped from the difficulties in his life. Half an hour or so each week that was filled with flippant fun and happiness.

Now, more than ever, I understood that feeling.

The more I fixated on films and shows, the more obsessed with the detail I became. Like boxing, I could see this slapstick form of acting was an art. It required the understanding of human emotions, of physiology and timing.

I had all of that straight out of the ring.

What's more, I began to realise that it was empathy that did me in with Tony Sykes. It was what made the things I saw with Susanna, Mark, Danny and Callum so hard to deal with.

Empathy had been my weakness, but in acting I could make it my strength.

At first I dismissed it. I'd never been into acting at school. At best, I was chosen to be an angel or a sheep in the nativity play. Once I played an apple in *James and the Giant Peach*. Hardly the makings of a star.

What's more, in Halifax, men didn't do acting. It was seen as something for girls or the gays. It definitely wasn't something that anyone would expect Chris 'Cocky' Cockcroft to do.

I'd be laughed out of town – or worse.

I tried to suppress the idea, but it refused to be shut down.

I binge-watched old classics, and the spotlight beckoned me seductively.

One day, I gave in.

I'd heard about an actors' workshop in town run by a guy called Mike Ward. I searched for the number and picked up the phone, hands shaking as I punched in the digits.

You're just calling to ask some questions. No big deal, I told myself.

As the call connected my palms started sweating. *He'll recognise your voice. He'll tell everyone! Everyone will think you're a poof!*

'Hello, Mike Ward speaking,' a congenial voice said.

I slammed down the receiver and slumped on the couch. I couldn't do it. Instead, I pulled on my jacket and went to a local pub. I hadn't been out properly for a little while. Maybe that was what I needed? I probably had cabin fever stuck inside those four shabby walls.

Surrounded by the usual crowd, with women and booze to hold my attention, it was the best place to escape my niggling intrigue about acting.

Or so I thought.

Even through the haze of alcohol and drugs, it was there, like someone gently but incessantly tapping on a windowpane.

I could see I was a fucking caricature.

We all were.

Looking around at all the bravado, the shouting and swearing and acting like our antics were revolutionary, I felt a sudden sense of despair.

There were blokes who'd sink ten pints before going home to beat up the wife, there were cheating spouses and people so desolate they couldn't have a good night without a sprinkling of party dust.

It wasn't a revolution, it was bullshit.

We were standing in the same spot of the same pub that our parents did, and their parents before them and… well, you get the picture.

Time moved on, but nothing changed in this town.

I was searching for something different. Something more.

It took three more failed attempts before I plucked up the courage to speak to Mike. Even when I did, I felt awkward and shifty, in the same way you do buying a dirty magazine as a teenager.

'Hello, Mike Ward speaking,' a voice said.

I was stood on my own, behind a locked door with my curtains drawn, but I still found myself glancing over my shoulder before I spoke.

'Hi, I think I might want to be an actor,' I said, my voice barely a whisper. 'Can anyone join your workshop?'

'What makes you think you want to be an actor?' he asked.

That was all it took.

All of the reasons that had been playing on my mind poured out. My unorthodox background, my time in the children's home, my love of the art of boxing that I was certain had saved me. Those Saturdays on the couch with Dad and now feeling lost with no idea what to do with my life.

Poor Mike got it all.

To my surprise, rather than laugh or hastily decide on my behalf that the acting life wasn't one for a fucked-up ex-boxer from the wrong end of town, he listened.

'Sometimes people with the most baggage make the best actors,' he said gently. 'They can better absorb the vulnerability of a character.'

I didn't have a clue what he was going on about, but at least I was in.

He invited me to meet with him personally at his drama school on West Grove Terrace. I told him more about my life and explained that I was risking my reputation to be there.

'People like me don't do this stuff,' I said. 'I'll have to be discreet.'

'We won't tell anyone,' he said.

A week later, I attended my first class.

I was shaking like a leaf as I sat at the back of the room, watching my new classmates file in. They all seemed to have an air of refinement and spoke eloquently. They were educated, talented, and they terrified me.

It was bizarre. I was a former boxer. Most of my friends were in prison before they were 19 and I counted dangerous criminals as genuine acquaintances.

What could these people do to me?

The answer was everything.

They could reject me.

They could laugh at me.

They could destroy my reputation, if word got out.

On the streets I had a name, a rep. I was someone. Here, I was just some tattooed bloke with a thick accent who was loitering around awkwardly. They had no idea that I was risking all I had left to be there.

For weeks I sat silently at the back of class, watching as the other actors performed scenes from famous books and plays and films.

I didn't even make eye contact, let alone speak to people. I just sat there and observed.

I absorbed vocabulary and intonation, picked up flourishes and movements from the performances.

The more I took in, the more comfortable I became. It just felt right.

Outside the theatre in my day-to-day life I felt like I was playing a part. 'Cocky the Rogue' – I just didn't connect with the old me any more.

Soon, I was so immersed in the sessions that when drugs and alcohol lowered my inhibitions, I'd break character involuntarily.

I'd started having singing lessons as a way to try and shake off my thick Yorkshire accent. As I learned to enunciate correctly, I stopped dropping my T's.

The lads thought I'd gone mad.

While I'd been exploring the lives of famous actors, I'd read that James Dean carried a dictionary around with him so he could have intellectual conversations with his peers and understand what they were saying.

So I did the same. I swapped my 'normal' words for 'big' words.

I tried to confine it to my theatre circle, but as the habit became deeply ingrained, learned words and gestures would come spilling out in the pub.

'What a lugubrious situation,' I'd sighed after hearing a friend of the group had passed away.

'You what, mate?' one mate spluttered.

'What's wrong with you, are you taking it up the arse, Cocky?' another one laughed.

Instantly I snapped back into character. 'It's fucking sad.'

They just thought I was doing too much gear.

Maybe that was true, but the coke only heightened my desire to show off the 'new me'. Be someone better, not a vacuous lad from the shit end of Halifax.

As the weeks turned into months, I went from sitting at the back of acting class looking over my shoulder every two seconds to relaxing and enjoying the atmosphere. Mike never pushed me. I respected him for that. Eventually the workshop felt like a safe space.

It took eight months, but when the time came for me to participate, I was more ready than I'd ever been for anything.

It was a scene from a play set in 1171 called *Four Nights in Knaresborough* by Paul Corcoran. I was selected to play Fitz, one of four knights sent to arrest Thomas Becket, the Archbishop of Canterbury, who accidentally kills him.

I stepped onto the stage with the other actors and took a deep breath.

You've got this, Chris.

All the other players in the scene exuded confidence and experience. They'd done this a thousand times before.

I was terrified.

My voice shaking and cheeks burning pink, I stumbled nervously through my lines, couldn't even get some words out.

When the scene concluded, I looked round the room, from audience to actors waiting for a response.

I really messed that up, I thought.

But slowly applause rippled around the room. I felt my spirits lift slightly. As we stepped down from the stage the actors I'd shared the scene with patted me on the back.

'Well done, Chris,' said one.

'First one is always the toughest,' said another. 'You did well.'

I glanced over at Mike: he was grinning from ear to ear.

Maybe I wasn't so bad after all? And even if I was, these people understood. It took time to perfect your art.

Invigorated by the positive feedback, I immersed myself more deeply in the arts, spending even more time in my grubby bedsit poring over books, poetry and films.

Harry Lloyd, James Dean and Marlon Brando were my mentors.

I started writing poems and sketching, mainly notes and observations about the things I saw occurring around me, as well as sketches of people I came across. At the same time I also continued to develop my skill of switching characters.

A pint-swilling, back-slapping Jack the lad with one crowd, and an educated thespian completely au fait with the air-kiss with the other.

Each time I took to the stage, I felt a deeper sense of belonging. Like I was meant to be there.

Although it had its similarities, acting had one big difference from boxing: self-reflection.

Boxing was self-discipline, focus and physical exertion.

You could punch out your anger as a boxer, but you couldn't look back on it and make sense of it.

Acting was altogether more cathartic. Every scene allowed me to explore a feeling, a hidden emotion or experience long-buried deep inside me.

Once it was out, it was gone.

One day in class I had to perform scenes from *Carlito's Way*. I was playing Al Pacino's character Carlito, a Puerto Rican gangster trying to go straight.

It was like Mike had handpicked the scenes for me.

I felt emotion growing like a bubble inside me as I acted out the scene where Carlito explains his past to his girl-friend, Gail.

'It's who I am, Gail. It's what I am,' I said. I felt every pair of eyes in the room on me, entranced. 'Right or wrong, I can't change that.'

I might have taken a while to understand some of the plays we studied, but this screenplay? This I understood.

I'd never meant to end up where I did. I'd just survived the best I could. I'd done things I was ashamed of and I'd seen things that had horrified me. I'd seen kids suffering violence and abuse on the streets and in the home.

I'd been lucky and I knew it.

As we moved through the scene the bubble of emotion grew and grew. I couldn't change my past, but I was the master of my own future.

As the scene closed the emotions spilled over. Shocked by the waves of emotion washing over me, I rushed back to my bedsit to be alone.

Back at home I sobbed and wrote down everything I was feeling until there was nothing left in me.

Like I'd been jet washed from the inside, cleansed.

Suddenly I realised the power of my newfound passion.

* * *

As my confidence grew, I knew I'd chosen the right direction. But that meant at some point, I'd have to break my cover.

Right now, with no reputation or circle of trust in the acting world, revealing all to my current friends would be like jumping off a building without a safety net. I didn't know who would be there to catch me if they all disowned me.

But I had a plan.

I was going to build a successful reputation in the acting world. Gain some respect and get some good gigs under my belt. Only then would I reveal the real me.

While I worked on my master plan, I more or less managed to avoid the two worlds colliding – not even my closest friends knew what I was up to. But there were some close shaves.

I was in a pub on the outskirts of town one day. It was a little place I'd found by accident that no one from either crowd had reason to be in. I'd taken James Brown, one of my tough guy mates from Halifax, there for a drink.

I was standing at the bar chatting with Browny, as we all called him, over a cold pint, when an excitable voice shouted my name.

'Oh my God, Christopher!' the voice squeaked.

I turned around and the blood drained from my cheeks.

It was a guy called Ollie from the workshop. Camp as Christmas and as eccentrically dressed as ever, he walked flamboyantly towards me, wearing what I could only describe as a girl's blouse.

'*What* are you doing here, Christopher?' he said, arms aloft, ready to throw them around me.

I wanted to ask him the same thing.

I looked at Browny. He was staring at me, slack-jawed.

Instinctively, I stepped back from Ollie and stuck my hand out for him to shake. He jolted to a halt and looked at me bemused for a second.

I wasn't surprised. He was used to Christopher the thespian. The thespian wasn't afraid of a hug. But Chris the rogue, the one he'd bumped into just now, he would have knocked his teeth out.

At least I hadn't gone that far.

'All right?' I said, my accent thickening for emphasis as we shook hands awkwardly.

I glared at him coldly, but inside my stomach was in knots.

I could see the hurt and confusion in his eyes and I felt dreadful. He didn't deserve this. He was a lovely man and a talented actor. But I couldn't blow my cover.

It didn't take long for Ollie to get the message.

'Well, nice to see you anyway,' he said briskly, dropping my hand before sashaying away to another part of the pub.

'Is this a fucking gay bar?' Browny uttered, as soon as Ollie was out of earshot.

'Fucking seems that way,' I said, rolling my eyes.

I was fully engaged in my street kid character again. Embracing the prejudice and talking like a caveman. I hoped that would be it, but Browny pressed on.

'So how does he know you?' he goaded, lifting his chin.

Shit. Shit. Shit.

I knew just one drop of poison could pollute my reputation. I wasn't ready for that yet. Caught off guard, I searched the corners of my brain for a believable response.

Then it came to me.

'Oh, just some friend of my sister's,' I said dismissively.

Browny backed down instantly. 'Ah, right,' he said, returning to swigging his pint. 'Makes sense.'

Inside I heaved a sigh of relief. *Thank God.*

That night I made sure I reined in my drinking. I knew if my mask slipped again, I'd be exposed.

The following week at class, I tried to make amends with Ollie, but the damage was done: he'd have nothing to do with me.

'Homophobic prick,' I heard him mutter under his breath.

I'll admit, that stung; it was the last thing I was. A homophobe, that was.

My dad might have been a man's man, but he was ahead of his time. His opinion was always 'live and let live'. Gay, straight, black, white – none of it mattered to him. That was how he brought us up and I was proud to have inherited that attitude, especially in the place where I grew up. But maintaining my cover was of the utmost importance. I couldn't let this upset derail my plans.

Suck it up, Chris.

Soon it wasn't just the workshop I was sloping off to. I'd enrolled myself in Calderdale College of Performing and was learning about music and art, as well as plays and poetry.

The way I felt about *everything* in my life changed. Brawls and banter in the local pub no longer entertained or fuelled my emotions. Instead of feeling bitter and angry about Dad's death and allowing my grief to feed off the undercurrent of small-town aggression that oozed from every doorway and pavement crack in Halifax, I became more reflective.

Everything happens for a reason.

Maybe Dad had to go so I could find my way here?

The words of the plays I performed and the poets I studied opened up a new way to channel my emotions. I didn't want to hurt myself or anyone else any more.

So instead of fighting or fucking or drinking, I grabbed a pen and let the words in my heart spill out onto a blank page. I soon found it was a lot easier to decipher that than the aftermath of a reckless bender, with all its blank spaces, questions and broken hearts.

I was bursting with love for my new outlet and it was getting harder and harder to be discreet.

Suddenly, my 'coming out' as an actor became imminent.

The Halifax Playhouse, one of West Yorkshire's leading theatre venues, invited me to join the Halifax Thespians and take the lead in its production of Richard Brinsley Sheridan's *A School for Scandal*.

I was taking the place of a rising star called Matthew Wolfenden, who'd pulled out of the show three weeks before it was due to start after he'd been offered a professional job in the West End.

Who could blame him? It was a way out of this town.

The part of the lead character, Joseph Surface, was significant. I had to learn thousands and thousands of words in just three weeks. At first the task seemed insurmountable. But calmly, I approached it like I had done boxing – with a passion and focus that bordered on obsession.

Daytime was for learning, reciting, repeating and perfecting. If I took breaks, I nourished myself with classical music and more literature.

Evenings were for rehearsal.

I lived and breathed the part.

The director of the play, John Eastwood, invited me to his mansion on the outskirts of Halifax to rehearse.

My bedsit was just round the corner from the theatre, a couple of minutes' brisk walk, which was handy for the evening rehearsals. Even so, I was careful to remain incognito. Every time I stepped out of the door I'd pull on a grey flat cap, a peaky blinder that obscured my face, but allowed me to see who was about. Made it easy to duck into a doorway if I spotted anyone I knew.

I was nervous, but my confidence was growing. I was ready to reveal the thespian, show the town what I could do. The cloud of depression that had enveloped me started to dissipate. I could see again. I had a purpose.

Eventually, opening night arrived.

Waiting in the wings for my cue, my heart was pounding. Looking out past the edge of the stage I could see hundreds of discerning theatregoers in their maroon velvet seats, framed by the elegant but faded glamour of the Playhouse. The lights went down.

As I watched as the opening scene between Mr Snake and Lady Sneerwell unfold, I felt a familiar sensation in the pit of my stomach. It was the same one I felt before I stepped into the ring with Tony Sykes.

Fear.

Only this time it was different.

I didn't feel like a dead man walking. Far from it. In fact, I'd never felt more alive.

I watched as the actor playing the servant scurried on stage in a subservient manner.

'Mr Surface,' the servant announced.

'Show him up,' replied Lady Sneerwell, before turning back to Mr Snake to continue their conversation.

That was my cue. My heart was pounding.

This is it, Chris.

Her words became the backing track to the blood pumping in my ears as I stepped out onto the stage. My whole body was tingling.

'He generally calls about this time. I don't wonder at people giving him to me for a lover,' Lady Sneerwell finished.

I took a deep breath, and then opened my mouth.

'My dear Lady Sneerwell, how do you do today?' I boomed confidently, before nodding towards the other actor. 'Mr Snake, your most obedient.'

I'd never heard myself sound more together, more powerful.

Act after act was performed flawlessly, if I do say so myself.

I could see the faces of the first few rows of the audience and they were hanging onto my every word. I had them in the palm of my hand.

It didn't even dawn on me that I was in a precarious position regarding my hardman reputation. I was laid bare, exposed to the bone, but I wasn't bothered. That feeling of captivating a group of people, hundreds of emotional beings with hopes and dreams and fears, set my soul on fire. No, I wasn't worried about what people would say. I felt indestructible. Omnipotent even.

Every applause and gasp, every laugh and tear stoked the flames burning inside me. It was a near-sensual experience. By the time it was over, I felt ten feet tall.

'This is incredible,' I said to my co-star Helen Forsyth, who had played Lady Sneerwell as we returned to the stage to receive a standing ovation. 'I've never felt anything like this before.'

She didn't say a word, just turned to me and smiled knowingly as we bowed.

It was true, though. Nothing had ever given me a high like this before.

I soaked up the applause and cheers, every clap feeding my new addiction.

Theatre was now my drug of choice. I was hooked and I wanted more.

A School for Scandal was a huge success and it left me yearning for people to share it with. It didn't take long for that to happen.

The success of the show meant word got around.

You heard Cocky's poncing around in some play?

I held my head high, even invited a few ex-con mates to see me in my next play, *Silly Cow* by Ben Elton.

In it I played Eduardo, a gay character struggling with his creative identity. Far from holding back, I gave it my absolute all.

It wasn't hard to spot my lot in the bar after the show. They stood out like sore thumbs, all rough edges and dirty fingernails.

I wound my way through the crowds towards them.

'Wonderful performance, Christopher, sublime,' said one gentleman as I passed by.

'Why, thank you,' I replied, graciously.

People were applauding me and stopping me to shake my hand, and it took an age to reach my friends. When I did, I was keen to hear their reviews. 'So, what did you think?'

Despite my bravado, a little part of me wanted my old friends to understand my new life.

My cousin Andy was the first to speak. 'You looked gay,' he mumbled. 'But good.'

I rolled my eyes. I guess a rave review would have been too much to ask. The fact they'd come was good enough for me.

My guests had accepted me as an actor. And soon so too did the rest of the town. Talk died down and aside from the occasional ribbing in the pub, it was business as usual. But that was Halifax for you. There was drama and scandal, tragedy and surprise, but nothing ever changed. Life always returned to what it had been.

I began to feel like I was stuck in a basin. Always moving, spinning round and round, but always ending up in the same place.

After my success at the Halifax Playhouse, I honestly thought the West End would come knocking, but it didn't take me long to realise it didn't work like that.

The local amateur gigs kept rolling in, but they didn't pay and they were only going to keep me trapped in this town, working as a labourer to earn money to live in between shows.

I needed a break to catapult me over the hills and out of Halifax.

There was only one person I could think of who'd managed it. An old friend called Adam Fogerty. Adam was a former heavyweight boxer, ex-Rugby League player and an actor.

He played 'Gorgeous George' in *Snatch* alongside Brad Pitt. His build and professional background meant he was always cast as real bruisers in proper bloke's films. No prancing around in pink tights in *The Merchant of Venice* for him. I called him to ask for some advice.

'I'll put you in touch with an agent in Leeds,' he said.

I went through all the usual rigmarole. I did my audition with ATS casting agency and had a chat with one of their agents, a guy called Michael.

'I think we'll be able to work together, Chris,' he said, shaking my hand.

And with that, I was signed.

Good old Adam.

It wasn't long before Michael rang me with my first fully paid, professional gig.

'It's a stand-in role,' he explained. 'But it's a good one.'

'Great,' I said. 'What's it for?'

'It's for *A Touch of Frost*,' he said. 'With David Jason.'

I swear I almost dropped the receiver.

David Jason?

Detective Jack Frost.

Del Boy.

I was going to be working with a true TV legend and one my dad had adored.

'Thank you so much,' I said, as I took down the details before hanging up.

I sat silently as I absorbed what had just happened. Then I glanced at the phone.

There was only one person I wanted to call with this news. Dad.

I had countless memories of being sat on the sofa with him watching *Only Fools and Horses*.

He'd belly laugh and shout 'Rodney, you plonker!' out loud. I didn't get it at the time, I just knew that it made Dad happy.

Why don't they have a hotline to heaven?

I could just imagine his face. His jaw would be on the floor.

'This is it, Dad,' I whispered into thin air, 'my big break. I'm getting out of here.'

CHAPTER TEN

Escape

It was six o'clock in the morning and the air had cold bite that took your breath away. I was shivering as I waited outside David Jason's trailer just behind the Yorkshire TV studios on Kirkstall Road in Leeds.

Suddenly a gold Mercedes rolled up the pathway. I snapped to attention like a Grenadier Guard. My stomach was filled with butterflies.

It must be him.

My role as a stand-in was to not only act as substitute for the main actor during set up, running through scenes for lighting and cameras, I was also expected to get David his breakfast in the morning.

I'd been read the list of requirements.

He likes kippers and tomatoes.

Make sure there's no old tea stains on the spout or edges of the pot.

He prefers not to talk in the morning.

Speak only when you're spoken to.

Do this.

Don't do that.

My head was swimming by the time he stepped out of the back seat of his car. I looked him up and down. He felt like an old friend and an untouchable stranger all at the same time.

My legs went to jelly as he walked towards me.

He looked grumpy.

'Now then, young man, what's your name?' he asked sharply.

'Chris Cockcroft, sir,' I replied, instinctively, like I was in some military line-up.

Why the fuck did I say my surname?

Outside of Halifax, it meant nothing.

A playful smile danced across David's lips. 'Cock-trott?' he teased.

'No sir, Cock*croft*. It's a very old Yorkshire surname from the 15th century,' I stumbled.

There I went. Keen to prove I wasn't some thick Yorkshire idiot. Like David Jason would even care.

'Anyone ever call you cockhead in school?' David asked, laughing.

I should have laughed along. It wasn't the first time someone had made fun of my surname, but that would usually end up with someone getting a smack in the teeth.

'No, sir. I'm an ex-pro boxer, I wouldn't have allowed it,' I said, still responding like I was talking to a drill sergeant.

What the hell, Chris?

I'd basically just threatened Sir David Jason. Surely I was done here?

I pursed my lips and held my breath as David paused for what seemed like an eternity. Then he spoke.

'Ah,' he laughed boisterously. 'We have a fighting cock.'

This time I kept quiet, even swallowing back my laugh at his joke.

Once again I found a routine as I worked on the set of *A Touch of Frost*. For eight weeks I was on set at the crack of dawn, David's breakfast immaculately plated each morning.

The days were long and gruelling. I ran through scene after scene, over and over, while the crew prepared the set for David's arrival.

Even though my performance would never grace a TV screen, I gave it everything I had, learned every line to perfection.

I couldn't help but think how excited Dad would be to see me stood on the set, surrounded by cameras and lights and professional actors – not to mention chatting away with David Jason like we were old mates.

I should have felt like I'd arrived – but it was far more than that.

I'd spent the last few years, striving. Pushing to become someone, achieve something. I'd thought I'd been striving to be a boxing champion or a famous actor, but in reality what I *was* didn't matter.

It was *where* I was.

I hadn't been fighting to make it big, I'd been fighting to escape.

And now, pouring tea for David Jason in a trailer on location in Leeds, I felt like I might be on the cusp of getting out of Halifax and escaping my past.

Word of my new job spread around town and suddenly the people who had been mocking me sat up and took notice. *A Touch of Frost* was one of those programmes that everyone watched.

People still had a pop, of course.

'Is he playing the plonker?' they'd mock, in a Del Boy voice.

By now I didn't care. I hadn't felt as comfortable and happy in myself for years, inside and out. I shed my branded sports-wear and grew my hair longer. My uniform of choice became blue jeans, rugged old brown boots and a big black overcoat like the one James Dean wore in the famous pictures of him walking round New York.

I didn't even watch which pubs I went into now – The Ivy House, The Shant, even the Ring O' Bells – my secret was out and it was liberating.

There was name-calling and a few altercations in the street and my grandad was now absolutely convinced I was gay.

I shrugged it off. His old-school mentality was pervasive in Halifax. People there just couldn't compute anything outside what was perceived as 'normal' for a man there.

The scope was narrow.

Boxing, crime, addiction, manual jobs, being in the local boozer.

I just didn't fit that mould any more. What's more, I didn't want to.

No one could see it, but I could now. It was killing them slowly. If not physically, then metaphorically. Crushing their hopes and dreams.

This was brought home to me one day when I was filling up my Nissan MICRA at the petrol station near Boothtown Road. I was walking back to my car after paying when I noticed a figure crouched in the back of my car.

Someone was in my car!

I crept over and peered in, fists at the ready for whoever might burst out.

There was no need. A pungent smell took a swing at me first.

I retched. The stench of shit took me instantly back to the night I met Mark.

A man with long hair and a beard matted with sick and stale food was hunched in my backseat. He looked 40 years older than me, but I recognised him instantly.

'Danny?' I said.

What the hell happened to him? He was a mess.

He must have seen me and waited until I was in the garage to slip into my car.

Maybe he needed help. Instinctively, I reached out to him. Then I recoiled. In his right hand he was holding a knife.

This wasn't the Danny I knew. The focused and dedicated athlete. The man I admired, idolised even. This was an addict, someone willing to do anything for a hit. He was a threat. A danger to me – I switched to 'street mode'.

'Get out of my car, you crazy bastard,' I yelled.

I braced for the attack, guard up, but it never came. Danny just broke down.

'Take me to my mum's grave,' he sobbed. 'Please.'

I softened. 'Danny, I can't.'

I'd barely finished my sentence when Danny raised his knife. My heart was in my throat. Was he threatening me?

'Danny—'

Without flinching he sliced the knife deep through his wrist. Crimson blood squirted from his arteries, all over the windows.

'DANNY!' I screamed.

Inside I was hysterical but I knew if I lost it, Danny would die.

'Take me to the cemetery. I want to die. I want to be with Mum,' he sobbed.

Panting with fear, adrenalin coursing through my body, I jumped in the car.

'Hold your wrist tight,' I ordered. 'If you don't, you'll die before I get you there.'

He was sobbing uncontrollably as I flew through every red light to the cemetery. If I argued the point with him now, he'd be sure to die.

He started to slip in and out of consciousness.

As I glanced over at him, I realised it was the first time I'd seen him since he'd quit boxing. Waves of guilt washed over me. How could I have just abandoned him? He quit for a reason. He probably needed help then.

I deserted him, not the other way around.

Somehow he managed to direct me to his mum's grave, weaving up the steep inclines of the cemetery, searching through the headstones that were piled on top of one another. Faces and names I remembered jumping out at me.

I shuddered. This town was full of ghosts.

We arrived at a grubby headstone with a grave-length stone border protruding below it. Looking around, that was where people usually laid flowers and tributes. But Danny's mother's was bare, just dirt and pebbles strewn in the space.

Danny pulled out a wad of blood-stained cash and threw it at me before dragging himself out of the car.

'Thank you, Cocky,' he said faintly.

I paused as the sheer horror of the scene unfolded. Danny crawled onto his mum's gravestone and began sobbing, forcing himself into the outline of the grave and curling deeper and deeper into the cold ground. His whole body heaved as he wailed like a wild animal, blood spewing from his arteries.

He was waiting to die.

I'd abandoned him once; I wasn't going to do it again.

'You're better than this, champ,' I said. 'I'm going to get help.'

I jumped back in my car and put my foot down. Sped back off to the local police station on Richmond Close. Panicked and covered in blood, I told the officer on the desk everything.

Thankfully, an ambulance reached Danny in time; the paramedics saved him.

It turned out he'd been living in a tent in the cemetery for two years. He'd succumbed to addiction just like Susanna had. Like so many had.

Homeless and aching to fill the void that the death of his mother had left inside him, he'd pitched up behind one of the old stone chapels in the cemetery and stayed there. He'd fallen out of society with no one to care for him.

Even though he'd quit boxing, once my anger towards him had faded, Danny had remained invincible in my mind. I'd conned myself that he'd found another way out. But it seemed that care-home kids didn't get happy endings. Not in this town anyway.

Was I going to end up the same?

After *Frost* I was sure it would only be a matter of time before I'd be plucked out of obscurity, lifted from the belly of Halifax's hills to a new life.

But it hadn't happened yet.

I'd imagined Danny as a superhero, but today he'd proved he was just human.

What if I failed too?

Would I end up the same, hunched over Dad's grave?

It didn't even bear thinking about.

As the days and weeks passed by, I tried to push those images of Danny to the back of my mind. But with every rejection and every day that went by without a peep from my agent, I began to crumble.

Like Danny, I forgot how to stand up and fight.

Halifax's gravitational pull sucked me back in. *You can take the boy out of the town…*

My dealer mates were there for me with conciliatory cocaine – at a cost, of course. I self-medicated my depression with whatever substance I could get hold of.

I was all but ready to give up, until I received a phone call.

It was from a theatre director called Peter Benedict, who I had met on the set of *Frost*.

'I'm directing a touring pantomime,' he explained. '*Mother Goose.*'

'Okay,' I listened. Truthfully, it wasn't exactly the role I'd been waiting for.

But if it got me out of this shithole of a town…

'I'd like you to play the debt collector, Jasper Grasping,' he finished. 'The tour begins in London.'

London.

It was music to my ears.

A place rich with culture and art, where artistic people gravitate to drink fine wine and discuss literature and poetry.

A place that wasn't hemmed in by towering hills and filled with abject poverty and despair.

Danny had a chance and he'd wasted it. That title fight would have got him out of this town. But he chose to stay and now this town was killing him.

Well, I wasn't going to make the same mistake.

I packed my bags and headed to London.

The next few months passed in a blur. The pantomime was gruelling but fun. Its cast was filled with people from all kinds of walks of life I'd never encountered before. I'd never been in more diverse company: openly gay men, transvestites, actors and actresses from around the globe. Before long I could count at least six gay men as some of my best friends.

I once again found myself with a new family, just like I had at the boxing gym. However, instead of sparring with weather-beaten hardmen, I was sipping fine wine with a group of genteel, sometimes eccentric, and always intellectual homosexuals.

I have to admit I wasn't immediately comfortable with it.

You only had to take my grandad's reaction to my new career of choice to understand the world I'd come from. The attitude in Halifax to homosexuality was stuck in the dark ages. They were fearful and suspicious of what they didn't understand and didn't have the intelligence to make sense of.

Sad thing was, it rubbed off on you.

I guess it also didn't help that before acting my only experience of men being interested in people of the same gender had been negative, sinister even.

Like Callum's story.

How he'd been raped until he bled by his grandad's mates.

Nor could I forget being 12 years old and hanging out with older men with powerful cars.

'If you sit on my knee, I'll let you drive,' one had said. He was easily 20 years older than me.

'Fuck off, you queer,' I'd snapped.

On the street, paedophiles inhabited the dark fringes, waiting in the shadows to pick off the weakest. The lost, the addicted, the starving.

Then there were the stories from the care homes, where men in power took advantage of vulnerable boys.

I was one of the lucky ones; I always had been.

I'd constructed a new identity as a worldly-wise actor, yet my small-town experience still constrained me at times.

Thankfully, once I stepped out into the world, it didn't take long for me to separate those experiences and observations of abuse from what homosexuality actually was.

The vibrant and intelligent men I was socialising with had nothing in common with the monsters I feared from my past.

As my confidence in the group grew, I admitted my feelings to Peter Benedict. After *Frost* he'd become my closest friend.

'I used to think that all gay men would try and bum me,' I said. Well, I could only go on what I'd seen.

'Chris, darling, I wouldn't touch you with a bargepole,' chuckled Pete, gently tapping my wrist.

Back in the day, I was sure I would have recoiled in horror or even thrown a punch. But not any more.

'Err, excuse me, am I not fit enough for you?' I joked, as I poured myself another glass of Cabernet Sauvignon.

The tour came to an end and as my money ran out, I was forced to return to Halifax and Mum's bedsit once again, drawn back like a magnet to the hills of doom and the soot-covered yellow stone buildings. When Dad was alive, the hills had always looked so green and lush, beautiful natural boundaries protecting our little bubble from the outside world. But now, more than ever, they felt like towering jail keepers.

They'd contained Danny and look what had happened to him.

I knew that wasn't what I wanted for myself, but I was stuck between two worlds.

I'd revert to type at home. Drinking, partying and sleeping around, just like the old crowd did. But I escaped to London at least twice a week for auditions and castings.

Each visit was like coming up for air, taking in a deep breath of culture and life that cleared the soot and grime from my lungs and saw me through the dark days back home.

I never got the parts, but I knew now that I had to keep going. I was choosing to live.

'You have to stay on the scene,' advised Pete. 'Something will come up, eventually.'

If you weren't on the scene you might as well be dead.

I loved London, but I was conflicted. As much as it attracted me, it also intimidated me.

In Halifax I was a big fish swimming in a very small, very toxic pond. It was slowly poisoning me, sucking the life out of me. But I was the BEST swimmer.

London was like an ocean filled with millions of sharks that could all swim better than me, or so it felt. I was trapped at the edge of my old life, gazing over to my new life and was desperately in need of a bridge across the valley.

I felt alienated by everything, even being in the pub – a place that had always felt comfortable to me. One time, I was with my mate, Ben. 'I'll have a glass of white wine, mate,' I'd said.

'Okay,' he'd said, laughing so hard he almost fell off his chair.

A few minutes later he returned from the bar and plonked a pint in front of me.

'I asked for a wine,' I said.

Ben looked blankly at me. 'I thought you were kidding.'

I was done. I was living in a town where your choice of beverage was intrinsically linked to your masculinity, or lack thereof.

I had to go somewhere that I couldn't just ricochet straight back from.

But where?

Later that night, intoxicated by the mix of beer and wine, I fell into bed. My heavy eyelids drooped shut almost instantly as I curled into my warm duvet.

Moments later my eyes fluttered open again. I was still enveloped by warmth, but my duvet had disappeared and a bright light was shining in my eyes.

I squeezed my eyes shut and then opened them wide.

That wasn't a light – it was the sun.

I used my hands to push myself upright, but they sank into a soft, grainy surface.

Sand?

As my vision focused, the landscape around me came into view. I could see the ocean in front of me. Around me, beautiful people were sat in swimwear, reading, scribbling in notebooks, playing guitar.

Where the hell was I?

I stood up and looked down. I was in swimwear too.

Confused, I walked from the beach towards a nearby pathway. A crumpled newspaper rolled like tumbleweed in front of me.

The *Los Angeles Times.*

I had no idea where I was going, but I felt confident. Lighter.

My feet led me to a building with an unmarked door.

I pushed the handle and walked through the frame. The room I stepped into was bright, white and stark.

There were desks and chairs, but not much else. The only place that had ever felt that stark was parts of Skircoat Lodge – stark and stinking of bleach.

But this felt different. Was it a classroom?

A door opened behind me. Footsteps tapped on the wooden floor and I began to turn around, but before I could see who had entered, I snapped awake.

I was back in my bedsit in Halifax.

I allowed the gloom to close in around me again. Where the hell had that come from? I'd known people who had been to LA to study, or just headed over there on a wing and a prayer to find stardom. But I had no real knowledge of it.

How could the image in my mind be so vivid?

For weeks after my dream, LA was the only place I could think of. I read everything I could about the place. It felt like somewhere I could *really* break free from my old life.

A place where I could hone my craft.

I got in touch with my mum's cousin Marcus, who had moved over there when I was a child. When I told Mum what I was doing, she emptied her bank account and kissed me goodbye.

'Good luck, son,' she said.

I couldn't decide if she was just happy to get rid of me, or she was genuinely supportive of me following my dream.

I hugged her tightly. Viv was still hanging around, still using her, but she refused to leave him.

I felt a pang of guilt, but what could I do?

All I could do was try and make a success of myself, like Dad wanted me to. Come back and sort everything out. Leaving the country felt like the only way to break the chains that bound me to my hometown.

The only way I could be truly free of my past and escape the shadow of the Halifax hills.

CHAPTER ELEVEN

Paradise

It didn't take me long to settle into life in America.

From the moment I touched down at LAX and I felt the glorious sunshine on my skin, I felt at home.

Maybe that's because it was such a weird place. All kinds of people from all over the world colliding in one beautiful, transient city.

Back in Halifax, if you wore a shirt that was more flamboyant than a standard check, you were the talk of the town. But not in LA. LA embraced the alternative, welcomed the lost and the broken.

Especially Venice Beach.

If art is life, then life is the art of capturing experience.

That's what Venice Beach was all about.

It wasn't obviously beautiful and it certainly wasn't clean, but its golden sands carried the footprints of legends past.

To be honest, a tiny part of me just wanted to stop striving and join the legions of well-tanned homeless folk, all of whom had come to this place with a dream at some point.

But I'd come with a purpose. I was here to study acting and break free once and for all.

Once again fortune smiled on me. A friend of Marcus' wife recommended a good acting class.

'I know just the place. He wants to go to Larry Moss Studio,' she advised. 'Tell him to mention my name.'

So I did. The course was led by a renowned Hollywood acting coach, Michelle Danner, and her previous students included John Franco, Seth MacFarlane, Salma Hayek, Zooey Deschanel, Penelope Cruz and many more.

Of course, it wasn't all glamour. I had to live and eat too.

To pay my way I found a live-in job at the Venice Beach Cotel, a travellers' hostel. I cleaned the toilets in the day and ran the bar by night, fitting acting classes and time to write poetry in between.

I'd found a place where my past couldn't touch me any more and where my creativity flowed freely. For the first time in years, I felt at ease.

* * *

One night I was behind the bar when I spotted a beautiful woman across the room. Her dark hair was knotted loosely on her head, a few strands falling across her wide brown eyes.

Our eyes made contact. I couldn't tear mine away, it was like a magnetic force dragging me towards her.

I'd been practising my American accent all day. It wasn't getting any better, but it seemed like a good way to strike up a conversation.

'Hi,' I said.

I cringed as I heard my accent: South African, mixed with Australian, from Texas.

'My name is Chris…' I started saying, before trailing off slightly.

Don't say Cockcroft, for God's sake.

As if my accent wasn't off-putting enough!

'…Thomas.' I finished. Plucking Dad's birth surname out of the air. 'And you are?'

'Adel,' she replied with a wry smile. 'Your American accent is shit.'

I offered her a drink. She was from Cumbria and was travelling the West Coast of the US while on a gap year from university. The bar was quiet that night and Adel was alone.

I explained I had moved to LA to try and make it as an actor. We were 3,000 miles from our motherland, yet there on Venice Beach we spoke for hours about our travels and studies, our homes and heartbreaks. We spoke about everything and nothing.

It wasn't that we got on, it was more than that. It felt like we connected on a deeper level.

But why? Why was she so special?

The night blurred under the influence of potent cocktails.

I can't remember the detail, but I know tears were shed.

Then she told me, and everything made sense.

'My family life wasn't the happiest,' she sobbed. 'I even had to spend time in a children's home.'

'Me too,' I gasped.

It was like a light bulb illuminating.

That was the connection.

It was the same sense of empathy and affinity that I'd felt for Callum, Mark, Terry, Susanna and Danny.

I didn't know her story yet, but I knew enough to know that she'd been let down. By her family, the system – somewhere along the way, her journey had been interrupted. Now she was searching, just like I was.

'I've lived in the shadows of my past for too long,' she said. 'I'm trying to break free.'

I looked out towards the beach and took in the stars and the gentle waves on the shore. We had all night.

'Tell me about it,' I said.

* * *

ADEL

'I couldn't hold onto the darkness of my past.'

'I got taken into care when I was 13,' Adel explained as she cradled her can of Asahi beer. 'But I'd already been born into a nightmare.'

She told me how her family were considered a nice, normal family. Her dad had a good job on the railways and her mum worked on the checkout at Tesco.

Her dad's shift pattern meant he could share care duties with her mum. It seemed like a situation most families would relish.

'We were the Joneses,' Adel said. 'I know people wanted to be like us, but behind closed doors Mum and Dad didn't get on.'

'How come?' I asked.

Adel shrugged. 'He was always tired and stressed about paying the bills. When things got really bad he'd just hide away in his den.'

'What was his den?' I asked.

Adel's eyes darkened and a shadow crossed her face. There was something she wasn't yet ready to tell me.

It turned out the den was a little room in the attic that neither Adel nor her mum were allowed into. His own little private sanctuary.

'When I was nine, something happened,' Adel said, looking at her feet. 'I woke up in the middle of the night and Dad was stood over me.'

I nodded, listening intently.

Adel paused and then she looked me in the eye.

'He was naked, Chris,' she said. 'He was hunched like a monster over his nine-year-old daughter.'

Maybe she expected me to shift uncomfortably. Make my excuses and leave. But she didn't know where I'd come from, what I'd seen.

'What did you do?' I asked calmly.

Of course she did what any scared little girl would do.

'I squeezed my eyes tight shut. I counted to 100 in my head,' she said. 'Then I opened my eyelids a crack. He was gone.'

'What happened the next day?' I ventured.

'Dad was his normal self,' she said. 'When we were sat at the breakfast table, I wondered if I'd dreamed it all. But I couldn't ask, could I? What kind of a freak would I look like if I'd been wrong? *Morning, Daddy, is it me or were you naked in my room last night?*'

Not a great topic of conversation over breakfast.

'I tried to convince myself it was a bad dream,' Adel said, her voice shaking. 'But even nightmares don't come every night.'

I felt physically sick as she told me how he would come into her room every night without fail. Sometimes he would just stand and watch her, other times she'd open her eyes to see him masturbating over her head, while she was tucked up in her pretty pink bedding.

'He always kept himself slightly in the shadows,' Adel said. 'I couldn't make out his face. I didn't want to. But I couldn't block out his eyes.'

'Did you tell anyone?' I asked gently.

Adel shook her head. 'It went on for years. The older I got, the more I understood how wrong it was. But I still tried to search for excuses to exonerate him.'

Hallucinations.

Somnambulism.

Maybe it was the early signs of a brain tumour. That changed behaviour, right?

'He never raped me,' said Adel. 'But it felt like he had. He stripped me of my innocence and childhood.'

I held Adel's hand as she explained how she'd spend nights lying awake, paralysed with fear.

'I was scared that if he knew I was awake, he'd touch me,' she said, tears flooding out of her beautiful brown eyes. 'Sometimes I would just see him stood in the corner of my room, staring straight at me through his malicious eyes,' she sobbed. 'I taught myself how to breathe as if I was asleep. I thought if I covered up any signs of consciousness, I'd be okay.'

I listened as Adel told me how her behaviour changed. She grew up quickly, exposed to things she should never have seen, and the years of sleep depravation left her wide brown eyes darkened with fear and her pink fresh skin pale and dry.

Concerned by her deterioration from fresh-faced schoolgirl to faded zombie child, Adel's school alerted the authorities.

The police raided their picturesque four-bedroom home in their nice, normal, affluent area.

'It must have happened while I was in school,' she said. 'They probably didn't want to cause me any more trauma.'

What they found was horrific.

Adel's dad's den in the attic had been converted into a darkroom and was home to a computer filled with images of her tiny, naked body.

'He'd processed all the pictures of me in his den and uploaded them to his computer,' Adel said numbly. 'I wasn't the only child on there and he was sharing the images with thousands of other perverts on the Internet.'

I was aghast. How could her own father have done that to her? Laid her out for the wolves to feast on? He was meant to protect her.

'What did your mum do when she found out?' I asked, my voice trembling with shock.

Adel stared stonily into the distance. 'She knew all along. She was too weak to do anything. Didn't want to shatter her own world. She wanted us to be the Joneses. We were the Addams Family.'

Turns out Adel's Mum had a breakdown. It was no surprise, I guess.

I thought of my own parents. Dad was our fiercest protector. He'd have died before seeing us hurt or abused. Before he died, Mum was the same. How could you move on after such a wicked betrayal of trust?

'The children's home saved me,' Adel said. 'I know that isn't the same for lots of care-home kids, but they rescued me from a nightmare and gave me another chance.'

I poured us another drink as Adel told me how she couldn't sleep with the lights off for years.

'I wanted to make sure he wasn't there any more,' she said. 'I needed to know he wasn't lurking in the shadows.'

The staff would oblige, but turn them off once she'd gone to sleep.

As she settled into life at the home Adel experienced waking nightmares.

'I'd open my eyes and be back in my room. Fear would immobilise me. If I needed the toilet I'd hold myself, because I was convinced he would be on the landing,' she explained. 'I had a routine. If I was scared, the corner of my room was my safe space. I'd curl up there and wait, desperately trying my best to make no noise, holding my pee in. All I could think was what if he sees me? What then? Eventually I'd just let go and wet myself.'

Typically, from my experience at least, some of the care-home staff were less than understanding. Adel told me how they'd chastise her and shout, *Why are you still doing this? He's not here!*

They didn't understand how deep her scars ran. No one did, until Gabrielle arrived.

Gabrielle was a new staff member and she understood Adel.

'She was so beautiful inside that it shone out of her eyes,' Adel explained. 'She was the kindest person I had ever met.'

'It's okay,' she told Adel. 'You're safe and you can keep your light on. I won't turn it out.'

In the end, staff gave Adel a police radio, so she could have contact with Gabrielle at all times of the day and night.

As Adel spoke of her, the light reappeared in her eyes. 'Her heart stretched beyond the boundaries of her job. She was my angel.' With the support of Gabrielle, she continued her education, even got into university. With her help she remained strong as her dad was jailed for a lengthy period for his crimes and her mum was sectioned under the Mental Health Act.

'Despite all that, she made me like myself again,' Adel smiled. 'The fear that had been paralysing me lifted. I felt free to learn who I was again.'

She paused.

'She was the light that blocked the shadow of darkness once and for all,' she said finally.

Immediately, the tone of our conversation lightened again. Adel excitedly told me about her next planned stops on her travels, and how she was excited to return to university the following year.

'There's this guy that I met,' she said with a twinkle. 'I think we might get back in touch.'

'Do you think you'll ever trust anyone again?' I asked.

'I'm not defined by my past any more. I chose to forget and move on,' she said.

Then she smiled at me.

'Going into care saved my life, Chris,' she said. 'I'm not going to waste that chance.'

As the sun rose we hugged one another tightly.

It felt like we'd left a tiny part of ourselves with one another. A year or so after our meeting, I heard from Adel. She'd gone on that date with the guy she mentioned and they'd fallen in love.

She'd escaped the shadow in her room once and for all.

CHAPTER TWELVE

All That Glitters...

The best thing about LA was that everyone was fucked up. No British stiff upper lip, no Yorkshire machismo, no shame. Just gloriously, openly fucked up.

People with mental health problems and abandonment issues, abuse survivors, addicts recovering and everything else in between.

Out here it was okay to have problems. NOT being broken in some way was an oddity.

It was fine to talk about your issues, too. Not just a few mumbled words over a pint that could be brushed off with a slap on the back and a 'chin up, mate'.

In LA, laying your soul bare was the norm.

In fact, it was what most of our acting classes revolved around – accessing your emotions. It didn't take me long to realise that it wasn't just an acting class.

It was therapy.

It was something back home that no one talked about. A few people had suggested 'getting help' – Jonny Stewart, my nan, even Mum at one point.

But never therapy.

Therapy in the UK was seen as a joke by the working classes. A rich-kid extravagance or ridiculous Americanism.

I knew that I needed to do something to address my past. My reactions to any kind of failure were proof enough of that. When something didn't go right, I reached for my self-destruct button. Poisoned myself with alcohol and drugs and meaningless sex.

I knew the claws of my past were still deeply buried in me, but I didn't want to lie on a couch and tell some prick with five degrees about it. What would they know about my life? How could they understand when they'd never experienced anything like my hardships?

Acting class was different.

It didn't feel like therapy. It was just people being interested in people.

'How did you get here?'

That was the main topic of conversation. All everyone wanted to know was what had happened in your life to bring you to this room in LA, to this class.

Everyone's situation was wildly different.

The rich American girl who had all the material possessions in the world, but whose parents were never around to care for her.

The Brazilians born in the favelas of Rio who'd been begging on the street since they were four years old.

And me, the care-home kid from a small town in the UK, struggling to find my place in the world.

You see, that was the one thing that really united us: we were all looking for somewhere to belong.

One day we were put into pairs for an exercise.

'Tell your partner something deeply personal about yourself. Something private and painful,' said Michelle, as she led the class. 'Make sure you pay attention to how your bodies react to the emotion.'

I knew there was only one thing I could talk about. It was at the heart of every bit of pain in my life.

It was how I lost my family. How I ended up in care, then on the streets. It was the reason I'd spent the last ten years searching for an as-yet-unknown holy grail. It was the sole reason I was about to pour my heart out to the ageing divorcee actress opposite me, who I had met just minutes earlier.

Losing Dad.

'I'm Chris. I'm from Halifax. It's this grim little town in England. That's where we lived when my dad died,' I looked up nervously. 'I was 11. It was completely out of the blue. Chickenpox, of all things.'

I felt a boiling sensation in the pit of my stomach. Rage at the injustice of how Dad was taken from me.

Fucking chickenpox.

I looked at the lady nodding intensely back at me and realised I didn't even know her name.

'I thought it was a joke when my uncle rang,' I continued. 'It was April Fools' Day. I can still remember the sound of my mum wailing.'

Heat rose in my cheeks and all the hairs on my arms stood on end. I could feel a lump forming in my throat.

That sound still haunted my dreams.

I hadn't realised it until that moment, but that guttural moan pinpointed the exact moment that my mum's heart broke.

When our family broke.

When I broke inside.

My steady breaths turned into a pant.

Hot tears began to stream down my face.

Every sense was suddenly more vibrant and clear to me.

I was shaking as I clasped my hands together.

Images of my perfect childhood flickered through my mind. The warmth, the laughter. The safety.

My home.

The only place I had ever truly belonged.

'He was my hero,' I said, sobbing freely. 'He was the best man. More than I could ever be. Better than I could ever be.'

Words flooded out of me. It was like I'd lanced a boil that I'd been carrying around with me for years. All the poison was flowing out.

'I miss my dad,' I wailed, years of desperation finally allowed to escape.

It was painful, but fuck it, it felt incredible.

When the time came to swap roles, I was like a deflated balloon.

I know that at the time I listened intently to my partner. Her name was Dakota and she had lost her mother. I helped point out her physiological responses to her pain, but I can't remember much else.

The session was the single most cathartic experience of my life. After that acting class became as much about overcoming my past as learning my art.

Fear from that night in Susanna's.

Guilt after seeing Danny back at home.

Everything revolved around experience, and that didn't stop in the classroom – not for me, at least.

Cleansed of my past, I wanted to experience more and create a new story for myself. I wanted to meet new people, touch and taste everything that LA had to offer, and that involved a lot of partying, drugs and sex.

'Look out, it's Chris Wild,' my friends would joke, as I'd slip out of yet another guest's bedroom in the morning.

The nickname stuck.

I stopped using Cockcroft and began using Wild as my surname instead. Much more Hollywood.

For my acting school friends I was an accessory, the English actor with a funny accent. I didn't sound like Hugh Grant so I was an enigma to them.

I shared their level of fucked up. The emotional damage and the trauma. What I didn't have was their money. The affluence was undeniable – you only had to attend one of their parties to understand that.

After one acting session we headed to the expansive home of one of my classmates. It looked like a spaceship nestled in picturesque hills and came complete with a butler, swimming pool and in-house drug dealer.

I was like a kid in a sweet shop as I was served four fat lines of the purest, whitest cocaine I'd ever seen. It wasn't the shit mixed with rat poison you got in Halifax. I did all four in a row, then immediately stripped naked and jumped into the pool.

This is the life of a star, I thought.

One minute I'd been dreaming of this life in my bedsit in Halifax, the next I was living it. At least that's how it felt.

I wasn't constrained by the ominous hills of home any more, the narrow-minded attitudes and limited opportunities.

I guess in a way I was just indulging my fantasies. Playing another part – the role of the famous actor with unlimited wealth – not living the reality of a man that would have to return to scrubbing toilets the next day.

I pushed that thought to the back of my mind as champagne flowed and I was served beautiful glazed sushi by a topless model with the most perfect breasts I had ever seen.

It was Technicolor perfection, a feast for all of the senses. A million miles from Halifax and the film of soot that obscured every hint of colour, beauty or hope.

This was the movie of my life that I'd imaged. Now I was playing the leading role.

Drink after drink and line after line, the party lasted for days.

I wasn't unaccustomed to a bender, but in LA, it was different.

In Halifax, you'd wake up with a dirty hangover, head pounding from the shit your drugs were cut with and stomach torn apart by the dodgy kebabs you feasted on.

Everything here was pure and perfect.

All you needed was a dip in the ocean and you were fresh as a daisy, ready to start all over again. Finally, I felt like I was in a place where my past couldn't touch me.

Until of course, it did.

* * *

The notification pinged on Facebook. It was from my cousin Andy.

Weird, I thought. *He's not usually in touch.*

I opened the message.

Sophie is pregnant, mate.

My jaw dropped and I watched the three dots bounce across my screen as Andy continued typing. Sophie was a local girl I knew. Just before I'd left for LA, I'd been out and we'd ended up having drunken sex.

I couldn't remember if we'd been careful, I was way too out of it for that.

All I remember is waking up with her in my flat.

Another message appeared.

She's saying it's yours.

Palms sweating, I started typing back. I had a million questions but I could only manage one line.

You're kidding me?

This had to be a joke.

I'm not, mate.

He wasn't. Not long after I received an email from Sophie confirming it.

It's true, Chris. I'm pregnant and it's yours.

My heart raced. How could she be sure it was mine?

As I knew all too well, there wasn't much else to do in Halifax except drink and fuck. I replied to her email.

I'm sorry, Sophie, there's no way it's mine.

A day later my phone rang. I could tell from the dialling code it was a Halifax number.

'Hello?' I answered.

'Chris,' a female Yorkshire accent snapped. I knew instantly who it was: Sophie. 'It's yours whether you like it or not. It can only be yours.'

'It can't be,' I spluttered.

'I'm serious, Chris,' she said angrily. 'It's—'

I hung up. Whether I was the father or not, deep down, I knew I was acting like an arsehole.

But I didn't want to hear it. I didn't want anything to risk dragging me back to that shithole of a town.

I buried my head in the beautiful sands of Venice Beach, lurching from acting class to party to bed, on repeat.

But unlike my peers, my funding wasn't infinite.

My money ran out periodically and then I had to return to Halifax. I told myself I was returning to remind myself who I was. Really, I was coming back cap in hand for cash.

Halifax was a stark contrast to LA.

Everything in Hollywood glittered. Everything in Halifax was grey and tarnished. Even the water tasted dirty.

Every corner was filled with unwelcome memories of my past. Not to mention a few ongoing issues.

By the time I returned, Sophie had given birth to a little boy called Bobby. I still didn't believe he was mine. I was in denial, but rather than have that confrontation, I just avoided her.

I had bigger concerns with Mum and Viv.

I'd been in town barely five minutes when I bumped into an old mate. As we'd chatted, he mentioned that he was surprised to hear Viv was trying to sell the cottage.

'You what?' I'd gasped.

There was no way Mum would agree to that. That place was all she had. The only thing left that was truly hers. It didn't take me long to get to the bottom of things.

Turned out Viv had been trying to sell Mum's house for cash. She was so beaten down by his abuse that she'd agreed.

'If you allow this, Mum, you'll be left with nothing,' I pleaded.

'If Viv thinks it's a good idea...' she trailed off weakly.

I was seething. The bastard had crushed every bit of fight out of her.

I'd threatened him myself over and again, told him to leave Mum alone, but he always crawled back the minute I had my back turned.

I knew I had to take action.

'You need to get out of here,' I hissed at Viv as I left Mum's.

'Make me,' he goaded.

Oh, I will, old man.

I made a call to an old school friend, Tommy Riordan.

'I need to speak to your dad,' I said in a hushed voice. 'Can you set it up?'

'Consider it done,' he said.

Tommy was the son of Connor Riordan, a local gangster with a fearsome reputation. Rumour had it that he'd had something to do with more than a handful of mysterious disappearances. He'd known my dad, so I was sure he'd be willing to help.

People always had time for Dave Cockcroft.

A few days later, I met Connor at a pub in Bradford. I didn't know its real name, but everyone called it The Nest.

'This man is bleeding my mum dry,' I explained. 'He's taken everything from her. Now he's trying to sell the family home. It's all she has. I just need him gone.'

Connor thought deeply for a moment. 'I don't usually get involved in domestics, you know that.'

My heart sank.

'But I'll see what I can do.'

'Thank you,' I exclaimed. I didn't ask what; I didn't want to know. Quite frankly, I didn't care. I just needed Viv's claws out of my mum's back.

True to his word, some of Connor's men paid Viv a visit. The next day he came to the house, collected his stuff and was gone in a flash.

Whatever they said, it worked.

It was like a weight lifted off Mum's shoulders and it certainly did off mine.

* * *

Knowing Mum and her livelihood were safe made my return to LA even easier.

I was looking and feeling great, living the life of 'Chris Wild, British Actor'.

Study.

Work.

Party.

Sleep.

Repeat.

All I needed now was my big break; I was ready.

I'd heard all the stories of how famous film stars had been 'found' in LA. If it was going to happen anywhere, it would happen in this city. I dreamed every night of one day being catapulted into the limelight.

Then one day, I was jogging down Hollywood Boulevard in just my shorts. My tanned skin was glistening with sweat as I was going at quite a pace.

Suddenly, a big old-style red Cadillac pulled up alongside me. I slowed down and came to a halt as the window rolled down.

I looked inside.

A man with shiny white hair and a mahogany tan not dissimilar to Donald Trump's was staring back at me.

He must have been in his sixties, but he was well preserved. Body tubby and face pumped full of collagen so his skin was smooth and even.

He looked like he lived a good life.

'Good afternoon,' I said, with a polite nod as I caught my breath.

'Afternoon,' he said in a pinched accent, looking me up and down. 'Are you an actor, dear boy? You must be with a body like that!'

Still a little breathless from my run, I half-wheezed and half-laughed.

'Yes, sir,' I said, trying to regain my composure.

'Well, then,' he said, handing me a business card, 'take my card and call me in the next few days. We should meet to discuss your career.'

I grasped the card, speechless. *Had I just been discovered?*

I didn't have time to ask questions. The man waved at his driver and the car shot off into the distance.

I stared at the card, scrutinising every aspect.

It was plain and didn't say much, just his name – Mitch – and an address in Brentwood.

Brentwood!

This wasn't Brentwood in Essex – this was one of West Hollywood's most affluent neighbourhoods. You couldn't find a home there for less than half a million dollars. He had to be the real deal. A real Hollywood producer.

I sprinted to the nearest bus stop and made my way back to the beach. I needed to get my body in mint condition. I was going to be a big movie star after all!

For the next few days I worked out constantly and deprived myself of food and water, so I dehydrated. Okay, it wasn't the safest method – Alan would have flipped. But it meant my body looked ripped, and fast.

Only then did I call Mitch, the mysterious Hollywood producer.

'Come tomorrow at noon,' he said.

'I'll look forward to it,' I replied.

I couldn't sleep that night. I rehearsed favourite scenes, which showed the breadth of my repertoire and displayed the techniques I'd learned at the Larry Moss Studio. I selected headshots and worked out some more.

I felt like I was teetering on the precipice of fame, and I was excited and terrified all at the same time. I'd done auditions out here, but never a private audience with a producer.

What would happen?

Would others be there?

Would I just perform or would there be an interview?

I was so nervous and eager to please that I arrived in Mitch's neighbourhood three hours early.

I found a coffee shop where I swigged back six black coffees impatiently, willing the clock on the wall to speed up. The smell of food was tickling my nostrils and seducing me: an orgy of chocolate croissants, French fries, tacos and fried chicken. I was starving. But I didn't give in, I had to look perfect.

It seemed to take a lifetime, but eventually it was time for my appointment.

I buzzed at the gate and was advised to go through the door and to the top floor of the apartment block.

It was 12 floors and there was no lift.

I was so hungry I could barely stand, let alone climb stairs.

Come on, Chris, this is your big chance.

I willed myself up the stairs. When I reached the top, Mitch was standing there holding a tiny dog. The thing was ugly, a cross between a cat, a rat and a koala bear.

'Chris,' he said, shaking my hand and planting a kiss on my cheek. 'Do come in.'

I was used to the world of theatre and art now – everyone kissed everyone. I didn't even flinch.

What I did notice were his hands. When he'd grasped mine, I thought he was wearing gloves, but he wasn't. His hands were just covered in hair, like a werewolf.

The dog yapped as Mitch showed me into his spacious apartment. 'Would you like a drink, boy?' he asked.

My bladder was bursting, but I didn't want to be rude.

'Yes, please,' I said.

Mitch rummaged around in his cabinet, fixing my drink.

I frowned. From what I'd seen, big shots usually had staff to do that for them. I shrugged it off. People had their eccentricities. Maybe he liked the ritual of making a drink?

'Thank you,' I said as Mitch handed me a wine glass, half-full of clear liquid, with what looked like a giant pea floating in it.

The expression on my face must have given away my lack of familiarity with the drink I had been presented.

'Martini, extra dry,' he smiled. 'It's delicious, darling.'

'Oh, I know,' I said, trying to regain face. 'It's my favourite drink.'

'Mine too,' said Mitch, playfully tapping me on the shoulder.

He watched as I took a tiny sip.

My insides lurched.

Fuck me.

It was vile.

And potent.

Between the dehydration and the starvation, this thing would have me out cold. I looked around and searched for something to detract attention from the drink.

His apartment was ostentatious. Pink cushions, leopard-print sofas and bright yellow curtains.

I asked the only question that popped into my mind.

'Have you ever seen *Only Fools and Horses*?' I asked.

Del Boy would love this gaff.

'No, dear,' he said, sitting on the sofa.

It was probably for the best.

His rolls of fat spread out on the seat like butter. In fact, he resembled a large block of lard, melting in the heat.

I was starting to get anxious. When would the audition start? I hadn't come here for a drink and a chat.

Mitch leaned forward and slipped his hand behind one of the pink satin cushions. Never losing eye contact with me, he whipped a pile of papers from behind it and waved them in my direction, like it was a magic trick.

And a shit one at that.

'Ta-dah,' he said.

I guessed it was the script he wanted me to read.

Maybe it was the 'hanger' setting in, but I was starting to lose patience. I reached for the script, but Mitch snatched the pages away from me.

'I have a question for you,' he said.

'Go on,' I said.

'How do you feel about taking your clothes off?' he said, flicking his eyebrow.

I pulled back, startled.

'What, do you mean in general?' I asked.

Maybe he meant for a role, if it was required?

'No, I mean right now,' he said.

Suddenly his face changed. His smile began to look more like he was snarling. Baring his teeth.

'Not very comfortable at all,' I said firmly.

I might not have had an audience with a producer before, but I knew enough to know that nudity was not the professional norm. Mitch leapt to his feet.

I gasped.

I could see through his flimsy linen pants that he was erect.

'If you don't take your clothes off right now, you'll never make it in Hollywood,' he bellowed. 'NEVER.'

In an instant everything fell into place. He was going to try and get me to have sex with him. He was at least 40 years my senior.

God knows if he was actually a producer or not. But his home suggested he was in a position of power or status. He'd used that to convince me that he could make me a star, in the hope that I'd let him fuck me.

My stomach lurched.

I had to get out of there.

I stood up slowly and started walking backwards towards the door.

'Where are you going?' he shouted.

'Getting out of here, you pervert,' I growled, grabbing his pathetic excuse for a dog as I spoke. 'Try to stop me and the dog gets it.'

Instantly, Mitch relented, shrinking back to the meek old man I'd first met.

'Please don't hurt her. I was just testing you,' he begged. 'This is Hollywood, Chris.'

Like that was some kind of excuse?

'Let's talk this over,' he continued calmly. 'I have cocaine, would you like some?'

He was the kind of man that trawled the streets looking for broken souls trying to find their way. A wolf waiting to pounce and have his fill.

It was a scene that felt distantly familiar, in a way that caused a tight unmovable knot in my stomach.

Where had I seen this before?

Suddenly, it hit me.

The children's home.

Claire.

The sweets and chocolate cake and girlie magazines all laid out for her on the Boss Man's bed. The promise of an easier life, privileges others didn't get.

Mitch's actions were exactly the same.

He was no different to the Boss Man, or Tariq or the drug dealers that Susanna sold her body to.

I thought I'd left the wolves behind in Halifax.

Yet here I was, staring one in the eye.

'Open the fucking door,' I yelled. No amount of cocaine in the world could have got me to stay, not now I'd seen his real face.

Mitch scurried over and obliged. I dropped the dog and sprinted off, didn't stop until I reached my bus stop.

Adrenalin had carried me to that point. Now safely away from Mitch, I slumped into a bus seat and stared into space.

Maybe the saying was true: *all that glitters isn't gold.*

Suddenly, the streets of LA that had shone so brightly to me that morning seemed faded and tarnished. The faces of people strolling up and down Hollywood Boulevard changed. Once again, I could see the wolves, teeth out, hunting down their prey. A shadow had been cast over my Venice Beach.

I was lost again.

CHAPTER THIRTEEN

Broken

After the encounter with Mitch, I tried to carry on as normal, get back to my glittering LA life – *Chris Wild: actor, lothario, life and soul of every party* – but something deep within me had changed. It was as if a chamber in my heart had cracked open.

Out of it poured a stream of worms, black and writhing before me, each one representing something, or *someone*, from my past.

I couldn't contain the blackness any more.

LA had lost its golden shimmer.

In my classes, I found myself revisiting people and scenes from my childhood, from the home, from my years of running away from myself. Things that I'd locked away long ago.

The way Callum would get beaten to a pulp while I looked the other way.

Watching Viv drag my mum from her bed and beat her black and blue.

That man injecting Susanna's vein on the blood-stained bed.

And Danny. My idol. My hero.

He'd fallen deep into addiction. Word from home was he'd been murdered in the street like an animal.

I was heartbroken when I found out. And overcome by guilt. *Could I have done more? Could I have saved him?*

To think I believed I'd dealt with all these demons. Who had I been kidding?

Did I think I'd really sweated them out on a punch bag? Or exorcised them on stage? No, I'd never addressed it. I'd just pushed it down. Deep down into one chamber of my heart and locked it away, letting it all fester and rot.

Now it was poisoning me, flowing into my bloodstream.

Trouble was, as a method actor, you didn't just revisit scenes. You had to *relive* them. Touch it, taste it, feel every single bit of pain like it was the first time.

My life in Halifax was like a wound. One I kept patching up. But it kept re-opening. Fresh and raw each time.

I still couldn't shake the similarity between what Mitch had tried to do to me in his fancy apartment and what I'd seen that night with Claire in the Boss Man's room, all those years ago.

It was as clear as if it were happening in front of me. I had so many questions. I had to know the answers.

Fortunately, a friend of a friend still had contact with her, so he gave me her number. I was amazed that she agreed to speak to me when I called out of the blue, more than ten years after we'd last spoken.

If I was honest, the image of her face just before she slammed the Boss Man's door on me had been etched on my mind for years. Claire never looked like the other care-home kids. She looked too well groomed; too well looked after. Her attitude of superiority got right up everyone's noses too, especially when she flaunted her privileges. The sweets, her choice on the TV and later bedtimes.

From what we could all see, she had it better than most. But something always seemed odd about the situation. I guess she had a different kind of vulnerability. While I fought back against the system, she'd accepted her life and just did what she had to in order to survive.

We spoke for hours, surprisingly candidly. She'd had a child very young and ended up a drug addict, reliant on heroin. She used her body to feed her habit and men abused her.

My time in LA had confirmed what I'd seen at home. These were all common traits in abuse victims. I asked her about the night I'd brought the paperwork to the Boss Man's room.

'Did you tell me the truth?' I asked.

'I told you then and I'll tell you again now,' she said. 'I always stayed there when he was away. It was a privilege he allowed me for being good.'

'I know he was there that night,' I said. 'You can tell me.'

'I know what you think,' she said. 'But he didn't touch me.'

I didn't believe her, but I didn't say anything. Instead, I remembered the beautiful 15-year-old girl she was, lounging in that room surrounded by sweets and pornographic magazines. It was abundantly clear exactly what had been happening. I respected her decision not to tell me and tried to find out where she'd come from.

'What was your life like before the home?' I asked.

'It was violent and abusive,' she said.

'Were you sexually abused at home?' I asked.

'No,' she said, flatly.

She denied it in the same way she did about the Boss Man. But I could tell by her tone she was hiding something deeper. Regret washed over me. We'd been cruel to her because we thought she was a snob, but she was not privileged at all. She had been preyed upon like we all were.

'Were you scared when we lived in the home?' I asked. She'd certainly never seemed to be, not to me.

'Every single day,' she admitted.

'Why didn't you run away then?' I asked. 'We all tried to.'

'Where could I have gone?'

'Do you think you could have asked for help?'

'Who would have listened to a kid like me?' she replied.

The realisation collapsed on me like a tonne of bricks. She was right. Back then, everyone who had ears also had teeth and, although she didn't admit it, I knew she'd learned the hard way that they weren't afraid to use them.

* * *

I soon regretted lifting the lid on my past, both in classes and through contacting Claire. Nightmares I hadn't had in years came back.

One took me back to being a child in the home, lying on my bed swaddled so tightly in my covers that I couldn't move. I couldn't speak either. I couldn't scream for help as darkness in the room closed in on me.

In the other I was an adult running away from darkness – shadows that had presence and movement, chasing me. The harder I ran, the heavier my shoes became, dragging me backwards, while I sweated and shouted until I was sucked into the abyss. That's when I'd wake up, wringing and panting.

I became too afraid to sleep. I turned to cocaine for solace. Being the token Brit in LA gave me a passport to as much of the stuff as I wanted.

'Chris loves getting fucked up,' they'd all say.

It was true. Because it was the only way I could block it all out. *It was the only way we all coped with it.*

I was doing nothing more than playing a part – the actor having the time of his life; the high-rolling, coke-sniffing movie star.

The reality? I was a damaged care-home kid seeking comfort in drugs. Hiding from my past in hours of chemically induced hedonism. Trying to find some relief from the pain.

I was no different to Susanna, Mark or Callum. I was exactly the same as any of the broken kids that had been tossed out of Skircoat Lodge onto the streets of Halifax, dishevelled and damaged.

I was still trying to escape.

Memories of my past started to collide with the realisation of how unnatural and unhealthy LA was. Traumatised people latching on to one another to try and normalise the horrors they had experienced or witnessed.

Some of the stories were so extreme that when I'd come round after a big night I'd lie in bed chastising myself.

I'd had it easy.

Some of my colleagues in acting class had been abandoned by parents who didn't want them, been physically hurt and sexually abused.

Remember what Adel's father did to her.

Claire had been born into violence and hate.

Callum had been raped by his own grandfather.

Susanna's mother left her to rot the moment she was born.

I'd been lucky. I had no right to be this fucked up. I'd had a chance, at least. More than one, in fact. And why?

I'd had something none of these people had – a family, a home and a solid foundation. Especially because of my dad, I knew right from wrong.

I'd learned survival instincts on the street through circumstance, but something else had carried me through.

Serendipity, maybe?

Or was it Dad's guiding hand?

Not in a religious or spiritual way, I didn't believe in all that.

But in what he'd taught me as I grew up. What I'd learned from his actions?

Dad might have been a rogue, a scrapper and occasionally on the wrong side of the law, but he stood up for people. Did the right thing. Where he saw injustice and bad behaviour he spoke out.

I suddenly realised I'd been looking the other way my whole life.

And just like that, I felt the magnetic pull of my hometown once again. Dragging me back by my feet as I dug my nails into the sands of Venice Beach, clutching and grasping, holding on for dear life.

CHAPTER FOURTEEN

Persona Non Grata

I returned to Halifax broke.

I was an actor of the finest calibre, highly trained but without work.

The false promises of LA had made me precious.

I wouldn't take a role unless it was the lead.

Panto?

That was beneath me now.

My arrogance meant the few phone calls I did get from agents dried up as I turned down jobs while I waited for 'the big one'.

It never came. Eventually, I was forced to go on the dole.

Dad would have been mortified. He grafted every day of his life. Provided for himself and his family.

They say pride comes before a fall. I was a living example, a joke around town. I'd made the mistake of lording it around on my previous visits home, talking like I was already a big movie star. I'd riled people, gotten too big for my small-town boots.

Now I was back, tail between my legs. A no one with nothing.

Nothing had changed, apart from the fact that Skircoat Lodge had been flattened and turned into fancy new flats. The small-town hive-mind still loved to gloat at failure and pull you back into the town's grimy clutches.

'We knew you'd never make it,' people sneered. 'No one from this town goes anywhere.'

Even my so-called friends, the ones from the street and the gym, were merciless. 'At least we respected you as a boxer,' they laughed. 'Now you're just a failed fairy.'

Defeated, I laughed along and sniffed whatever I could get my hands on to mask the pain.

I stayed with friends and family. Anyone who still had the heart to have me around.

I could always count on Jonny for a place to lay my head and an old boxing friend, Mick Rose, invited me to help him work on a new gym he was setting up. They could both see that my behaviour was masking deep emotions.

'I want you to help me set up a gym for local kids,' Mick said. 'Like the one you started at.'

'I'd love to,' I said.

It didn't stop my partying, but it curbed it. For about three months it gave me focus, but before long I fell spectacularly off the wagon once again.

I was out of control and people started to lose patience.

Jonny couldn't cope with me any more so I moved out, created a bolthole for myself in Mum's old cottage off Shay Lane.

It was a grade-two listed building, built from the remains of a ship. Outside, I guess it was picturesque, white walls and black window frames, situated in a little cobbled courtyard. Inside, it was dark, damp and abandoned, but the beams from the old ship still stood firm.

There was nothing there. Just the abandoned detritus of a life previously lived there, along with a TV gingerly placed on a broken table, a chair and a small oil heater.

Those were my additions.

I'd obliterate myself with drink and drugs and crawl back there at the end of each night, allowing the darkness to envelop me. It wasn't like I got much sleep though.

My dreams were haunted by faces from the past.

The ones who'd never had a chance and had fallen by the wayside.

Those whose unfortunate existence had been torn from the planet.

Terry, Danny, Mark.

Those who continued to live the nightmare.

Susanna, Claire, Callum.

Then there were the people who had given me a chance to be something.

Alan, Peter, Mike, Jonny and his family…

I'd failed them all, I'd failed myself and, worst of all, I'd failed my dad.

The sense of guilt was all-consuming.

My old 'friends' took advantage of my downward spiral. Drunk, I'd beg them to give me coke and promise them I'd pay them back the next day.

They knew I had nothing, but still they obliged.

'We'll sort you out, Chris. You're one of us,' they'd say.

The next morning…

BANG, BANG, BANG!

I'd jolt awake and my body would contort with fear immediately.

The wolves were at my door.

They'd be there to collect whatever the going rate for six bags of coke was at the time.

Soon I had no friends.

I had no food.

I'd borrowed money off just about everyone I knew, and every drug dealer in town was after me so I couldn't even leave my house.

There was only one place left to go.

'Mum, I just need a few quid,' I begged.

'No, Chris,' she said. 'I've already given you everything.'

A phone call to Donna was equally fruitless. Even my family were turning their backs on me. And who could blame them?

I was nothing but a burden, a waste of space, and a *persona non grata* – unwelcome to everyone.

I returned to Jonny's house. I knew he didn't want me there, but he was a good man with a caring soul. He looked in my eyes and knew I was broken deep inside. He wasn't one to turn someone in need away. It wasn't how he'd been brought up. Without saying a word, he let me back in.

Lying on the bed, buried among my covers and sobbing, I remembered the story Dad had told me as a child. The one where he came off his motorbike and snapped his ankle on the way to work.

'I didn't want to die shaking like a dog on a park bench,' he said. 'That job was my escape.'

'So what did you do, Dad?' I'd asked in awe.

'I strapped my ankle up with a stick and my bootlaces, lad,' he said. 'Got back on my bike and rode to work.'

'But didn't it hurt?' I'd asked.

'Of course it did. But what choice did I have?' he said. 'No show, no pay.'

Live or die. That was the choice.

Dad always chose life.

Just the thought of my dad caused the tears to fall harder and faster.

I'd experienced a fraction of the injustice at the hands of the system that Dad had. But Dad had never ended up like me. I was pathetic.

I felt physically sick when I wondered what he would say if he could see me.

'A pebble in a puddle doesn't even make a splash,' Dad used to say.

I knew what I was an experiencing would be a pebble to Dad. *A blip*, he'd call it.

I knew he'd find a way out, but I couldn't.

He'd made sure Donna and I believed we could be anything we wanted. Although his playground was Halifax, he'd encouraged us to peek over the hills and see that there was more to life than staying in this suffocating valley.

It was the reason I'd travelled to London and LA.

My sister Donna dealt with Dad's death in her own way. She also travelled, and met her partner and moved to Australia.

But the cold hard truth was that I'd failed. I was penniless, alone, addicted to drugs and alcohol.

I'd become Danny the loser, the thing that had motivated me to try and escape Halifax, my past and myself.

I'd thought I could live up to my father's name. But now I was an embarrassment to it. I didn't deserve the life I'd been given.

I'd thrown away too many chances. I was weighing too heavily on my family. I was broken inside and nothing could fix it.

Not boxing, not London, not LA.

Nothing.

It was time for me to go.

Live or die?

The best option for me – and for everyone else – was death.

I was decided.

Tomorrow, I would go back to where my decline started.

Mum's old house, now my derelict bolthole.

There, I would end it for good.

* * *

I must have eventually drifted off. Slipped into the blackness of sleep in yet another intoxicated haze. Despite the drugs and alcohol still pumping through my system, I woke up with a clear head.

It was a strange sensation.

I hadn't felt so happy and focused in years.

It was 30th December 2007 – my twenty-eighth birthday.

And my last ever.

I had it all planned out in my head.

I was going to hang myself.

If I took pills, I might change my mind. Or maybe they wouldn't work and I'd just end up getting my stomach pumped.

Imagine failing at ending my own life too?

No, hanging would make certain I'd be finished off.

By now, I'd made my peace with the idea.

Life didn't want me. My constant failures were my cue to exit this world.

In a few hours my burden, my problems and my lack of success – they'd be irrelevant.

The emotions that had been consuming me for months, years even, disappeared. Fear, shame, guilt, pride, anger – they all just evaporated into nothing.

I felt instantly lighter.

As I stepped out of Jonny's house wearing old jeans and a clean white T-shirt that he had given me, I didn't even bother to put my hat on to hide my face from the dealers I owed money to.

Won't be an issue much longer.

I had a spring in my step like Zebedee from *The Magic Roundabout*.

My cheery demeanour must have endeared me to some, because I managed to convince my old actor friend, Alan Stockdale, to lend me some cash. I told him it was for food and rent. Really, it was for a large bottle of vodka and two bags of cocaine.

If I was going out, I was going out on a high.

Although I'd made my decision, I was still scared. I figured that if I was drunk, I'd just drift away and the coke would numb any pain.

Next stop was the dole office to pick up my dole money.

Usually I'd be scrabbling around to pay my most urgent debt off, but not today. Today I went straight to the Ivy House, sat down and sank a few pints while chatting to the lads. I don't even recall what about, I just remember feeling on cloud nine.

After that I hit the rest of my locals, every single one.

For the first time in years my life felt effortless.

Faces old and new came in and out. Some ignored me, some spoke to me, while others stood laughing at me.

I didn't care. I was about to go on a one-way journey. A journey that was irreversible.

It sounds weird, but as I walked through the winding streets back to Mum's old house, I felt excited.

I smiled broadly at anyone I knew. Called out their names and waved at them cheerfully. They probably thought I was high or that I'd finally cracked.

But I didn't care.

Soon I wasn't going to feel pain any more.

I wasn't going to feel the unbearable weight of my own existence crushing me down, always forcing me back here. To this damned valley.

I shuffled briskly through the backstreets. I was safe under the dreary grey canopy of tree branches intertwined above me as I followed the old stone wall down to the house.

It was a route I'd travelled so many times before in my life. Always in the shadows, always trying to slip away from someone – the police, dealers, even my own friends.

This would be the last time.

Inside, I felt at peace.

It took me 40 minutes to get there. When I arrived, I pushed open the creaky wooden door, its black paint peeling away in stark contrast to the grubby white exterior walls.

I shut the door behind me and popped the TV on to create some background noise. I didn't want to risk any nosy neighbours hearing anything and ruining my plan.

I'd already found a length of rope and all that was left to do was create the noose.

I carefully tied a simple running knot and then coiled the rope around several times, before looping it back through to create a hangman's knot.

I'm not even sure where I'd learned to do it. I guess I'd seen enough movies to understand the basics.

1, 2, 3, 4, 5, 6…

That should do it.

It wasn't perfect, but no one was going to be marking my efforts out of ten. I knew the more coils I made would make it less easy for me to loosen if I panicked.

Next, I tied the rope to one of the old oak beams in the ceiling. They were damp but still strong as anything – they'd once been part of the Armada sent out to battle against the Spanish.

They'd easily hold my feeble weight.

I looked around. It wasn't like our old house on Ripon Terrace.

This place held no good memories, just pain and anger and violence.

It was the place where my life had veered off course. Where my descent into chaos and failure began. It seemed fitting, poetic even, to end it here.

I did my best not to think about who might find me.

I remember being horrified at hearing how Terry's family had found him hanging.

But I was no loss.

Terry was a great man. I was weak and pathetic. *It won't be any great shock.*

Once the noose was in place, I started swigging back vodka, only breaking to snort fat lines of cocaine. In the background there was a programme about Harry Potter author J.K. Rowling on the telly. I could vaguely hear her voice, but I wasn't listening, my mind was focused on other things.

I was ready.

I placed the lone chair under the noose and climbed onto it. Then I picked up the noose and slipped it around my neck.

By now my vision was fuzzy from the alcohol and the rough bristle of the rope scratching against my skin was almost comforting.

This is it, Chris. Time to escape.

I tightened the knot around my neck until it restricted my ability to breathe normally.

The room seemed to be spinning around me. I couldn't distinguish the noises I could hear. Was it the TV or the echoes of my memories ringing in my ears?

I guess it didn't matter.

Heart pounding, I looked down to the wooden floor below.

Just jump and you're dead, Chris. It's over.

I'd pulled the noose so tight that my breathing was already becoming erratic and spots were dancing in front of my eyes, just like before you pass out.

It's that easy. Just jump, I urged myself.

I went to lunge forward, but every time I did, it felt like something was holding me firmly in place. A mysterious force field that I couldn't break through.

'What the hell?' I choked angrily.

Why couldn't I just do it? Was I too scared?

So many times in my life, I'd felt like a hand was guiding me, nudging me in the right direction. Pulling me this way and that.

Training in the boxing gym, starting my theatre career, going to LA.

There was never any planning involved, I'd always just been driven by some invisible force.

Now I could feel that force again, but instead of waving me on, it felt like a hand on my chest fighting against the momentum of my intended fall.

Dad?

Suddenly the peace inside me was broken. The calmness I felt gave way to a rising panic. What the hell was I doing?

Spluttering, I brought my hands up to my neck and started pulling at the coils to loosen the noose.

1, 2, 3, 4, 5, 6…

As each coil loosened I felt the pressure release. I swallowed the air hungrily, gasping in big mouthfuls before I collapsed on the seat of the wooden chair.

Momentarily, I felt a stab of disappointment.

I was still alive; I'd failed again.

Then I brought my hand to my chest, the imprint of that imagined force still tingling against my skin.

Reality collapsed in on me like a tonne of bricks.

I hadn't failed.

I had tried to kill myself and I couldn't.

Not didn't.

Couldn't.

There was a reason for that.

This was rock bottom.

I'd thought I'd been there after my knockout by Tony Sykes, then the fake Hollywood producer who'd tried to take advantage of me.

But now I knew.

This. This was rock bottom.

This was the place I'd been heading to since Dad died.

I'd got here. And I'd survived.

*   *   *

It was like someone had altered the contrast on a TV set.

Everything around me looked brighter and clearer, the world was more full of colour. Even sounds were more crisp and sharp.

I collapsed on the floor, physically and emotionally drained, my eyes glued to the TV screen. The J.K. Rowling documentary was still on.

I'd never read a Harry Potter book in my life, but she captivated me.

I could sense her tenacious spirit and survival instincts as she spoke about how she'd considered taking her own life in her mid-twenties after a failed relationship and the pressure of becoming a single mother, struggling to make ends meet.

Maybe it was the drugs kicking in, but I swear that I could feel her power seeping through the screen and lighting up the room. It was like Harry Potter himself had brandished his wand at me and willed hope back into my heart.

Suddenly filled with energy, I sat up and scrabbled round for a pen and paper. Then I started scribbling, as if my life depended on it.

> *Dear Ms J.K. Rowling,*
>
> *My name is Chris C Wild and I'm an actor from Halifax in West Yorkshire. It's 30th December 2007 and it's my birthday. I'm the old age of 28. Anyway, let me tell you about the experience I have just had…*

I wrote about my acting experiences, how I'd come to realise I wanted to be an actor. How it gave me life. I explained how, when I'd been watching her documentary, I'd been feeling lost and hopeless; down about my life and career. I glossed over the suicide attempt. I trusted she was a smart enough woman to read between the lines.

I never thought just listening to you would relight the flame inside of me to carry on with chasing my dream. Thank you for being you, for being around in the same era as me.

As soon as I was done I fell into a deep sleep. I have no idea how long I slept for, but when I woke, covered in sweat and moisture hanging in the damp air of the derelict house, I felt more alive than I had done in years.

* * *

It was like I was emerging into the light from a deep, dark cave. If yesterday I'd felt elation at the idea of ending it all, today I felt the ecstasy of relief that I hadn't succeeded.

The first thing I did was walk into town to post the letter I had written. I didn't expect a reply, but I wanted to thank her. In part, she'd saved my life.

I guess I must have looked a mess, not least because of the thick red welt across my neck where the rope had cut deep into me. But it didn't matter.

All that mattered was that I was alive. Now, I had the chance to live.

I walked back to town following the exact same route that I had when I was on my death march a day earlier.

This time, everything looked different, felt different.

It was like my stomach had been tied in painful knots, restricting everything in my life, cutting me off from clarity, colour, beauty and true happiness.

Everything before this had been false, saccharine-sweet experiences and gilded visions that blinded me to the truth around me.

Walking back to town, once again through the quiet back-streets, the warren of old stone buildings and cobbled streets, the bare winter trees screamed life. Hints of green moss punctuated their branches swaying in the wind, which no longer looked grey but glistening sliver. I spotted pots of flowers in windows and birds darting through the sky.

Had these signs of life been here before?

Even the hills that were visible along the road seemed bright and alive, despite it being the depths of winter.

As I drew closer to the town centre, my newfound appreciation of life gave me a very different nudge.

A lot of people wanted to hurt me. I owed them.

I had to be careful. I valued my life now.

I slipped my hand in my pocket and pulled out a woolly hat that I pulled down, almost over my eyes.

I couldn't change the mistakes I had made, but I had to try and do everything I could to make my life better from this moment on.

Almost as soon as I'd done this, I noticed two men walking straight for me.

Something isn't right.

I picked up the pace until I reached a side street. Then I broke into a sprint, didn't stop until I reached the Lloyds Bank in the town centre.

They'd never follow me in there, would they?

I darted inside and then waited for them to burst in, but nothing happened.

Am I still paranoid from the drugs?

I began to realise people were staring at me.

Act normal, Chris.

I walked up to the front desk and gave a friendly nod to the clerk at the desk. She was sunbed tanned and peroxide blonde, but her eyes looked tired and drawn.

'I want to open a bank account,' I said. 'But I haven't got any money.'

'That's fine,' she replied, a broad smile adding wrinkles to her face. 'You just need to fill in a few forms.'

'You don't understand,' I explained. 'I'm in serious debt.'

'Just fill in the forms,' she said gently, passing me a pile of papers.

Dutifully, I did. Partially because I didn't want to go back onto the streets, partially out of sheer curiosity. Would they give a loser like me a bank account?

I handed the papers back to her and ten minutes later I had my answer.

'You qualify for our gold account, Mr Cockfroff,' she said, squinting at the paper.

This bloody name.

'Cockcroft,' I corrected her.

'The account has an overdraft of one thousand pounds, Mr… Cockcroft,' she continued carefully. She went on to explain that she'd ordered me a debit card that would be sent via post within the next week; I'd get a PIN number too.

'Then you'll be able to take money out at a cashpoint, or pay in stores,' she said.

'Up to a thousand pounds?' I gawped. She just nodded, seemingly unaffected by my surprise.

I sprinted back to the house, carried along by the breeze rustling through the trees. The first thing I did was climb back onto the chair and cut the noose down.

I watched as it fell to the floor, landing in a crumpled heap. I couldn't help but wonder if that was indicative of how my death might have been received if I'd succeeded.

Quietly slipping off the face of the earth, leaving no trace.

I shook the thought off immediately.

It was irrelevant.

I was alive and I was going to live loud. Not partying or pandering to my own ego, I was going to make amends. I was going to make a difference.

And that had to start with me.

I had to follow my passion.

I had to leave Halifax behind. So I did.

I spoke to my mum and Jonny Stewart.

'I'm moving to London,' I told them. I didn't explain why and wore a scarf to hide the red line that still marked the skin on my neck.

'Go for it,' said Jonny. 'This town isn't doing you any favours.'

It was time for me to let the wound of my past heal.

I was ready to go. I was ready to let the blood flow and embrace it. Understand what the pain was and deal with it.

But I couldn't do it here. The risk of reinfection was too great.

There was one place I had to visit before I left: the old gym.

I climbed up the creaky steep staircase to the top floor of the boxing gym. The boxing posters showing famous fights from years gone by were peeling off the walls and covered with dust, Danny's face still dominating every inch of them.

The gym itself was empty and a mess, but that smell still hung in the air.

Sweat, adrenalin, survival.

Alan had retired years ago. No one gave the place the love it deserved any more. I picked up a brush and started to sweep the floor, slowly and rhythmically until it began to resemble the place I'd once loved so much.

As I swept, I spotted a pair of boxing gloves on the side of the ring. I hadn't worn a pair since my fight with Tony Sykes, almost a decade earlier. I pulled them on and laced them up.

As I approached the bag I inhaled deeply, the scent of the gym igniting a thousand memories in my mind.

Danny appeared in the corner on the speedball in front of the window, the green hills visible through the soot-covered glass lurking over his shoulder.

This town killed him.

Alan was nearby on the pads, teaching some scrawny-looking street kid how to throw a left, right, left.

A kid just like me. I wonder if he made it out?

Before I knew it, I was back in the room, punching forcefully and sweating profusely until I was gasping for breath and clinging onto the bag.

Sadness washed over me.

I'm sorry, Danny.

A few days after my debit card arrived, the PIN number dropped through my letterbox.

Time to go.

I packed some clothes, toiletries and a copy of *Hamlet*, and headed to the bus station. There I withdrew £350 from the nearest cashpoint and jumped on the 564 to London.

This time I knew it was for good. That piece of emotional elastic that had been attached to me for so many years had been cut. It had been cut the moment I returned to Mum's and cut that noose down.

I had escaped the town, now it was time to live.

CHAPTER FIFTEEN

London Calling

Away from the oppressive hills of Halifax, free from the footsteps of my childhood – and my father's before mine – with my newfound will to live, London was a sea of opportunity.

This time I wasn't running; I was evolving.

The eight-hour National Express coach trip down to Victoria Station had given me plenty of time to think. To work out my strategy and make sure that this time I didn't waste my umpteenth chance. Even cats only have nine lives. Who knew if I would get another one?

It had taken standing on the edge of death to make me realise that I couldn't run away from my past. Nor could I bury it or mask it with drink and drugs.

My past – Halifax, my life on the streets, the care home – was a wound. Wounds needed time and attention to heal.

You'd always carry the scars, but you'd be able to move on in a positive way. Ignore them and you risked an infection that would seep into your blood and poison your whole being.

The latter hadn't led me to a good place. So I made a promise to myself.

I was going to tend my wound. I was going to deal with my past. Understand when the failures weren't mine and make peace with the times when they were.

Humility was a good starting point.

When I thought back to the lives of Callum, Mark, Danny, Terry, Susanna and even Adel, I knew I was blessed.

The reality is that they were dead before they were even born. Born into broken worlds of cyclical abuse and violence, failed by a system that was supposed to protect them, they never stood a chance.

In the homes, the majority found uninterested care staff working for a payday in a culture of fear and silence, controlled by powerful men like the Boss Man. Eager to protect their own lives – when they should have been protecting ours – they bowed to the authorities and became their henchmen.

The tiny amount of care workers who did give a damn, the Mr Jacksons and Gabrielles of the world, well, they couldn't save everybody. Especially not after the system unceremoniously booted you out into the world at 16.

That's when the wolves would be waiting.

I was different.

Although a tragic twist of fate meant my family ended up broken, it was never going to be possible for me to fall as far as they had. I'd grown up in a home filled with love and laughter. We didn't have much, but we had one another.

Much of this, I credited to Dad.

But I couldn't forget Mum either.

Even after Dad died and Viv got his claws into her, Mum still did her best to support me. I guess in my years of anger and despair, I'd forgotten her pain. Poisoned by my infected wound, I only saw my own.

Her and Dad were a proper Romeo and Juliet. Losing him broke her heart in a way few people could understand. It was like she lost part of her own being.

I thought she was weak for letting Viv into her life, but I realised then that he had been poisoning her. But she survived. Why? Because of her own strength and her family's love.

I knew we would never return to those blissfully happy days on Ripon Terrace, her and Dad watching peacefully from our front wall as Donna and I played with other kids from the street on the grassy, green park across the road.

But deep down I felt my love and respect for her return.

Without her, I wouldn't have had the strength to pick myself up at rock bottom and give life another go.

It's a family trait.

That said, I realised the Cockcroft name weighed heavy on me. Others expected me to live up to my dad's hardman reputation; I expected it of myself. I thought about having more kids of my own. Even if we lived on the moon I was sure the burden of the family name would catch up with them somehow.

As much as I loved my dad and everything he stood for, I didn't want anyone to ever have to carry that weight again.

It stops with me.

I changed my name legally to Chris Wild.

* * *

Life in London got off to a great start. My friend Peter Benedict came up trumps again and introduced me to a friend of his who had a spare room in a luxury flat in Clapham and was looking for a lodger.

Mike Baldwin was flamboyant, warm and the most intellectual man I had ever met. Already in his late seventies when I arrived, it was like he'd lived a million lifetimes.

He'd been a costume designer who had worked with some of the biggest music stars in the world, including the Beatles, Freddie Mercury and Tina Turner. But his talents didn't end there – throughout his life, he'd been a writer, actor, photographer, illustrator, interior designer, theatrical jewellery maker, choreographer, model agent, theatrical agent *and* he'd even managed a male strip club in the 1970s.

I have to admit that I was a bit nervous meeting him.

He was looking for another lodger to join him and his other housemate – a male stripper who everyone knew as 'Foxy G'.

'He's just looking for someone creative and energetic,' said Pete. 'Someone who'll inject fun into the household.'

It was a million light years from my life in Halifax, but I hoped I fitted the bill.

'Hi, I'm Chris Wild,' I said, on the day I met Mike.

'Hello, beautiful,' he smiled, his sonorous voice ringing around the room. 'I'm Mike Baldwin, darling.'

He was very big, but carried it well. He walked elegantly with an old cane that helped him balance his weight. I liked him instantly.

It seems the feeling was mutual, as he offered the room to me. It was small with a single bed, but it was in Zone Two and the rent was minimal – I just had to help Mike with day-to-day housekeeping and chores.

I didn't mind.

I'd left my ego back in Halifax. I was starting again from the bottom. Although, on the surface, my new pad suggested otherwise.

I found work first as a waiter at a boutique restaurant just round the corner from Mike's. Before long, I was poached to be manager of an infamous gastropub in central London. I had a knack for understanding people, making them feel welcome and making them want to come back.

Of giving them somewhere to belong.

The pub was frequented by a broad client base, from day-tripper tourists and office workers to politicians, TV personalities and police chiefs.

The pub was renowned for its drug-fuelled lock-ins. After-hours parties where I'd have to engage in cigar smoking, shit talking nonsense and hours of boring conversations with celebrities stuck in monotonous marriages and dreaming of infidelity.

The things I saw during those parties would be enough to fill a tabloid rag for 20 years. I'd be lying if I said my partying ways were behind me – I still drank and took drugs recreationally, but I was no longer trying to mask anything.

If I was honest, the best times I had were those spent with Mike, learning about his life and being educated by him.

He taught me a new word every day. Soon I didn't need to carry my dictionary with me, my mind was broadened and my confidence burgeoning.

He had me reading William Faulkner, Virginia Woolf, George Orwell, Ernest Hemingway, Noël Coward, Emily Brontë… the list went on.

'I'd still be on colouring books if it wasn't for you,' I joked one day.

'Don't be silly, darling,' he'd smile.

Of course I had bad days. Times when my dark past would return to haunt me, or the previous night's hangover would throw me into a chemically induced depression. But rather than hold it in, or mask it with another line of coke, I'd offload to Mike and he'd put it all in perspective.

'Fuck it, darling. Who cares? You're better than all that,' he'd say.

His philosophy rubbed off on me.

I worked hard and played hard, while continuing to pursue my dream to become an actor. The pub paid the bills; the acting fed my soul.

Early on, I was offered a small part playing a boxer in a film called *Shank*. It was set in futuristic London and followed a teenage gang out to avenge the murder of one of their own. The film broke no records, but it made a headline back home:

CHRIS BEATS DRUGS TO LAND ROLE IN
NEW GANGSTER MOVIE SET IN FUTURE

It was a great start, but the reality of being an actor soon hit home. Getting parts was hard – you received so many rejections. At times it got too much.

One particular day, about four months after I had moved to London, after yet another rejection I was contemplating if it was all worth it when the post arrived. In it there was a bunch of letters that had been forwarded from my Halifax address.

One stood out. It was in a high-quality cream envelope – so not a bill or circular, and definitely not a letter from any of my family.

I opened it and pulled out the single sheet of paper. The letter was printed on the same heavy paper, bordered in navy blue and bearing a gold stamp at the top of the page.

A gold owl?

I read the first line and gasped.

'Dear Chris, thank you very much for your letter of 30th December – your birthday in fact – and I am so sorry it has taken me this long to answer it.'

I knew instantly who it was from – J.K. Rowling.

My eyes absorbed each word, where she sympathised with the situation I had found myself in and explained how she'd coped with feeling like there was no hope. Her words reinvigorated me.

'Keep acting. The only true happiness for people like us is to do the thing we were born to do. Everything else will fall into place around you. Good Luck.'

People like us. Fighters. Scrappers.

I framed the letter and placed it on my bedside table, and read it three times a day for inspiration. Weeks turned into months and the months into years. I had a few ill-fated relationships, dipped my pen in the company ink as it were, but they all ended in tears. I worked hard in the pub and continued auditioning for everything and anything, took on a few small parts.

I had faith in J.K. Rowling's words.

Keep acting. Everything else will fall into place around you...

London was so much more diverse and vibrant than Halifax. I'd once been afraid of giving up my place as the big fish dominating the small pool, coming to an ocean full of much bigger fish, but now I relished it.

It wasn't the celebrities and politicians that made the infamous pub interesting. It was the unknown customers with real lives and real problems, people like me with a past.

Over the years, many that I met had been in care. But one stood out.

Before we even spoke, I knew we shared an experience. It was in his eyes, slightly darker and slightly sadder than the other revellers in the bar.

His name was John. He was a lawyer from Scotland with a passionate love of musical theatre. He'd been in London for work, but had decided to stay for a few days extra to take in some shows.

'Do you have family down here?' I'd enquired. Pretty standard pub chat.

John just shook his head. 'I don't have any family, just lots of wonderful friends.'

It wasn't a response to shut down questions. This was an invitation. This man wanted to talk. I topped up his red wine and refused his attempt to pay.

* * *

JOHN

'It made me determined to make something of my life.'

'My mum wasn't a bad woman,' John said. 'She was sick. She had schizophrenia and was overweight to the point where she was bedridden.'

It was the early nineties and a time when mental health issues weren't taken as seriously as they are today – in fact, they were barely spoken about.

'I was her carer because she couldn't do anything for herself,' he said. 'It was a lot of responsibility. I missed a lot of school, but I didn't mind. She was my mum and she needed me.'

John's childhood was hard, but there was one glimmer of joy that he and his mother shared.

'Mother loved *The Sound of Music*,' he smiled, happy memories lighting up his dark eyes. 'Any musicals, really, but that one in particular. I'd curl up on her bed with her and we'd sing our hearts out.'

But, one day, social services found out that John was acting as his mother's carer.

'Apparently, it was called social neglect if a child looks after a parent,' he said. 'But there were no support services, so what choice did I have?'

John's care and devotion to his mother landed him in a children's home. The system decided that she was incompetent and lazy, fabricating her mental illness to profitably gain from the little bit more cash you get with disability benefits.

'They said she was just fat and more than capable of caring for me. Said she was feeding me shit because I was fat too,' he laughed. 'But it was me doing most of the cooking for both of us.'

'Did you have any choice about going into care?' I asked.

'There was just me and Mum. Nobody else.' He shrugged. 'I asked if we could get some home help instead, but that wasn't convenient for them financially.'

It was cheaper to put him in a home.

Short and rotund for his age, John was an instant target for care-home bullies.

'I hated the place because it wasn't a home. It wasn't my home,' he said, sipping his wine pensively. 'I was different to the others. They were born into a different world. My mum loved me, and I loved her. Our circumstances were unfortunate. She couldn't help being sick.'

My heartbeat picked up its pace. I thought of my mum and dad, of how I felt in Skircoat Lodge. That wasn't my home either.

'Was it really bad?' I asked. 'I was lucky, others in my home suffered a lot more.'

John went on to tell me how the kids mocked his size and played humiliating games at his expense: find-a-fatty, pick-on-a-fatty, twist-a-fatty's nipples…

'Tuesdays were the worst,' he said. 'That was shit-dunking day. They'd force my head down a toilet full of freshly deposited shit. I wasn't allowed up until I'd successfully managed to pick up a turd with my mouth.'

Instinctively, I retched, before apologising profusely.
He'd actually lived this.

'It's fine,' he smiled. 'My initial reaction was the same too. At first I struggled, I fought and screamed, but that just made it worse. So I resigned myself.'

'You did it?' I asked.

'The first two times I passed out, holding my breath to try and block out the putrid stench. They just kept putting me back in. The third time, I did it. After that I went all in – I started to swallow the shit, lick it, come back up with it all over my face and laugh hysterically at them,' he said. 'What kind of person eats shit? A crazy person who's had *enough* shit. That's who.'

I was speechless. But I understood. It was reverse psychology: he wanted to show them he wasn't afraid.

'They thought I was mentally unwell and became a little apprehensive of me after that,' he said.

But the bullying didn't stop. In fact, members of staff joined in, heckling the bullies on as they rode around the grounds on his back like a pig while he was forced to make grunting noises.

'When I told the housemaster I was being bullied I was told to "grow some balls",' he said, anger flickering in his eyes. 'Can you imagine? I was a child who had just been torn away from his mother.'

I understood completely.

John gave up asking for help and put his head down. He took the bullying and said nothing. But inside a fire was burning. He knew a life of love and compassion and he wasn't going to let the home break him.

On his thirteenth birthday, his mother committed suicide. He received a notification from social services two weeks later, along with a birthday card from her.

> *Dear John,*
>
> *Today is your birthday, Happy Birthday. I lit 13 candles to celebrate your birth. I'm sorry I can't be with you as I am sick. You're a good boy. Remember that. Please make sure you change your socks every day, brush your teeth, wash, and say a prayer for me as I do you.*
>
> *Love always, Mum.*

The letter became John's driving force. He tolerated the abuse and focused on the benefits of the home. Three square meals a day and the chance to go to school.

'All around me kids were ending up on the streets, in jail or with substance issues. I knew my mother didn't want that for me, so I didn't let it happen.'

'Do you begrudge the system?' I asked.

'For what happened to Mother, yes. They didn't understand her illness, or at least they didn't care enough to. She could have still been here today. Maybe we would have been reunited,' he said wistfully.

'And for you?' I probed.

'Not really,' he said. 'I understand why they put me in care. If I'd stayed with Mother, I'd have missed out on a lot of things. I can see now that she *wasn't* able to care for me, but I don't blame her either. It just made me determined to make something of my life, so I did.'

Turns out he used his education well. Managed to get a degree and become a lawyer specialising in helping victims of child abuse.

I had no idea such a thing existed.

'What I see day-to-day makes it even more clear to me that the home I was in was more guilty of child abuse than my mother ever was,' he said.

'Does it still happen today?' I asked.

'Things are changing, but there are still too many vulnerable children suffering as a result of a failed system,' he said. 'That's for sure.'

CHAPTER SIXTEEN

A Place to Belong

John's story kick-started something inside of me. I was taken aback by the clarity of his emotions towards his time in care. I recognised our similarities – we both came from loving homes – and our differences – he'd suffered far more in care than I had. But I was so impressed at how he had turned his pain and suffering into something so positive.

What could I do to make a difference?

I'd certainly never be a lawyer, but maybe I could use my acting in some way?

I shook my head.

What a daft idea.

I put the thought to the back of my mind, but my attitude switched. I cut back my party habits and got myself back in the gym. I still liked my job, but all of a sudden the social scene became a lot less seductive and enjoyable. It started to feel vacuous. Just another place for broken people to hide.

I felt like I needed more, a true purpose.

A few weeks later, *more* walked into that pub and into my life.

I was hosting a comedy night that was run by one of our regular comedians. His wife worked in fashion and she'd brought a whole load of her friends with her. They all looked like they'd stepped straight off the pages of *Vogue* and ordi-narily, I'd have been like a kid in a sweet shop.

But not that night, that night my eyes were drawn only to one woman.

It was her eyes that got me. Beautiful and bright, they were so wide that I physically felt her gaze envelop me.

She was laughing and talking with friends, pouring wine and flicking her long, dark hair absent-mindedly away from her flawless olive complexion.

I'd never seen a woman that looked so alive, so at ease in her own skin.

She glanced over and spotted me staring. I sucked in a sharp intake of breath.

Shit.

Quickly, I spun back round to the bar, gasping for breath.

Be cool, Chris.

Nothing escaped the notice of my team.

'You okay there, Chris?' one of the bartenders smirked.

They were in no doubt as to who had caught my eye, so I didn't try to hide it.

'Where do you think she's from?' I pondered, gazing over at her: a vision of perfection, with fastidiously applied make-up and chic, sparkling nails.

Arabian, maybe? Egyptian? Palestinian? I thought, as I walked towards her table. I had to know; I had to speak to her.

'Excuse me,' I blurted out.

The beauty turned to me with a surprised expression on her face and a waft of Coco Mademoiselle drifted towards me.

Bloody hell, she was even more stunning up close, and that fragrance…

'Yes?' she replied politely.

I composed myself, despite the aroma of Chanel teasing my senses.

'Can I ask where you're from?' I said, my voice trembling slightly with nerves.

'I'm Greek Cypriot,' she smiled.

'Ah, you're Greek,' I said, my curiosity now sated.

Big mistake. A look of anger crossed her face.

'I said I was Greek Cypriot,' she snapped.

I was stunned and not entirely sure what I'd done wrong, but I got the feeling I'd just insulted generations of her family. I pulled a seat up alongside her and fumbled around for an apology.

'I… I… I…' I stuttered, unsure where to start.

I needn't have worried. She knew exactly where to start. It was a verbal slam down, full of detailed historical facts and expressive hand gestures. Her intellect seduced me even more than her looks.

It took all I had to tear myself away from her, but I had an evening to host and the show was about to start. I excused myself and walked back towards the bar. As I did so, I caught a glimpse of myself in the mirror.

I gasped in horror.

I was wearing a Gap T-shirt so tight that it looked like it had been sprayed onto my skin. It wasn't my intended look, but the top had shrunk in the wash and I'd put on a bit of muscle.

I looked ridiculous.

There was no way that—

My brain stopped mid-flow.

Dammit, Chris, you didn't even get her name!

No, this modern-day Aphrodite couldn't possibly be attracted to me.

Tail between my legs, I went back to my work until the interval.

As the mob stampeded to the bar for top-ups, I spotted her again. An angelic apparition among a sea of thirsty faces.

What happened next was like an out-of-body experience. I could only enjoy the ride my brain was, for some reason, taking me on, powerless to stop it. I waltzed cockily over to her, lassoed in by her beaming smile. Then I opened my mouth.

'I forgot to tell you I'm Irish,' I said, in the broadest Northern Irish accent I'd ever heard. 'What can I get you to drink?'

Why the hell did you tell her that?

Okay, so I *was* third generation Irish, but I'd never even set foot in the country.

And you weren't Irish when you were speaking to her before.

I watched in horror from my out-of-body vantage point as I pratted about.

You're blowing this, Chris…

I could almost hear my dad mimicking Del Boy. *'Chris, you dipstick.'*

Before I knew it, I was hiding in the kitchen, trying to cool down by the fridges.

What the hell was this?

I'd felt lust before. Been driven wild and left speechless by women.

But this was something else entirely.

And I'd almost certainly blown it.

Or so I thought, until I returned to the bar and was approached by another woman. I recognised her from the group.

'Her name is Androulla,' she said smiling. 'Androulla Ashikka. You should ask her out. She likes you.'

I shook my head in disbelief as her friend walked back to her seat for the second part of the show.

Androulla Ashikka.

Her name rolled off my tongue. It was the most beautiful sound I'd ever heard.

Was there anything about this woman that wasn't celestial?

It was clear I wasn't going to regain my composure that night.

And I was still wearing this ridiculous T-shirt.

So instead of approaching her again, I just kept the free drinks flowing over to her party, sending my number over to her with her final drink.

As she left, she looked over her shoulder and smiled at me.

I felt like I'd been shot. Must have been the Cupid's arrow people always speak of.

All I could do after that was wait. I'd left our fate in her heavenly hands.

It's an understatement to say that I was a wreck.

I watched my phone day in and day out, willing a response. For five days nothing came. Then finally…

BEEP.

My hands shook as I clicked the message open.

Sorry I haven't been in touch, I've been busy with work.

It didn't say much, but it meant that we were on and I couldn't have been happier. We messaged back and forth for days, finally setting a date to meet up.

Still, fortune didn't seem to be on my side. I had to cancel the first date when I couldn't get anyone to cover my shift at work. A second date, I got sick and once again had to let her down. Finally, we arranged to meet on New Year's Day,

1st January 2012. I knew that if I missed a third date, I wouldn't be getting another chance.

So you'd have thought that, since I was working New Year's Eve in the infamous pub, I'd have done my shift and gone home, got my beauty sleep.

Played it cool.

As if. I was Chris Wild.

I woke up at 2pm on New Year's Day with a throbbing head and a nose stuffed with drug bogies. I'd been working – and partying – until 6am and had no idea how I'd got home.

Mike made me a cup of tea and a slice of toast.

'You've got your big date today,' he said. 'Up and at 'em!'

I had five hours until I was due to meet Androulla.

Come on, Chris.

I tried a bath, a Sunday roast and 'hair of dog' in the form of two pints of lager, but nothing was shifting the fug of the night before. I looked shocking – sallow skin and eyes like piss holes in the snow.

I was nervous too. In the weeks that had passed since we first met, I'd heard she'd been asking around about me, digging to find out where I'd come from, if I was to be trusted.

She was a smart girl. A smart girl who could have anyone, so why would she risk wasting her time on a loser like me?

God knows what people had told her. While I'd left my life in Halifax behind, I'd been honest about my origins. The kind of life I'd lived.

And on this day I looked like I still lived the life of a scumbag on the streets of Halifax.

What would a goddess with a successful career in fashion want with me?

I called my mate Anthony King for some advice. In a way, I was probably trying to self-sabotage, to circumvent the rejection before it happened. I'd told him all about Androulla and even showed him a picture.

'I'll just call her and explain it was a rough shift,' I reasoned. 'She'll understand, right?'

'No chance. Three strikes and you're out,' he said. 'You'll never meet a girl like this again, I promise you, Chris. Don't mess this up.'

He was right.

I made a decision. It was clear she'd done her homework. If she didn't like what she found, well, what could I do?

I was too tired to fight it.

I waited and waited outside in the cold. The agreed time of seven thirty came around and there was still no sign of her.

I'd blown it. She wasn't coming.

I was about to turn and walk away, when I heard the precise click of expensive heels. I looked up and saw her face beaming at mine.

'I'm sorry I'm late,' she gasped. 'I stopped to get you this.'

She extended her arms and I looked down. Cupped in her hands was a pretty pink box tied with a delicate ribbon. Inside was a single cake.

'It's a cupcake for your birthday,' she said.

She'd remembered my birthday? My heart felt as if it was about to burst. It was such a small gesture, but it told me all I needed to know about her heart. She was loving, giving, perfect.

I threw my arms around her in a warm embrace.

'I love you,' I said.

I spoke the words so tenderly that they barely left my lips, tumbling into her sweet-scented hair as I hugged her.

'Pardon?' she said.

'I said thank you,' I replied quickly.

Play it cool, Rodney.

We sat down and ordered drinks. We'd barely taken a sip when she took a deep breath and spoke.

'Right, Chris,' she said. 'I just want you to know that I know all about you.'

My stomach sank. *Here we go. This was a pity drink, wasn't it?*

'I want to make it clear from the outset. I'm not into drugs, or excessive partying. I *certainly* don't do being a "fuck buddy" and I just want to draw the boundaries now,' she said. 'Can I ask you some questions?'

I paused for a moment, filled with trepidation. Then I heaved a sigh.

Fuck it, why not?

'Of course,' I said.

The questions were personal and intrusive. For a moment I hesitated. I could lie or soften the truth. But what would be the point of that? I'd already decided I wanted to marry this woman. You can't build a marriage on lies.

I let her hit me with them.

Have you taken drugs? Do you now? How often?

Yes. Yes. Quite a lot, not as much as in the past.

Are you seeing other women? Have you ever slept with a prostitute? Do you have any kids?

Not recently. Yes.

The last one made me pause. I hadn't thought of Sophie for a long while. I don't even know why I said it, but the word slipped from my lips.

Maybe.

Androulla's eyes widened, but instead of fleeing, she leaned in closer, and put a soft hand on top of mine.

That was it. The floodgates opened. Over dinner, I told her all about my family, Dad's death, Skircoat Lodge, the things I'd seen, the people I'd hurt and abandoned, and those who had hurt and abandoned me. I told her that countless numbers of people from my past life had killed themselves or committed suicide. I told her about Sophie and Bobby. How I'd denied being the father and shut her out. Truth be told, I'd seen some pictures on social media and there was an undeniable resemblance to me around Bobby's eyes.

After a few hours, it was all out. Purged.

It was as if I'd just dumped a bag full of stinking, awful rubbish on the table between us. It was everywhere and it was a mess.

Why had I done this? Who was I kidding?

No one had wanted to stay around before to clean up this mess, so why would this angel? She was too good for me. I'd destroy her and drag her down with me.

I expected the end of my story to be her cue to get up and leave.

Thanks for dinner, but not interested.

Androulla had other ideas.

'That's okay,' she said gently. 'We can deal with all of that.'

Then she leaned over and kissed me.

With those few words and with that kiss, it was like she picked up all of my rubbish, the secrets and skeletons in my closet, and packed them neatly back into my bag of hope. I knew then she would be the one who would bring order to my chaos.

For the rest of the date, we remained entwined. Her soft lips tasted like strawberries. Before we knew it, we were being asked to leave by an irritated waiter. I glanced at my watch: it was 4am.

Things moved pretty fast from that night. We were head-over-heels in love and spoke to each other about 20 times a day.

I quit my job as manager at the pub and extracted myself from the drugs and negative influences around me. I'd never really experienced dating. I'd had strings of one-night stands or crazy 'all-in' infatuations. But Androulla insisted on it.

I'm glad she did, because I loved it. Slowly peeling back her layers to discover more and more about her, it was a beautiful journey full of joy, every single day. Piece by piece, she healed each part of me.

'You have to acknowledge your son,' she told me.

Strong enough to do the right thing, even though it meant taking partial responsibility for a child that wasn't hers. I got back in touch with Sophie, poured out my story and apologised for being a narcissistic prick. I apologised to her family and asked for the chance to make it right.

I was handed yet another chance.

By the time I was united with Bobby, he was six years old. I was racked with guilt. My dad would have killed me. I'd done to Bobby what Taffy – Dad's father – did to him. Abandoned him.

Lucky for me, Sophie had done an incredible job. She had a strong family around her. They'd stepped in when I'd dismissed her and made sure that Bobby had everything he needed. He was healthy and bright and had never had a sniff of a children's home.

'You're making it right now,' Androulla would soothe when I broke down over my failings. 'You can be a great father for the rest of your life.'

It was times like that that made me realise I never wanted a day without her by my side. So eight months after first meeting, I proposed.

I didn't have enough money for a ring, but I didn't want to waste time. I knew better than anyone how precious that was. I applied for a credit card and bought her the best solitaire diamond my limit would allow me to.

I knew she loved the walk along the river Thames towards the Tower of London, so I took her for lunch and suggested that we head to the Tower. As soon as we got there, I dropped to one knee.

'Androulla, will you marry me?' I said, heart leaping out of my throat.

She paused for what seemed like an eternity and I started to sweat.

Then she broke the silence.

'Yes, yes, yes,' she said. Then she bolted in the direction of the nearest loo. I sprinted after her and stood outside.

She was being sick!

'Are you okay?' I asked as she emerged.

'It was just such a shock...' she said, half-embarrassed. 'And I don't think lunch agreed with me.'

I threw my arms around her. We'd deal with it together. A few months later, we bought a home together and Androulla met my family in Halifax.

Like so many people, she was surprised by its beauty given the stories I'd told her about the place.

Soon after we travelled to Cyprus to meet her family. After just a few hours with her parents I felt I understood Androulla on an even deeper level.

Stella and Tony's eyes conveyed a deep emotional loss, similar to the shadowed eyes of the many care-home kids I had encountered over the years. Later, Androulla explained that they had been refugees in the Cypriot war of 1974. They'd been torn from their homes and everything they'd ever known without warning. Their families had been ripped apart and they'd been left with nothing.

Like being a care-home kid, but on a different scale.

Still, they had overcome their adversity to meet and have a family. Both were forgiving souls, choosing to move on rather than fight.

'Fighting gets you nowhere,' Tony would say, with a smile.

Androulla carried their history in her heart. It gave her the ability to understand, forgive and heal. It was what made her so special.

That was what had captured me that night in the pub.

She was the first person I'd never had to lie to and it was the first time I'd felt true love and protection since my dad had died.

I was convinced he'd sent this angel to me.

* * *

On 1st December 2012, at 2:30pm, I was waiting nervously at the altar of St Sophia's Church in Bayswater with my best man, Jonny Stewart, at my side.

'Did we really need to get here two hours early?' he ribbed.

In the short run-up to the wedding, poor Jonny had been the call centre of curiosity in Halifax.

Is he really getting married? Has he really calmed down? Have the drugs finally fried his brain?

Mum did have her doubts.

'I'm proud of how well you're doing, son,' she said. 'But it's very fast. Are you sure this is what you want? Are you sure she's the one?'

'I've never been more sure of anything,' I said.

Our guests were a hotchpotch of Androulla's expansive Greek-Cypriot family, a shifty-looking bunch from Halifax and Androulla's glamorous fashion friends – the Prince and Princess of Saudi Arabia even turned up.

My stomach was just filled with excited butterflies, waiting for Androulla to arrive. As the time drew nearer, nerves began to gnaw at me. I'd done over 100 stage shows and I'd never gotten stage fright, but I was terrified it was about to kick in.

Then the doors flew open and the room lit up.

It was like a chorus of angels began singing in my brain. *My love, my saviour, my everything.*

Tears pricked my eyes as she walked towards me down the aisle, sparkling on Tony's arm. You'd be hard-pushed to say who looked more proud.

Emotion completely overwhelmed me as the service began.

Lip quivering, I stuttered my way through the exchange of rings and the joining of hands, hands still shaking as we drank from the common cup.

How could this woman want me, for ever?

Whatever her reasons, she did. An hour later, we were man and wife.

Our reception took place in the Rosendale Pub. Booze and food flowing, it was Jonny's turn to take centre stage.

Please, Jonny, be kind, I begged silently. I needn't have worried. Jonny, solid as ever, gave what I still think is one of the finest best man's speeches I'd ever heard.

'Why do they say,' he joked, 'for better or for worse? It's true, really, because Chris couldn't have done any better and Androulla couldn't have done much worse!'

The room exploded into laughter. Myself included. I knew how lucky I was, punching well above my weight.

Jokes about my childhood followed, but then the tone changed.

'The ambition he has always had is now paying off. It took a lot of guts to up sticks and move to London to chase his dream,' he said, putting a hand on my shoulder. 'And he found more than his dream. He found his Androulla.'

I felt a lump rise in my throat.

Later that night we took to the dance floor for our first dance to Elton John's 'Something About the Way You Look Tonight'. I pulled her close.

'You're the most beautiful woman in the world,' I told her. 'Inside and out.'

Androulla looked up at me, her eyes as wide and captivating as the very first time I caught sight of her, and let the happy tears flow.

My own tears weren't far behind.

* * *

We were happy, but our first months of marriage weren't easy. I was building a home with Androulla, a place to belong. We were even expecting our first baby.

But I still wasn't completely settled or content. After leaving the pub I'd had three nine-to-five jobs, each only lasting a few weeks. I just wasn't built for the monotony and purposelessness of working for a pay day, a slave to the salary.

What's more, I was still waking up in the middle of the night in cold sweats, thinking about faces from my past. Most recently, it had been Callum.

We'd been so cruel to him. He was mentally damaged. I'd betrayed my friend in front of older kids. I'd join in when they taunted him and made him do dangerous things for our entertainment. Sometimes he'd get hurt, but he wouldn't care as long as he got his cigarettes. Each time that memories of days I allowed him to be preyed upon by the wolves came back to me I heard John's words: *There are still too many vulnerable children suffering as a result of a failed system.*

For years I'd been searching for a reason for being. Now finally, I felt like I'd found it.

'I want to go back into the care system,' I told Androulla over dinner one night. 'I can't help the people from my past, but I can help people suffering now.'

I'd done all my research. There was a social care course at the College of Haringey and Enfield that would allow me to work in a children's home. I already had a book of knowledge on survival that I could make good use of when I got there.

Androulla put her head in her hands. I knew it wasn't the money that she was worried about. I was fortunate that Androulla's job paid our bills and kept a roof over our heads. She was worried about me.

'Are you sure you can handle it?' she said. 'You care too much. You get too emotionally attached.'

'I just want to make a difference. Do something important with my life.'

'Then I support you,' she said.

I enrolled on the course, which was due to start later in the year. I could have been sat twiddling my thumbs, but one day my phone rang. It was an old friend, Lee Barnes, with whom I had studied performing arts, back in Halifax.

'We're making a short film about an autistic boy who gets abused by his older brother,' he said. 'We thought of you while we were casting.'

Instantly, I expected to be offered the part of the bully, I usually was in TV or film, the muscle or the bad lad.

'We'd love you to play the part of Carl, the autistic boy,' he finished.

I read the story overview. It was disturbing, sent shivers down my spine.

Set in and around the hills of Halifax, it follows autistic Carl and his violent and abusive older brother Robert on an out-of-the-blue camping trip, examining the relationship between the two brothers – Carl having always been the family favourite – and encouraging the audience to examine what they would do in the shoes of the short film's handful of characters.

I was elated. It was gritty and raw and would allow me to tap into the physicality of my emotions, just like I had in LA.

As I started researching the part, the more I learned about Carl's character, the more I was reminded of Callum.

I wonder what had happened to him? What was he doing now?

I hadn't seen him since that last cigarette we shared behind the walls at Beaconsfield Reform School.

That must have been 15 years ago, maybe more.

I set about trying to find him. I wanted to make my peace with him. Apologise for not helping him when I should have done, for not being stronger and defending him.

I was the lucky one, the stronger one. I was never damned like you.

But there was no trace of him. Then I remembered: he had a cousin, a girl called Samantha who had been in care herself. I remember someone saying that she'd set up a group to help other girls who'd been in care, but I didn't know much about it.

I managed to track down her address and I wrote her a letter. I explained how I'd started working on a film and it stirred up memories of guilt. I told her I was trying to get in touch with Callum so I could make amends. Before long, I received a reply.

Dear Chris Wild,

Thank you for your letter.

It saddens me to inform you that my cousin, Callum, took his own life in 1998. He was 18 years old. We weren't close but what I do know is that Callum had suffered all his life. When he left school he got involved with the wrong crowd and became a drug addict. Please do not feel bad for what you did as a child. You were not to blame for his death.

I wish you all the luck with the film.

Samantha

I must have read it 50 times before it sank in. He'd been dead for 15 years. While I'd been sweating it out in the gym and prancing around LA and London, Callum had been lying stone cold among all the other bodies in Stoney Royd Cemetery. He'd been part of the ghost town of Halifax every time I'd returned home.

That night I sobbed and I discovered more details. Turned out he'd hung himself from the swings next to Beaconsfield Reform School. Where we used to laugh and smoke and play.

What other horrors had I missed while I'd been tying myself in knots trying to 'find' myself?

I wrote to Samantha and asked if we could meet. I wanted to understand her experience of the care system too, compare what I had seen in the hope that it would help me make more of a difference when I finally became a care worker.

She agreed. So a few weeks later I travelled back up to Halifax and met her in a small greasy spoon café near North Bridge.

* * *

SAMANTHA

'Wolves always work in packs.'

'I wasn't close to Callum,' she said. 'I just know how he died. I know he was a victim of the care system. That's why I know you weren't to blame.'

'How so?' I asked.

'Because you're just like us,' she said. 'You're a victim of it too.'

Inside my stomach knotted, tight with guilt. *I've been through nothing compared to some.*

Samantha stared into space as she ran her teaspoon across the rim of coffee cup, back and forth, creating a low, satisfying ringing sound. I didn't mind because it seemed to be helping her to think.

Suddenly she stopped and placed the spoon on the table, before looking me dead in the eye.

'You have to remember that these people—' Samantha stopped abruptly and snorted. 'Sorry, these *animals*, that ran the care homes were masters of manipulation. We were told every second of the day that we were unwanted, trash, left abandoned by our parents because we were pure evil or worthless.'

I nodded in agreement. It was exactly how the Boss Man and The Bear had run Skircoat Lodge.

'We were made to feel grateful that *someone* would have us. Like there was no other choice for us.'

Samantha had already told me how she'd been taken into care because her parents couldn't handle her.

'I started out like many others,' she said. 'I was neglected from birth, and grew up having to fend for myself. My parents had better things to be doing.'

I didn't ask what; I already knew. I'd seen it so many times.

'Of course, that led to stealing, causing fights and mayhem wherever I went. They didn't want to take responsibility for that.'

'But it was a cry for help?' I probed.

'Of course it was, I was a child,' she said. 'But social services never saw it that way. They never tried to help you sort it out. Vulnerable kids like me were great fodder.'

I nodded, understanding exactly what she meant.

Fresh meat for the hungry wolves.

Samantha was put into a children's home in Calderdale in 1992. She was 13 years old. Her mum hugged her and said goodbye when they came for her but her dad was too stoned to even notice she'd gone.

For the next three years, she was handed over into the care of the children's home principal, Mr Brown.

'I remember standing the doorway looking down at his shadow,' she said. 'He was six foot tall, huge to a teenage girl. I remember feeling a lump in my throat. Sheer fear rising. I swallowed it and made a loud gulping noise. He knew that I was…'

'That you were vulnerable?' I cut in.

'That I was ideal for his home,' she sneered, memories clearly fleeting through her mind.

Samantha was stripped of her clothes and belongings and in return was given a scruffy grey tracksuit with the number two on the back.

'It stank of damp and mould. Like it had been passed down for years.'

From the start, she knew something wasn't right. She'd not been dragged up on the streets or ended up there like I had, but she was streetwise.

The first signs were clear over supper, which took place in a dining room external to the main part of the home. All these weird-looking girls were staring at me with sad eyes,' she said. 'They looked kind of like broken dolls, vacant and glassy-eyed.'

They had good intentions though, each of them whispering warnings to the unfortunate new resident as they crossed from dining room over to bed.

Watch out for Mr Brown.

Avoid him at night.

Mind your back door.

'I was confused. There was only one "back door" I could think of,' she said. 'My backside. I couldn't understand what a grown man would want with a young girl's "back door".'

She decided they were just trying to scare her. But being streetwise, she didn't take any chances.

'I ran to my room and slammed my door shut,' she said. 'I was in a room on my own in a single bed with plastic mattress sheets that creaked every time I moved. It seemed weird, considering how many of us were crammed into the home. I soon found out why.'

The next morning Samantha rose and headed towards the dining room for breakfast, seduced by the smell of fresh baking.

As she was walking down the corridor she heard a voice shout: 'Number two, stay where you are, do not move!'

It was Mr Brown's right-hand woman, Miss Black. She was huge and hairy, with the stance of a Bulldog.

'I was still quite feisty. That day adrenalin got the better of me,' said Samantha. 'I had a name and I wanted them to use it, so I told her "My name's not number two, it's Samantha."'

It was a mistake she wouldn't make again. Mr Brown was also in the room and he did not take kindly to Samantha's cheek.

The six-foot-tall 'care'-home leader landed her with a punch square on the jaw.

'Everything went black because I'd been knocked out. The next thing I remember was the whitewash of the ceiling staring down at me. My jaw was locked and in agony as I picked myself up and made my way to the seating area by the kitchen,' Samantha explained. 'None of them had seen anything. Or at least they pretended they hadn't.'

'What happened next?' I asked.

'I saw Mr Brown in the kitchen whispering with one of the other girls. She was about the same age as me,' she said. 'She turned round and started walking towards me. I saw him pat her on the bum as she went. It turned my stomach but she didn't even flinch.'

'Did she say something to you?' I asked.

'Yes,' she nodded. 'She told me breakfast was over and that I was to go back upstairs to my room immediately and stay there until further notice. So I did.'

'Didn't you tell her what had just happened?' I questioned.

'Something in her eyes told me to do exactly as I was told. That if I didn't, it would get worse,' she replied.

Loose lips get you whipped.

That day Samantha went back to her room, scared, hungry and in agony.

'I knew I'd given a little attitude, but I couldn't work out why it warranted being punched out cold by a man three times my size,' she said, her eyes cold from having told the story a thousand times before.

No one came to get her from her room that day. She just curled up in bed and cried, too scared to venture out of her own accord.

'I got so hungry,' she explained. 'I'd barely eaten since I arrived and now I was banished to my room, destined to sit there and inhale all the cooking smells drifting in from the kitchen and local baker's.'

Stay there until further notice.

Soon, further notice arrived.

'I heard footsteps outside my door,' she said. 'I was elated. I jumped off my bed, ran to the door and threw it open.'

'Was it Mr Brown?' I asked.

'No, it was the girl from the kitchen in the morning again. She said that Mr Brown wanted to see me in his room as soon as possible. When I asked why, she didn't reply. In fact, she never took her eyes from the ground to look at me.'

Samantha scurried up to the thick wooden doors of Mr Brown's room and knocked twice. She didn't want to dawdle and make him angry again.

'I could hardly hear his booming voice through the thick wood, that's how thick it was. But I could just about make out that he'd told me to come in and close the door,' she said.

Samantha described the room to me: dark, with a small lamp on the bedside table, old-fashioned wooden furniture like on a Hollywood movie set from years ago.

I couldn't help but notice how similar it sounded to Boss Man's the night I'd found Claire in there.

'There was this huge chocolate cake on his desk. It was the biggest one I'd ever seen. I thought he was going to apologise for what he did to me that morning,' she said.

Mr Brown emerged from the bathroom in a black silk dressing gown, smothered in Old Spice.

'He smelled just like my grandad,' Samantha said. 'It took me back to moments of happiness and comfort. Looking back now, I'm sure it was part of his tactic. Everyone's grandad smelled of Old Spice in the eighties and nineties.

'He offered me a piece of the cake. Cut me a huge slice. It was three layers of sponge thick. I wolfed it down faster than I'd ever eaten anything because I was starving and scared he'd change his mind. He was laughing as I did it. I even apologised for eating like a pig.

'He asked me questions, like where I was from and my favourite movie. He wasn't booming at me now, his voice was gentle and I felt safe,' she said. 'But as we talked, my mouth became dry so he went to his wardrobe and pulled out lots of little bottles of liquid.'

Mr Brown poured two drinks. Two shots of vodka.

'I was thirsty so I drank it, even though it burned my throat,' Samantha said. 'One after the other, trying to quench the thirst. I lost count of how many I had.'

Then, for the second time that day, Samantha saw black.

Her eyes darkened as she continued telling me her story. I could see how the shadows of the past were torturing her soul.

'I remember waking up alone in my own room first,' she said. 'And then I remember the pain. I couldn't move my legs or lower spine without feeling like a dagger was being stuck in them.

'I managed to sit up and lift my covers to see what was going on down there. When I did, it was like that scene out of *The Godfather* – you know the one with the horse's head? There was blood everywhere. It was as if my legs had been amputated in the night.'

I gasped in horror. What had the animal done to her?

She explained how, as she'd sat up, she'd been hit by another wave of pain, a million times more agonising than the pain in her back or even her jaw from earlier that day.

'It shot up from my rectum right through my body. I vomited everywhere immediately, diluted brown chocolate cake mixing in with the crimson blood on my sheets. It was then I realised why we had plastic bedding,' she said. 'That was the day I was officially initiated into life at a children's home.'

I shook my head in horror as she described how her bath water had turned red as she was bleeding so heavily from her backside after Mr Brown had raped her.

She was 13 years old. And in his care.

How could he?

'Did you tell anyone?' I asked.

'Not at the time. I was a kid from a broken home. No one believed us about anything,' she said. 'He had standing in society. Powerful friends. Anyway, how do you tell someone you think you've been raped when you can't remember because you passed out? When talking about sex isn't the done thing anyway?'

She was right. It wasn't like now. Talking about even consensual sex was taboo. Let alone accusing a pillar of the community of rape.

And if you were just unwanted street trash, well…

'They weren't stupid,' Samantha said, interrupting my train of thought. 'They knew what they were doing. They knew who to groom.'

She was right. That's why I hadn't lasted five minutes in Skircoat Lodge. I was broken, but not broken *enough*. I was the type of kid who would eventually have exposed their behaviour. So they cast me out.

'I limped to breakfast. Mr Brown was there, told me to eat my bacon and eggs,' she said. 'But I was too sick and sore. I wanted to stick my fork in his eye but I was paralysed by pain and fear.'

Samantha caught the eye of the girl who had summoned her to Mr Brown's room.

'It was a look of indescribable sadness,' she said. 'After breakfast she came to my room again and handed me some bathing salts. "Bathe in these every day," she whispered. "The wounds will soon heal. I'm sorry." I understood then that she was speaking from experience.'

'Did it keep on happening?' I asked.

Samantha shook her head. 'Not with him. Once he'd "had you" you were officially trash. He had a few favourites who stayed in his quarters all the time. They used his predilections to get alcohol and cigarettes. That was how they chose to survive.'

Samantha chose another route, running away at any opportunity.

'The police always brought me back. Then I'd get given "the treatment",' she said.

'The treatment?' I asked.

'Solitary confinement for a week. No luxuries. Barely even the basic requirements for life. You got water and the occasional opportunity to take a piss,' she said.

'What about food?' I asked.

'You only got that in return for giving sexual favours to the wolves,' she said. 'Mr Brown's pack. Wolves always work in packs, you know.'

'What do you mean?' I pushed. 'There were others?'

Samantha laughed sarcastically as I realised the naivety of my question.

Of course there were. Callum's grandad had his pack. So did the Boss Man.

'Yes, there were others. Other male social workers, local politicians and celebrities,' she said. 'We were their fodder. Nothing but warm flesh. They loved underage girls. There were others who liked the boys.'

'You were easy prey,' I acknowledged, the reality lying heavy on my shoulders.

She nodded. 'No one was safe.'

'What about the police?' I asked. 'Surely they must have noticed something, queried why so many kids were trying to run away?'

'They didn't care,' Samantha said. 'They were there too. I remember opening my door and peeking through the crack to see uniformed officers taking full advantage of what was on offer. It was like a catalogue for paedophiles. Sometimes we would line up in the corridors for sexual perusal, praying that we wouldn't be picked.'

My blood boiled.

Mr Brown hadn't been running a children's home. It was a business, a brothel for the wolves. Like so many of the lost souls I had encountered over the years, Samantha turned to drink and drugs to block out the pain. She left the home at 16, after three years of torture and abuse, got a job in a greasy spoon and returned to live with her parents.

'Weren't you mad at them,' I asked, 'for what happened to you?'

'They needed help paying the rent and for Dad's drug habit,' Samantha shrugged. 'I needed a roof over my head while I waited to get to the top of the list for my own council flat.'

Needs must.

She waited two years. But it was worth it.

'It wasn't much, but for me it was a safe place,' she said. 'The first safe place I'd ever known. I made it a home. *My* home.'

Eventually, she started having counselling.

'I finally found the courage to speak to someone about the rape,' she said. 'But at first, when I gave my statement to the police, I was dismissed as a troublemaking whore.'

'What did they say?' I asked.

'They said Mr Brown was a respectable member of the council, a family man, credible. They pointed out that I was the daughter of a junkie,' Samantha said. 'They reminded me of all the great things that he'd done for the town. The lovely community parties he'd laid on, the donations to charities. Then they asked me if there was a chance I'd "misunderstood" the incident.'

Samantha said there was more, that she wasn't the only one.

'They kept asking me if I might have dreamt it. Telling me that there were no other complaints. If there were others,

they surely would have been reported? Surely the police would
have known?'

*How could she have dreamt the pain and the bleeding? The
physical scars?*

I felt sick to my stomach.

'I felt as powerless as I did during "the treatment", it was
horrific,' Samantha continued. 'But I wasn't going to back
down this time. I looked the officer in the eye and told him
that the police did know – but only because they were raping
girls, too. They were raping boys. Whatever took their fancy
– it was all on offer. All the people in power, the responsible
adults, they were the ones doing the abusing, or at least facili-
tating it. Wolves always work in packs.'

Eventually, an investigation was opened. Arrests were
made. Samantha's story made the local paper, though her name
was changed to ensure her privacy.

'After that, hundreds of other girls came forward and gave
evidence.'

Samantha had been right. Mr Brown had the whole
community in his pocket, right down to the local pharmacist
who supplied him with sleeping pills to crush and mix into his
chocolate cake.

That was what had knocked her out.

'Did they get him?' I asked.

'Oh, they got him,' she smiled. 'Him and a load of his pack.
Local celebrities, priests, you name it. He was put away for
seven years.'

Samantha didn't stop there. Justice for her alone wasn't
enough. Her experience in care may have shattered her, but it
didn't crush her spirit. She'd always been streetwise, was used

to causing mayhem. She put those skills to good use, setting up a charity to help young girls who had suffered abuse like she had.

'Some of the girls were as young as eight when they had been abused,' she said. 'So far, we have managed to get more than 50 of the bastards convicted of rape and sexual abuse and sent to jail. This is my life now, this is how I moved on.'

CHAPTER SEVENTEEN

Back to the Home

I knew things hadn't been right in the care system when I'd been growing up: my own experience in Skircoat Lodge and conversations with Susanna, Claire and John had proven that. But Samantha's story was like a spotlight shining on my life.

Suddenly, scenes behind closed doors were revealed, the missing blanks were filled in, and it was a horror story.

No wonder Dad had never wanted us to end up in care.

Outside of acting classes, I'd only gone to the past when my mind took me kicking and screaming on an unwanted trip into my history. But now I was ready. I stayed true to my promise to myself. I was going to tend to my wound so it would heal properly, even if that meant uncovering painful truths.

Our baby was about to arrive and I couldn't pass down a legacy of poison and uncertainty to her. I switched on my computer and started typing. I wanted to go right back to where it all began for me:

Child abuse Skircoat Lodge

The top results were like a punch to the stomach. There were stories in the *Yorkshire Post* and the *Halifax Courier*.

CHILD CARERS JAILED FOR DESPICABLE SEX CRIMES

IT MUST NEVER HAPPEN AGAIN

LIVES RUINED BY LEGACY OF SECRET ABUSE

I did a double take when I spotted the date.

November 2001.

Twelve years ago!

I scrolled down the page and there he was, older but still as domineering and imposing as when I'd known him. His eyes bored into me through the screen.

The Boss Man.

I felt just like I did on the day he belted me for not buttering my toast correctly – scared, angry and powerless. His full name was Malcolm Osric Phillips. He was 68 when he had been charged for his crimes. Turns out, the reason that Skircoat Lodge closed in 1996 was due to a report published by the NSPCC in 1994, criticising the home.

They said that bathroom doors were missing locks, staff walked into children's rooms unannounced, meals were eaten in silence and staff seemed dominated by Phillips.

All very accurate, by my recollection.

It was damning, but not damning enough. It took an allegation of rape against Phillips in 1995 for that. No charges were brought, but he was dismissed and the doors to Skircoat Lodge were shut for good.

After that, in 1997, the new director of Calderdale Social Services, Chris Brabbs, called for an independent investigation to be launched.

The paper said that they'd hoped the investigation would 'clear the air of long-standing suspicions'. As it turned out, it revealed a pack of wolves preying on the kids in their care.

It was called Operation Screen, and it ran until January 2002. Investigations went right back to the 1980s and focused on Phillips and his colleague, Andrew Shalders, who was 54 years old when he was convicted. Shalders was gone before I came to the home. I'd heard his name and whispers about him from the older lads around town, from people like Mark. Lucky for me he'd gone because, unlike Phillips, his preference was young boys.

In 1985, he'd even been suspended after a boy living at Skircoat Lodge and four former residents went to the police and accused him of sexually assaulting them. But the case was dropped because of insufficient evidence and Shalders was reinstated into his position.

No questions asked.

He left in 1988 to care for mentally handicapped adults. Apparently, no complaints ever came from there.

'No adults were believed to have been harmed,' the story said.

Maybe he only liked little boys. Then I shuddered. Or maybe his later victims didn't have the capacity to speak up.

In 2001, Phillips was jailed for seven years for 12 counts of Indecent Assault on a female under 14, one count of Indecent Assault on a female over 16 and one count of Gross Indecency with a girl under 16.

Shalders was locked up for 15 years for 11 counts of Indecent Assault on a male under 14, one count of Indecent Assault on a male under 16 and two counts of Gross Indecency with a boy under 16.

Another worker, Terence Thomas O'Hagan, was charged with Buggery of a male under 16 and Indecent Assault on a male under 16 years, but he died before he was convicted.

I was glued to my computer screen for hours, travelling down a rabbit hole of pain and abuse. The stories that came out in court were horrific.

One boy, abused by Shalders, was promised that he would be sent to another children's home, where his brothers were living, if he complied with his sick demands.

Of course he complied – he wanted to be with his family.

But it was all a ruse. Whenever the boy tried to refuse, Shalders threatened to go back on his promise. The boy was never reunited with his brothers.

My heart broke. The poor kid.

The fucking animal.

As I read about Phillips' catalogue of crimes, committed during his 18 years in charge, I thought of Claire and tears pricked my eyes. She'd been his victim, for sure.

The tactics he used were strikingly similar to the care home boss who had abused Samantha, plying his victims with treats, followed by booze or snacks laced with sleeping pills.

Children were shipped from one care home to another, passed around like sex toys between depraved 'care'-home workers.

Hadn't Lottie, Claire's friend, been sent to a home in Wales?

Had that been her fate too? Abuse and isolation?

It wasn't just Skircoat Lodge either; other children's homes were involved, like Dobroyd Castle in Todmorden. With every click, I found another home in another town with another abuser's name. I found evidence of warning signs missed – the director of Calderdale Social Services while I was in the system – Rod Ryall – was given a warning in 1982 for photographing boys in their running kit. Six years later he was convicted of abusing two boys over a four-year period.

Funnily enough, he and Phillips had worked in the same Birmingham authority in the 1970s.

Samantha was right: these people did work in packs.

Six other staff members from Skircoat Lodge were arrested on charges of sexual and physical abuse, but there was insufficient evidence for any of them to be put away.

My mind flashed back to my probation officer. The one who'd taken me out in the hills hunting for gems, trying to make me have fun and trust him. I had no doubt he'd been grooming me. I'd been so close to becoming prey to the wolves.

Suddenly, the chaos and mess of the lives of all those people who hadn't been as lucky as me made sense. I couldn't have put it better than the opening line of the *Yorkshire Post* article:

The reign of Malcolm Phillips and Andrew Shalders at Skircoat Lodge ruined lives and created damaged children who grew into scarred adults.

No wonder so many turned to drugs or took their own lives. By that point, I could count 22 old friends from the care system who had either killed themselves or died of a drug overdose. Callum was just one of them.

But again, it wasn't just Halifax. The first social worker involved in aiding the Skircoat Lodge investigation, Deborah Wortman, referenced a similar major inquiry in North Wales. In the run-up to the trials they lost 19 victims to suicide. Their past was too horrific to face.

I read her comments on the case, with tears in my eyes.

'It was a different world then. Children weren't listened to and they didn't have rights. We heard over and over again that they didn't know who to turn to. They were lost.'

I hoped with all my being that she was right. That it *was* a different world back then. It had to be.

Finally, I stopped scrolling and shut down my computer.

I sat in silence for a while, contemplating everything I'd just read. Part of me wanted to run away, shove it all back inside my brain in a folder marked 'do not open' and abandon my plans to study the social care course.

But I couldn't. I still carried with me the souls of all my lost friends, the ones that never had a chance. I owed it to them.

* * *

My sense of responsibility grew even stronger on 17th May 2013, when my daughter Antonia arrived. She was a healthy six pounds three ounces of perfection, staring back at me with big dark eyes, wide with innocence.

Although I'd been able to build a relationship with Bobby, and I knew I'd lay my life down to protect him, I'd not experienced this part of the journey with him. As I cradled Antonia in my arms, close to my bare chest, I could feel her tiny heart beating on my skin.

That moment it was like the whole world stopped.

It was potent and inexplicable. A bond like no other forming in seconds.

We were connected. She was my blood.

'You've got your grandad's eyes,' I smiled, looking up at Androulla, who nodded in agreement.

Well, I was the image of my dad, so it was entirely possible.

Antonia gurgled back at me, grasping at my finger. I closed my eyes.

Please, Dad – watch over her, like you have me.

He'd always been my guiding hand. He'd led me here to this place and this beautiful woman. He'd helped me find my home again. Now I needed his watchful eyes on my little girl.

'I wish Dad was here,' I said to Androulla. 'He'd be so proud.'

I swear at that point Antonia made a laughing sound. Something just above my head to the left had caught her attention and she was staring at it.

Dad?

Warmth spread through my body and I felt the ache of love in my heart as I imagined him standing behind me, arms on my shoulders and pulling silly faces at my brand-new daughter. If he was here, he wouldn't have missed it for the world.

Being parents came quite naturally to us. Yes, the sleepless nights were tough, but it was worth it to watch Antonia grow and thrive. Androulla was already the perfect wife, but motherhood turned her into a fierce lioness. My love for her deepened every day – it still does.

Surrounded by friends and family, I was able to continue with my plans to go back into the care system to work. In between studying, I returned briefly to Halifax to film *To Catch a Butterfly*.

We had five days to film and a £3,000 budget that mainly went on technical equipment. All the actors worked for free, it was a passion project. Now I was aware of the darkness that had been hidden under these hills, it felt even more important.

The local community got behind us too, providing free food and drink, as well as accommodation for those of us coming from out of town.

The piece was entirely improvised, so I devised a backstory with Dan Wilson, who was playing Carl's violent older brother, Robert. The last scene was dark, as it showed Robert beating Carl to death on the windy moors of Halifax, releasing years of resentment with his feet and fists – until fate intervenes.

'Don't go easy on me,' I said to Dan. 'I want to feel the pain. I want it to be real.'

'Why?' he said. 'The make-up girls can work their magic.'

I poured my story out to Dan. About Callum, about how I'd let him be hurt by others when we were kids. How, as I'd filtered through my memories, I remembered times when I'd joined in the kicking and the punching too.

I needed to be punished. To feel just a fraction of what he must have felt.

Dan was a complete pro. He kicked the absolute shit out of me.

I felt actual fear as I looked up at him while he rained blows down on me.

Before long, blood was running down my nose. Thank God we did it in one take!

I lay on the wet ground, cold, sore and hungry as the crew set up for the final shot of the film.

This one's for you, Callum, I thought.

After that, the film went into production and I went back to London and my studies. Making ends meet was hard. Androulla looked after the house and I lived on £70 a fortnight from the job centre, but it was worth it.

After studying for six months I received my NVQ Level 2 in Social Care. I knew I already had all the tools and passion to be a care worker, I just needed the legal document to get through the door. At first I found a job as a care worker at a private care home, which looked after kids from abandoned, abused and disadvantaged backgrounds until they were 18.

It felt great, seeing the kids I worked with growing in confidence and learning new skills. I was proud to teach them boxing and acting as an extra-curricular activity. Many of them went out into the world and got themselves jobs and homes.

Finally, I was making a difference. But although these children were damaged, they were nothing like the nightmares I had grown up around.

That's not to say I didn't think those nightmares no longer existed. It was coming up to two years after the news about Jimmy Savile had broken. He was no different to Phillips and Shalders – a rabid wolf wearing a mask of public respectability. Operation Yewtree was in full swing and it was becoming clear to me that the country was far from resolution when it came to child abuse.

Singers like Rebecca Ferguson had spoken up about their own experiences of abuse in the care system. Hollywood stars, footballers and all kinds of sportspeople came forward and said 'me too'.

Their bravery in speaking out impressed me, but then they were public figures. They had money and the support networks around them to do so – family, friends, counsellors and lawyers. What about all those faceless, penniless people that didn't have that support network?

A culture of abuse had permeated our society and now, with the Internet, it was getting worse. Paedophile rings were no longer just close-knit circles of influential perverts concentrated in one area like Phillips and his cronies, they were now a global network of people from all walks of life, connected by the dark web.

There were victims of the ring that Phillips had been involved in still fighting for justice, back in Yorkshire. All of this, fuelled by the words of Samantha and my memories of Callum kept pushing me towards my ultimate goal.

To work with kids like the ones who'd perished, their voices unheard, in my hometown.

I applied for another position that would train me to become a trauma therapist – a specialist care worker who helps people address, come to terms with and recover from traumatic events such as physical, mental and sexual abuse.

I filled in the application meticulously, listing all my experience – personal and professional. I outlined what I could bring to the team and explained how my own time in care had driven back to the system to try and help others.

Because I'd been lucky.

I was offered the job. Most of the kids I worked with came from dysfunctional families and had endured some of the worst kind of abuse imaginable. Nothing had changed in that respect. They were different to me, like all my friends had been, but I could relate to them because I knew what it was to feel unwanted and lost. Finally, I could put my experience to good use.

On the surface, everything seemed tighter, cleaner and safer. The home was modern and in good condition and the children and staff weren't ruled by an iron fist. There was the opportunity to make a difference. They were open to ideas.

As long as you were willing to take the responsibility on yourself, for no extra pay. I was more than willing – I knew the difference that escapism could have.

But it was a fragile façade. Every new staff member had a story to tell about previous homes, as did every new child.

It was two sides of the same negative story.

Workers complained how they were underpaid, tired, stressed and fed up with the young people in their care physically and verbally attacking them. The kids came with tales of abuse from previous homes, where care workers would either neglect their duties in favour of sitting in the office all day, or beat up and bully them.

Truth is, I didn't know who to believe. North or south, private or public, it all just sounded like the same old fucking mess. A catastrophe in every children's home, in every town.

In my job I had to visit other homes to carry out assessments, and some of the conditions I found, well, I wouldn't have left a dog in.

How was a grubby house with rotting carpets that stank of piss an appropriate 'home' for three vulnerable young people?

What's more, underneath the surface it didn't seem that much had changed. Historic cases of sexual abuse in children's homes were being revealed and revisited across the country, highlighting how kids were still potentially at risk.

More investigations and convictions from the already infamous Rochdale sex ring, Lambeth Council, paying tens of millions of pounds to victims of horrific abuse at Shirley Oaks children's home, and reports into seven decades of child abuse at homes in Jersey were being published.

There was an unspoken and uneasy acceptance.

Of course the abuse and mistreatment continued, but what could we do?

Undeterred, I did what I knew I could do: I focused on making a difference where I could. I introduced boxing lessons, creative writing classes, acting sessions and art therapy to the home. Seeing some of the residents embrace the things that had saved me gave me a real sense of hope and purpose. But support from other team members was minimal. No one else really stuck their neck out.

'Be careful, Chris,' they said. 'You'll slip up.'

I had no idea what they meant.

Before long, scratching below the surface, I found some familiar problems. Most of the staff had been there a lifetime.

Worn down by long hours, budget cuts and low pay, they had lost their motivation and passion to help kids and were just waiting it out for the pension.

A lot of them viewed the kids as lost causes.

'What's the point?' they'd moan, as they hid in the staff coffee room.

'The point is, these kids deserve a chance,' I'd state firmly. 'They deserve better attention.'

But there was another problem. A new one I'd never encountered before – a high turnover of young workers with a textbook education, and no life experience. They had floundered because there was no 'how-to' manual to fix these kids.

In the old days, the care home sector was a tight circle – everyone moved around from home to home. Once you were in, you were in. They were the instigators and the guardians of the horrors that went on behind closed doors.

Now, the kids ran the show. Bodies like Ofsted had put rules and regulations in place to keep them safe. But the kids had learned how to play those rules.

They'd spit and swear at staff workers, safe in the knowledge that they wouldn't be on the receiving end of a beating like we used to be with the Boss Man and The Bear.

As a result, no one wanted to work in the system. Private and public sector care homes alike had to scrape to find any willing recruits. New starters lasted a year, if we were lucky.

'Who'd stick with this shit for eight pound an hour?' reasoned one old-timer as we watched yet another new recruit walk out the door after just a few months. In one way, he was right: it was hard. When you learned what had happened to these kids it broke you. There was no way you couldn't take it home with you. It was like a thorn in your heart.

Neglect was always the common denominator. So many of the kids had been abandoned by their dads and left with mothers who were addicted to drink and drugs, just like Danny.

Whether they were babies or teenagers, Mum usually cared more about her next drink or fix than caring for her child. There was never food in the cupboards or clean clothes to wear, no one to give advice or walk them to school. They came from homes with revolving doors that allowed in a steady stream of drug dealers, pimps and paedophiles who could smell vulnerability a mile off.

The kids at the home had all experienced physical violence, and most had been raped or sexually abused as well. Sometimes it had been a one-off attack, but usually it was sustained sexual abuse, more often than not at the hands of a responsible 'trusted' adult or a family member.

The abuse kicked off a cycle. The kids would go off the rails, turn to drink and drugs to cope with what they'd experienced. Often they'd turn violent or sexually aggressive themselves.

It was the kids that had been systematically sexually abused from childhood we had to keep the closest eye on. One pair in particular – a teenage boy called John, who had been violently abused by an uncle and another called Francis, who had been repeatedly raped by his grandfather – were a huge risk to one another.

John had become a bully, physically and mentally intimidating even to the care-home staff, while Francis was so scared and damaged that he could be manipulated to do anyone's bidding.

Just like Callum.

If they were left alone in a room together even for a few minutes, John would force Francis to give him a blowjob or try to have sex with him. If you tried to stop them, John would invariably lash out.

I tried my best to keep my eye on them, but my colleagues didn't always monitor with the same vigour.

'They'll always find a way so just leave them to it,' one said. 'It's not worth the paperwork or the black eye.'

Of course, aggression directed at us wasn't acceptable. But it was our job as care workers to understand where they had come from and why they behaved that way. It was our job to educate them.

To help them – no matter what.

Of course, there were also less extreme cases, where a child was put in the home after being injured during a one-off domestic incident or because a parent was suffering from depression and couldn't care for them. But the system allocates places by location, so kids from relatively normal homes would be thrown in with kids with substance issues, from violent backgrounds that had been sexually abused.

They were vulnerable, but not damaged like some of the others. But before long they'd be led astray and go off the rails, exposed to drugs and sex well before they ever would have been in a home with similar cases.

The saddest thing was that sometimes the damage would be so great that by the time their parents had overcome their issues, they'd be too far gone to rescue.

As the weeks and months passed, I refused to stay silent. I questioned why cases weren't assessed for severity. I spoke out when I saw the service lacking, when the residents weren't getting the specialist psychological and medical help they needed as quickly as they should, *if at all*.

It didn't do much good.

'There's not enough money,' I'd be told time and again, until my managers were blue in the face.

I gained the reputation of being a bit of an upstart and a lot of people didn't like me. In many cases, the feeling was mutual. But I wasn't going to change my ways. I had returned to the system to make a difference. In my day, children didn't have a voice at all, and I was going to make sure that no broken soul in my care went unheard.

But the modern care system made it logistically difficult. It appeared to me that the volume of cases was crushing social workers and they were drowning in paperwork.

'How can I keep my eye on 30 kids?' one said, throwing her hands up in despair in the staffroom one day. 'It's impossible.'

She'd not been with us long but she was already starting to be weighed down.

The response from the old-timers made me seethe with rage.

'Don't worry too much,' one snorted. 'They'll all end up in jail or on the streets anyway.'

'Or dead,' interjected another. 'Fuck it, you're not going to save them.'

My blood boiled. These kids were just like I had been decades earlier. They had a right to start again. Yes, their backgrounds were broken and hopeless, but they weren't lost yet. They still had a chance.

If we chose to give it to them.

The attitude from the old days was still pervasive. Back then, we were already dead in the eyes of our care workers – me, Callum, Danny, Susanna, Samantha and all of the others – we were sacks of flesh existing as punch bags for their rage or toys for their entertainment.

Nowadays, abuse within homes themselves wasn't prevalent, but ambivalence to what was happening to residents outside the home or any signs that they might need more than just a babysitter? That was rife, either through apathy or incapacity due to the sheer workload.

I was shocked to discover that very few of the workers had ever been in care themselves. A lot of them came from good, solid families with college and university educations. They didn't understand coming from a world where you were born half-dead and had to fight to even have a glimmer of hope of survival.

Danny, Callum and Susanna hadn't made it out. But I had, and so had Samantha, John and Adel.

It was possible, but a struggle. And the kids needed help to make it.

I still felt the scars of my experience. I still carried my friends who'd been devoured by the wolves at the top of the feeding chain with me.

I could see myself in these kids' eyes and I wanted to save them.

If that meant being the resident upstart, I was fine with it.

*　*　*

The modern care system was still full of broken souls, but their journey to the children's home was different, usually much slower, if they made it at all.

Back in my day any unfortunate twist of fate could land you in the care of the authorities, as I knew only too well. But in the modern system there was so much more red tape, so much bureaucracy, and social services weren't as quick to take children away from their families.

I could understand the good intentions of this, working to keep families together, but learning about cases like the deaths of 'Baby P' and Victoria Climbié during training and through my own research, it appeared to me that understaffing, over-working and lack of interest in the profession was leading to incredible negligence across the country. Lessons still didn't seem to be being learned.

In my opinion, too, the old guard in the system – the ones sitting like geese with golden eggs waiting for their pensions – avoided complex and traumatic cases like the plague. They just couldn't be bothered.

Younger, newer key workers – the ones who filtered in and out of the revolving door on a regular basis – had these cases dumped on them. Overwhelmed by the workload and lacking the experience to deal with such cases, they either crumbled under the pressure or mistakes were made.

Most of the time they were fixable, but I personally was always waiting for a ball to drop.

One particular case I'd heard of chilled me to the bone, the story of a boy known only as 'Child A'. It was proof to me that the system – although different – wasn't fixed. Far from it.

Vulnerable children were still at risk.

* * *

CHILD A

'Condemned as evil, left to rot.'

Child A was the eldest son of a woman with substance and alcohol issues. She was used and abused by a string of men – Child A's 'uncles', as he knew them – each one adding a new sibling to the household.

It was like a production line: new man, new baby; new man, new baby.

She was trying to fill a void where love hadn't been bestowed on her in her life. Her addict parents had never given a damn about her and the men were off like a shot when she became pregnant. When she wasn't making babies, she was drinking to drown her sorrows.

Child A and his siblings barely existed in the eyes of society before they took him into care at 13 years old. Somehow, they fell below the radar. Maybe it was an administrative error?

At eight years old, Child A was responsible for looking after his four younger siblings – all girls. All of them were born at home. None of them had a formal education, instead Mum made them stay home to do the housework and look after one another, so she didn't have to.

Not that the social workers who dutifully paid their visits noticed, their minds racing ahead to their next appointment or the pile of paperwork waiting for them back at the office.

If they tried to go out to school or elsewhere, they would be locked up for three days and given the belt by their mother. Fear reigned and they all did as they were told.

They cleaned and cooked meals while their mother entertained the next man in the bedroom upstairs – their new 'uncle'.

They were perfect little workers because they knew nothing else. Child A had always been quiet, according to file notes. But he was never allowed out and never made friends, so it was no surprise.

Child A's only fun was being in charge of the TV: he was the boss of the remote.

Saturdays were great for cartoons, but when they finished they'd go through their mum's videos. One day, Child A found a video with a sticker on saying DO NOT TOUCH.

That was a red rag to the curiosity of a child.

He popped the video in the recorder and lined his four siblings up on the couch with him. He sat in the middle, with two girls either side.

'We're going to watch a movie that Mum's made for us,' he'd announced to them. Well, it was certainly a video homemade by their mum.

But it was never for her children's eyes.

It was a video of her having sex.

Child A, being the eldest, understood this was how his mum spent much of her time. But he barely interacted with the outside world and had no understanding of what was right and wrong when it came to sex.

At his age, with hormones raging, he found what he saw exciting, exhilarating… *arousing*. This was his sexual awakening.

The girls just found it funny, of course. Because Mummy was on TV with no clothes on, making funny noises.

At the time, Child A had never had an orgasm or even masturbated, but he was at that age where seeing things like this chemically affected your body.

Apparently, as he'd watched the video he'd become erect and ejaculated; he couldn't stop it. After that he learned to masturbate, like most boys his age.

Images of anyone else having sex would have done the same, but for him it was his mum.

He'd never had anyone to explain boundaries to him. To teach him that you're not supposed to have feelings like that towards your family.

It became his ritual to watch the video every day, while his mum was asleep or at the pub. He'd make all the girls play upstairs.

Apart from his eldest sister.

He thought he was learning about things that adults do. Grown-up stuff that they'd have to do one day. He thought he should teach his sister by making her watch the tape.

His sister wasn't interested, she got bored. So to try and show her the importance of it, he created a game, to make it interesting and fun.

'We need to practise what Mum does,' he'd said. The two siblings would take off their clothes and imitate everything they saw on that tape. She would laugh hysterically as he jumped up and down on top of her. There was never penetration or arousal, it was just fun and exciting. Once the tape stopped, they went back to normal life.

They did it every day for two months. After he was taken, Child A told social services it made him happy to make his sister laugh, as she was rarely very happy. Perhaps in a different home, with a different parent, this behaviour would have been noticed. A conversation about 'private parts' and the birds and the bees would have stopped the cycle.

At that point it was wrong, but it was the uneducated experimentation of children.

The horror hadn't yet begun.

One day, Child A and his sister were playing the game in the kitchen. Their mum had gone to the pub so they knew she wouldn't be back for hours. But today she had forgotten her cigarettes, so she came back early, with 'Uncle' whoever-her-latest boyfriend was.

They walked in to see her two eldest children naked and simulating sex on the kitchen table. They shouted at them, of course. Told them they were disgusting, but they didn't explain why. They just punished them.

Punishment was being forced to carry on playing their game after the video had stopped. To 'do it properly', as their mother goaded.

Punishment was to force Child A to rape his sister.

Child A's drunken mother, egged on and assisted by her lover, sexually assaulted him. Made him erect and forced him to penetrate his sister.

She begged them to stop because it was hurting her. It made her bleed.

But they didn't stop.

Uncle-whatever-his-name-was just watched with his hands down his trousers. Afterwards, he had sex with Child A's mother, right there and then.

It didn't stop there. This 'Uncle' seemed to stick around. For a couple of years, the couple forced Child A and his sister to play their version of 'the game' over and over. On a whim, whenever they wished.

In the end, Child A developed sexual feelings towards his sister. His sister didn't laugh any more when they had to play 'the game'. She sobbed instead. Child A wasn't able to control his own urges, but deep down he didn't want to hurt his sister. So one day, when his vile mother once again instigated 'the game' for the entertainment of her and her boyfriend, he refused. Clamped his hand tightly over the waistband of his trousers and wriggled as they tried to strip him.

In a drunken fury, she took the belt to Child A. Then she kicked him and punched him until he bled. In her rage, she hadn't realised that she'd left the kitchen door wide open. A neighbour saw her raining blows down on her 13-year-old son, who was limp on the floor.

She called the police. When they arrived, the whole story came out.

Child A's mother and her boyfriend were arrested immediately for their sick crimes. Both were sent to jail for six years for child abuse. All five siblings were taken to separate care homes.

It was too late for Child A and his sister. The damage was already done. There was no saving these broken souls. After lots of examinations and meetings with professionals, it was decided that Child A could not be put in a standard care home, instead he would go to a special Child Sexual Exploitation (CSE) resource centre for children who are sexually dangerous until he was an adult. The abuse had caused an unnatural attitude to sex with young girls, particularly in regards to his sister.

He was a boy with a heart clear of malice, transformed into a monster by his own mother.

How had the authorities not spotted it sooner?

He was ordered to remain under the care of an appropriate adult for the rest of his life. It was one of the worst examples of the failure of the system I had ever heard of. Why was no one watching the kids of the addict, the children whose eyes were always dark and never went to school?

Was it because no one cared, because they just weren't important?

I was told that the boy is now around 15. Still being passed from key worker to key worker and being avoided by those disgusted with his history that was not of his own making.

The system had turned its back on him again. A broken soul with an unthinkable past, condemned as evil and left to rot.

CHAPTER EIGHTEEN

For All the Broken Souls

I refused to be beaten down. No matter how many cases they threw at me. No matter how complex or traumatic, I vowed never to turn my back on a child.

I kept pushing to provide extracurricular sessions for kids at the home. The art therapy class was particularly popular. It wasn't your regular art class. The paintings created were dark and troubling, shadows lingering around the corners of the canvas. The shadows of their unfortunate pasts.

It would almost certainly be too painful to recount the meaning behind each picture. The paintings delineated their souls.

That's probably why they never displayed them, just tucked them away in their rooms.

It was rewarding at times, but it was exhausting too – I was working every hour I could and it was putting a strain on my relationship with Androulla.

'I told you you'd get too attached,' she said.

I withdrew into myself, like I was permanently walking around under a cloud. I was meticulous in my work, but also provocative. I asked more questions than others, reported more concerns, dutifully filling in all the required paperwork and hand-delivering it to the appropriate line manager. I followed up everything with an email.

I'd heard stories of care workers who were trying to invigorate the system marked out as trouble causers, and dismissed shortly after on administrative technicalities. I wasn't about to let that happen to me.

I received many emails from my superiors praising me for my commitment and 'fresh approach' and telling me I was going to go on to do great things. However, there was an undercurrent dragging in a different direction to their words. Smiling at me like hyenas. Silently noting my outspoken behaviour. Remembering the times that I kept on fighting when I was meant to sit down and be quiet.

The pack system was still alive and well, but it had a different agenda now.

To wrap everything in red tape so it was nice and secure for them – not the kids – obviously.

As the months passed, it wore me down. The hoops care workers had to jump through made it impossible to do anything at a pace, if at all. In my opinion, children's lives were at risk of slipping back into the gutter due to paperwork and needless bureaucracy. At times all I could do was make sure I was making a noise about my concerns.

I recommended behavioural therapists, trauma counsellors and psychological therapists. Programmes and treatments that I knew would make a difference and help these kids start to piece their broken souls back together again. To give them a fighting chance.

Sometimes the old-timers cheered me on.

'Go on, Chris,' they'd say. 'Go for it.'

More than one confessed to me that they wished they were as brave or that they had the energy. But they only had a few years left before they'd be retiring. They were worn down to a nub by the system.

Wouldn't want to rock the boat now, would I?

That was always the refrain.

It was different for me. They'd come into this as a job to pay the bills, while I'd come in with a life's mission. I wasn't hanging on for any pension, I was trying to make a difference.

So I kept pushing, trying to make changes. There were others like me, up and down the country, but they were being told the same.

There's no money.

Constantly hitting brick walls became physically and emotionally draining.

Frustrated and desperate to offer a glimmer of hope to the kids in my care – the kids in care *anywhere* – I put pen to paper and started writing about my past and how I'd felt when I'd been in care.

I think I was doing it for me too, to try and make sense of everything that had happened.

I talked about the people I had lost and the things that saved me.

I wrote about how everyone could escape past demons, like I had.

How everyone had a chance.

Soon my colleagues noticed me scribbling away in my notebook.

'You're not a journalist, are you?' they joked. 'Going to expose us all?'

I laughed and shook my head, masking my anger.

It's not about you, it's about the kids. It's for *the fucking kids.*

There were a few people I thought understood how a care-home story with a happy ending might help other kids. Inspire them.

I gave some of my colleagues a glimpse of my work. I was proud of it and, what's more, it was breathing life back into me, reinvigorating my original mission. Then one day, I was called into my manager's office.

'We are suspending you on full pay pending an investigation,' he said.

'What for?' I spluttered.

He refused to go into detail but I had to leave immediately. I drove home in a blur, sat on the couch and didn't move until Androulla came in from work. She only had to look at my ashen face to know something was wrong. Her eyes asked the question before her mouth did.

'I've been suspended,' I said.

'For what?' she gasped, popping Antonia on her playmat and sitting down beside me.

'I don't know,' I said. 'I'm under investigation.'

I had no idea what had happened. Although I was outspoken, I did everything by the book and I had great relationships with the kids in my care.

What could it be?

Then it dawned on me. The only thing that had changed in the past few weeks was that I'd started writing. I knew I couldn't write about the kids in my care and I wouldn't want to. Current cases and things that were ongoing in the care home were completely of bounds.

And rightly so.

But I was writing about my own experience in the care system, everyone knew that. It was years ago, far away in Halifax. Surely that wouldn't be a problem?

'Maybe you're overthinking it?' said Androulla, a loving hand placed firmly on top of mine.

'Maybe,' I said, stroking my chin as I scoured my memories for anything else it could be. There was nothing.

I couldn't work while I was being investigated, so I had plenty of time on my hands. An idle body makes for a busy mind and a busy mind goes digging around in corners that haven't had light shed on them for a long time. Usually for a good reason.

I spent time worrying about my kids. They'd be reassigned another key worker for the time being, but a lot of them thrived on consistency. This could be a difficult upheaval. It wasn't that I was exceptional, I was just what they knew.

I hope they're doing okay.

And what about the art and boxing classes? Who would pick them up while I wasn't there, would anyone? I thought of how the kids opened up when they painted, came alive and poured their souls out onto canvas for a few hours. You could see the negative energy draining out of them, as creativity bred hope.

Then my mind started to go back further. To Halifax, to my lost friends and the ones that still suffered. To the kids still in care.

I repeated their names over and over in my head like a sad mantra: *Dad, Callum, Mark, Terry, Susanna, Danny, Adel, John, Samantha, Child A.*

I was focused, concentrating on their plight and meditating on what might have been if someone had been there at the start to give a damn.

My mind went to some very dark places in those weeks. I became depressed and I know Androulla was worried about the impact the change in me might be having on Antonia. Kids absorb everything like a sponge, from language to pervasive atmospheres.

We argued more and it felt like my 'happy ending' was coming apart at the seams. I was contacted by work for interviews, emailed queries and I noticed senior people from my employer checking my LinkedIn profile time and time again.

What were they looking for?

I'd always been completely transparent. I'd told them all about my past and was convinced that it, in part, was why they'd employed me.

Pressure started to build up inside. The constant throb of expansion was like a headache that leaves your cranium fit to burst, but it was taking over my whole body.

Then one day I woke up and I knew I was full.

I had to let it out and I knew just how I was going to do it.

I was going to paint.

It worked for the kids I did art therapy with, so why not?

I had an easel, paints, brushes and a canvas that I'd bought from an art shop after I'd visited an exhibition of the artist Lincoln Townley's work. I'd been researching art as therapy for work and had gone to the Saatchi Gallery to see his paintings. They depicted the artist's time living and working in Soho. I'd never been moved by art before, but his paintings were alive with their subject's spirit. It inspired me to try, but I'd never got started.

Now I had no choice but to start. I didn't even feel like I was acting consciously. It was like my body had taken over and was acting of its own volition.

I took everything out to my little wooden shed in the garden and set up the easel and canvas. Next, I splodged a selection of paints out, grabbed a brush, dipped it in the viscous black pigment and raised it in the air. Momentarily, I paused. What was I doing?

I'd never painted in my life. Didn't have a clue what I was doing.

But then I felt it: gentle pressure from behind me, nudging my hand towards the canvas. As if to say, *It doesn't matter, just do it.*

It was like a presence from beyond was instructing me. Voices from a dark place making my hand move in whatever direction they willed.

I fell deeper into my own mind, driven by the words swirling in my head. They were the words of all the broken souls I had ever encountered.

I was doomed from the start… Social services dropped us like a sack of spuds… I'd been in pain all my life… the wolves always work in packs…

It was haunting but exhilarating all at the same time. There was no plan or sketch to follow. I hadn't even thought about what I was painting, I just allowed my subconscious to guide my hand, brushing broad strokes across the stark white canvas, changing colours and motion, speed and direction.

An image began to come into focus, like one of those magic eye pictures, where you have to stare at it for a while in a specific way to see what it is you're looking at.

Suddenly those other-worldly commands stopped. I was free to drop my brush. So I did.

It was like a hypnotist had just clicked his fingers and invited me to be 'back in the room' after making me unwittingly run a marathon.

Although it felt like I'd only been in there a few minutes, I was sweating, splattered in paint and breathless, like I'd been toiling for hours.

I stood back and let my eyes settle on the complete image. My brain took a moment to arrange the shapes and colours. Then I gasped and fell into the seat behind me.

Somehow a face was staring back at me. I thought I was seeing things. How could I have created that?

The face was a woman's. I recognised it straight away, but I couldn't understand how.

It was Susanna. Unmistakably, undeniably Susanna.

Had she been guiding me from beyond the grave?

I stared at the painting for a while, absorbing every detail. At first I was impressed with myself. I'd never lifted a paintbrush before that day. But then reality hit me around the head. But what did this mean? Why had I created it?

I always had so many questions, but you aren't always blessed with answers, or a neatly tied up ending.

That was true for many of the care-home kids I had encountered.

Why did my mother abandon me?

Why did my dad have to die?

What did no one stop those people from hurting me?

Since the night I'd tried to take my own life, I'd been striving to find my purpose, the reason that I outran the wolves when others didn't.

I'd been trying to absolve myself of the guilt of survival.

I'd thought going back into the care system was it, my end goal. But now that was under threat, for a reason I was not yet privy to.

But maybe I was wrong. Maybe I couldn't be the voice I wanted to be in the system. The system would always stifle voices.

Back in my day, it was the children who were silenced. Now it seemed that it was anyone trying to make the system work better.

Maybe I needed to be the voice of those lost souls from a bygone age, to speak to those broken children of today, to provide warnings and hope?

By the time I emerged from the shed it was dark. Androulla's face staring out at me from the kitchen, through the patio doors. Her brow was furrowed into a scowl. I pushed the door open and stepped into the kitchen. 'What time is it?'

'It's nine o'clock at night,' she snapped. 'Antonia is in bed. You didn't see her all day.'

I'd been in there for 11 hours?

'Why didn't you come and get me?' I asked.

'I did,' Androulla retorted. 'More than once. I was banging on the door. Antonia was shouting too. But you ignored us.'

I didn't hear a thing, I must have been in some kind of a trance.

'I'm so sorry,' I said, as we sat down to eat. As we chatted over dinner, I explained that I'd felt the urge to paint and had been swept up. As I spoke, I noticed that the pressure building up in my body had eased and my chest felt less tight, like something had been unblocked inside me. I told Androulla.

'You do look a little better,' she said. 'Can I see the painting?'

'Tomorrow,' I said.

I was exhausted by the whole experience and ready for bed, but sleep didn't come easily. I was still trying to figure out what had happened.

As I pieced together the day's events and took time to recognise the change in my mental and physical state, I felt a glimmer of happiness, a sense of relief as well as the physical sensation of pressure being released.

It was like my memories of Susanna had acted upon me like a toxin, poisoning my own body with guilt and forcing me into a state of inertia.

The guilt that I survived had sat inside me, silently gnawing away at my own soul. But now she was out, her spirit reincarnated on that canvas.

What did she want from me?

Suddenly it clicked. She wanted her voice heard.

Nothing more, nothing less.

The next day, I crept into the shed early in the morning. I pulled up a chair in front of Susanna and spoke to her.

'So, you want me to tell your story?' I asked. The movement created by the texture of the paints indicated yes.

'Well then, you need to trust me,' I said.

I was going to share her story, warts and all. No sanitising it or putting a halo where there wasn't one. But I was going to explain how she got there.

How her soul was shattered from the start.

Just like that, we made a silent pact. I signed my name on her top and then placed her to one side in the shed. At that moment Androulla knocked on the door. I shouted her in and she appeared, wearing her dressing gown. As soon as she laid eyes on the canvas, she recoiled.

'What the hell is that?' she gasped.

'It's a painting,' I replied with a smile. I think it was the first time I'd cracked a joke in weeks.

'I can see that,' she smirked back. 'But why is she so scary?'

I knew that would be how she'd react. How most people would react.

'She's not meant to be scary,' I said gently. 'She's just been through a lot.'

Over coffee, I explained Susanna's story. Androulla listened with tears in her eyes.

'There's more of them in me,' I explained. 'I've realised that I carry all of their souls with me.'

'Keep painting them,' she said, hugging me as she left for work. 'Just, maybe, don't let Antonia see them,' she added, sensitively.

I completely agreed. I wanted to protect Antonia from the horrors of the world for as long as I could. The protection that should have been offered to all of the souls that I carried inside of me.

Over the next few weeks, words would come to me in the night, words that would drive the next painting. I never planned anything, I just followed what my mind and body told me.

This was me, letting my open wound bleed out onto the canvas, the letting out of blood releasing years of pain and guilt.

I became obsessed. Controlled by their voices. Callum came next, then Mark.

Androulla made sure she was there to look after everything else. She knew that this was like 'going cold turkey' – horrific in the short term, but with greater long-term effects. She reminded me to eat and tried to make me rest the best she could.

I went days without sleeping. I ended up passing out and went to the doctor, who told me I was suffering from exhaustion and depression.

He prescribed Citalopram, an antidepressant, but I threw the prescription in the bin. I didn't need anything to numb my emotion right now, I needed to see and feel everything exactly as it was.

I kept painting and carried on my writing too. Samantha crept up on me in the middle of the night. Danny was painful, my affection for him made it hard for me to contemplate what I'd created. Terry, Adel, John and Child A, they all followed.

When they were all complete, I felt about two stone lighter. The colour returned to my cheeks and the weight that had sat on my chest for most of my adult life was gone. Vanished into the ether.

I'd exorcised all of my demons onto canvas. Now I just had to complete my promise to them: to make their voices heard.

Eventually, the decision came back from work.

I was to be summarily dismissed from my position as care worker at the home for Gross Misconduct. The reason?

'The serious breach of trust and confidence that has arisen from the falsification of your application form.'

Ten months into my employment, in a role where I had been outwardly praised for my work, it appeared that they'd found a mistake with a date on my application. I looked through the notes and back at the application. It was a genuine oversight. It hardly seemed real that it would be the reason they would sack a care worker when they were in such dire need of committed staff.

It appeared to me that this was just an excuse, a reason to get rid of a potential troublemaker. I accepted it, but before I packed that experience in a box and put it away on the shelf in my heart, I made sure I raised any concerns I'd had about the home to Ofsted.

My final gesture to the kids I'd cared for. Who I *still* cared for, but could no longer help directly. I was never informed of any outcome, but several senior people and a few of the old-timers were moved on a few months later.

Maybe it was sheer coincidence.

Or maybe it wasn't.

I started working with young people in less restrictive environments, giving talks in community centres and helping out at youth theatre groups designed for kids coming out of care.

Androulla said I was like a different person. Not angry or morbid any more, just positive and hopeful.

That said, I still lived with my guilt and often picked up broken souls to carry with me, like I always had done. I found myself drawn to homeless people on the street, keen to know what had brought them to this place in their lives. More often than not, they'd had some brush with the care sector.

One girl I met was living under the bridge at Waterloo Station. She was painting a portrait on a piece of her cardboard bedding. Her eyes reflected a sea of dark memories and the lines on her weather-beaten face aged her beyond her years. I got us both a coffee and sat down to talk to her.

* * *

ANNIE

'I was deemed an unfit mother.'

Her name was Annie. She'd been living on the streets for a few months after hitting 16 and being kicked out of the care system. All she had were the clothes on her back and a rucksack carrying two pairs of socks, a photo book and a towel. The coat she was wearing had been donated by a kind passer-by on Christmas Eve.

'I had nothing to give him, other than to say thank you, so I painted him a picture of London Bridge,' she smiled.

Annie didn't know any life other than the one in care. She was six years old when her parents abandoned her.

'I don't know why,' she said. 'They just went missing from my life.'

She told me that when people asked her what it was like growing up in care, she couldn't answer because she had no comparison.

'For me it was just growing up,' she said.

She was like the stray cat attached to a neighbour's house. No one knew who she belonged to – she didn't even have a name – so the home just gave her food, a place to sleep and her name.

'I liked the film, so it kind of grew on me,' she smiled, sipping her coffee.

Annie had a humble way about her. She acknowledged others' pain readily, but dismissed her own.

'My own story isn't particularly sad, but my memories are full of melancholic tales,' she said. 'Over the years I saw so many children come and go, each one carrying a bag full of dead hope. At first I'd hug them and try and make it better, but there were too many.'

Annie told me that she found the stories of sexual abuse hardest to deal with.

'One girl I befriended told me that her mum and dad would make her have sex with her brother,' she said, her face showing her repulsion. 'The saddest thing was that she had become accustomed to this evil abuse. She even told me she missed the attention. She said it was the only time her parents showed her any affection.'

Annie became the home's resident agony aunt and her heart became hardened by the stories told to her by broken children and crushed care workers.

'I often felt that my heart had turned so cold it must be blue,' she said. 'But that all changed when Thomas arrived.'

He was a care-home kid too, brought up through the system.

'He looked like butter wouldn't melt,' Annie said, blushing at the memory. 'But he was a right cocky bastard and I loved it.'

Annie recalled the night he was brought to the home. The night he thawed her heart.

'It was a Monday. The staff had forgotten a new person was due, as usual – they'd been too preoccupied with their coffee breaks and telly shows. They were scrabbling round to sort his room out, before the boss of the home found out.'

A car pulled up and Annie ran outside to see the new arrival.

'I had been at the home so long I even had my own private room. I was like part of the furniture. I pretended I knew all this history and would wind the newbies up with the scary stories I'd been told at six years old,' she said, chuckling. 'My favourite was telling them that the home was an old mental institution where children were said to have gone missing, when really they were buried in the cellar because they had misbehaved.'

She didn't go easy on new staff either.

'I told one that I came into the children's home because I murdered all my family while they were sleeping,' she laughed. 'Because the voices in my head told me to.'

The worker started on the Monday and left on the Tuesday.

This new arrival was different.

'What the fuck are you looking at?' Thomas said, as he swaggered towards the entrance of the home in his tracksuit and Nike trainers.

'If he'd have been a girl he would have been picking his teeth up off the concrete,' Annie said. 'But he wasn't. His presence and attitude just captivated me. Intoxicated me. My legs turned to jelly and I was in love.'

Like all teenage girls, Annie became obsessed with her crush.

'I was like a lovesick puppy, I barely left his side,' she smiled. 'I was so used to taking care of myself. Now this guy was taking good care of me. He made me feel beautiful, like a human being.'

Unabashedly, Annie told me how, before long, they were 'at it like dogs in heat'.

'We took full advantage of my private room privileges,' she said. 'I really didn't know a lot about sex. My sex education had come from those poor victims of sexual abuse.'

All the explicit information cried onto her shoulder was absorbed in her brain.

'I know it sounds horrible, but I felt like that knowledge had finally been put to some good use. Healthy, natural, intended use,' she shrugged. 'We would recreate acts that had been described to me as happening in an abusive setting. But it was different, we weren't quite adults, but were two non-related, consenting people in love. Our sex life was the only pleasurable memory I can recall from my time in a children's home.'

Of course Annie got pregnant. Mrs Townsend, the manager of the home, had Thomas removed from the house. Annie was transferred to an all-girls' care home in the middle of nowhere.

'We were like Romeo and Juliet being torn apart,' Annie told me. 'It broke my heart. He was my life, my escape, and we were now bonded by blood.'

'Did you speak before you left?' I asked.

'Briefly,' she said. 'He said he would come and get me. But I never saw him again.'

They sent Annie to a convent, a building in the middle of a big field with no roads, no station, nothing.

'Even if I'd ran away I wouldn't have gotten far,' she said. 'I gave birth to my little girl there. I remember her being very small. That's about it, as she was taken from me immediately. I'd barely touched her skin when the midwives tore her from me and put her in the arms of Derek and fucking Tracey.'

Derek and Tracey were the people who adopted Annie's baby.

'I don't know if that was their names,' she sighed. 'It's just what they looked like. Normal, run-of-the-mill Derek and Tracey.'

Annie wasn't given the chance to fight for the opportunity to become a mother. She was 15 years old so the system deemed her unfit.

'After the birth I just remember lying in bed, crying all night,' Annie said. Grey sadness tinged her eyes. 'She was my beautiful baby and I didn't even get a chance to kiss her goodbye. I left that convent with only her blanket as a memory.'

Her tears flowed as she explained how from then on her life careered off the rails.

'I went crazy, started drinking heavily and lost all my existing self-respect in the bed sheets of strangers,' she said. 'After I left the home, when I turned sixteen, I was living in a hostel full of drug addicts. I found it a bonus to have nothing. That way, no one could take anything from me ever again.'

'Derek and Tracey' made a home for her daughter and even sent Annie some photographs. It was a gesture that became her turning point.

'She had his smile and my eyes,' Annie said, opening her photo book. 'I saw these and realised that giving her up was the best decision for her. What could I have given her?'

Annie shook the photos in my face.

'These images made me want to change, to become something she could be proud of,' she said. 'But coming out of care is a shock. All of a sudden the roof over your head and the guaranteed three meals a day are gone. I'd never had to pay bills or anything like that. Now, I had to learn how to live on thirty-six pounds a week. It was impossible.'

'Is that how you ended up homeless?' I ventured.

'Sort of,' she said. 'You see, once you're out of the system you're expected to blend into society as a normal human being, just like that,' she said, clicking her fingers. But Annie wasn't bitter.

'I have to appreciate what I have,' she said. 'How lucky I had been.'

'So many of those who I knew in care have died,' she said. 'My life was shit. It's still not perfect, but to this day I count myself as one of the lucky ones. I'm still alive.'

It was a feeling that resonated deeply with me.

'I'm one of the lucky ones, too,' I said. 'Why are you on the streets now?'

'Because I can't afford a home,' she said.

'Is there no help?' I asked.

'Yes, there is,' she smiled. 'In eight months' time. That's the length of the waiting list. I put myself to the back of the queue when I spiralled out of control. I'm trying to save money so I can study to be a nurse. I want to build a safe home for my child – for when we are reunited.'

My heart felt like it was stretching open to this wonderful, positive human being. So much hope coming out of a place where there was none.

'What about your painting?' I asked.

'It's a hobby,' she said. 'It keeps me warm and busy. Kills the time before I can meet my girl.'

'When will that happen?' I asked gently.

Annie replied with fire and determination in her eyes: 'I can't see her until she is 18. I had her when I was 15.'

'How old are you now, Annie?' I asked, inflated like a balloon with hope and excitement.

Her next words were like a pin, piercing that hope.

'I'm 16. She'll be one now. So I have 17 years to go. More than my lifetime to this point,' her eyes turned a sad grey for a moment. But just like when clouds pass across bright sky, the light returned. 'But that's nothing when it's your child you're waiting for. I'd wait 20 lifetimes for just one moment with her.'

* * *

I sobbed the whole way home on the train. I'd seen hope and determination like that before, in Danny. But the shadows had caught up with him. Was that going to be Annie's fate too?

When I got home I retreated straight to my shed. Annie's soul was raw within me. I needed to recreate her spirit, take everything I'd absorbed that afternoon and wring myself like a sponge to ensure I captured the essence of her being – her pain, her light, everything.

Hours later, I added her to my wall of broken souls. I looked at each one. They were all so different, yet united by one thing: their dark eyes that reflected the pernicious life of their memories past.

I knew what I had to do and now there was no reason to hold back.

I grabbed my laptop and started typing.

*   *   *

This book is for all the broken children. The ones I couldn't save and the ones that still suffer today. It's for all the broken souls. It's for everyone. It's proof that there is always hope.

Afterword

I finished writing this book in January 2018. At that point, 22 people I'd known from my life in the care system in Halifax had either committed suicide or died of drug overdoses. It was the same week that the red carpet at the Golden Globes turned into a sea of black in protest against the Hollywood sex abuse scandal, after allegations against male movie moguls and stars like Harvey Weinstein and Kevin Spacey cracked the lid on years of assault and abuse. Oprah Winfrey – a survivor of sexual abuse herself – led the rallying cry that time was up for these men who had abused their positions of power to manipulate and silence the women they had harmed. No doubt by the time you read this, far more will have emerged from the shadows. It was also the same week that boxing legend Micky Ward, who inspired the Mark Wahlberg movie *The Fighter*, revealed in his autobiography that he'd been sexually abused by a family friend. Footballers abused by their coaches have bravely stood up and spoken out, as have those abused by politicians in the corridors of power in the UK.

Voices are being raised and, this time, are being heard. I add my voice to that noise all the time. But I also want to speak for those without profile or power. Not everyone is Oprah.

In a world where the sitting President of the United States of America says of women: 'You can do anything [to them]... Grab 'em by the pussy,' it's easy to become disheartened and wonder if any of us can make a difference. I know because I have been there, time and again.

But then when I look at my daughter, who is now five years old, I know I can't stop fighting. None of us can. As parents who want our children to be safe, to end up with loving and respectful partners, we have to sow the seeds in the next generation now. And not just the privileged ones, but those who have come from broken backgrounds, where what they've seen and learned will taint their future and continue cycles of abuse.

In the eighties and nineties in Halifax, where my soul was made and broken, the abuse was horrific, but contained. Now, it has seeped out of those narrow corridors and into the rest of society, in all professions and at all levels, from the bottom of the gutter to the top of the ivory towers. Nowhere is safe from the wolves now.

The care system is still broken. It hasn't stopped, but the abuse now lies hidden between the walls of power. During my two years working in modern children's homes, and through the interviews and research I conducted for this book, it's clear to me that all children in the care system are still exposed to danger, as no money is being invested in their care. The industry is in crisis because there are simply not enough engaged and passionate workers to meet these children's needs. The ones that do have the fire in their belly appear, to me, to either be crushed by unmanageable workloads or silenced by bureaucracy.

The level of risk could be about to get worse. The new Education Secretary, Damian Hinds, the man responsible for education and children's services, has a record of voting against the welfare and benefits that many care leavers will rely on, such as raising welfare benefits at least in line with inflation.

The majority of the money that is currently supporting young children in care, in both the private and public sectors, comes from Europe. With Brexit and the tremors of uncertainty it sent through the continent, the aftershock is already being felt now. And we haven't even had the big quake yet.

In my story, and the stories of many others in this book, the abuse was confined within the walls of a children's home and people looked the other way, sometimes too scared to speak up. Now it is everywhere, and too often people are still looking away. But now there is no need to. There is nothing to fear from speaking up about abuse witnessed. Ultimately, and sadly, there are more of us than them.

I recently returned to Halifax, to the site of Skircoat Lodge. The main building was razed and it's been a beautiful block of luxury flats for about 15 years. It still bears the name of the children's home, but I am sure that most residents don't have any clue about its significance and the ghosts of the past that tread there.

Maybe someone should remind them?

We can't forget these victims of the past, because if we do, we'll fail to see the victims that surround us today – the Hollywood actress whose films we adore, the quiet child in the classroom, the drunk on the train that we avoid on our commute home, our favourite footballer and the beggar in the street.

All of these broken souls, with their dark eyes and empty hearts, needs our help. Our voices.

Every day I look at my beautiful, loving family and I give thanks. I think about the extended family I have been blessed with through my union with Androulla, my mum – who is now happily remarried – and my sister, Donna. I think about the passionate and committed campaigners and activists I have the pleasure of working alongside, and I never take one single thing for granted. Because I know that I was lucky. Somehow, I was always one step ahead of the wolves and I escaped. The shadows may have nipped at my heels, but they never quite grasped hold. They never pulled me in like they did my old friends.

We're all born equal, but sometimes life chooses a road for us. For too many children in care, the road they are pushed down is dark, dangerous and abusive. But it's a road that can be avoided. Every child deserves to be loved and safe – it is possible to alter the course they may have been set on, due to unfortunate beginnings.

I think about that every day and remind myself that I have to keep on fighting for a better future for children in care and in dysfunctional abusive family settings, for gender and sexual equality, for hope.

For all the broken souls… Will you join me too?

Notes Found in a Children's Home
Written By Broken Souls

During my time both living and working in the system, I have discovered many a scribbled note revealing the innermost emotions of the kids trapped in Britain's broken care system. Teaching writing and therapeutic art classes to young people in the system, providing an alternative way to channel grief, pain and fear, I have also been privileged for them to share with me a glimpse of their beautiful, broken souls. These poems are a snapshot of the emotions of those living in the care system, as well as from those who got out.

A LETTER HOME TO MUM

I'm fed up of being branded unwanted, forgotten, disowned.

Tell the truth – reveal the real reasons I'm here. Put down that glass of vodka, cut down on the drugs, look at me – I'm here, I'm alive. You created this, do not ignore it.

I hope I'm nothing like you when I grow up. I hope I never see you ever again. You care more about him than your own children.

Remember that day when the two police cars came to collect me to bring me here? I saw him smiling through the window with his smug grin. He's beaten you, Mum. Everything you were is gone, and everything you have now belongs to him.

I'm stuck here surrounded by strangers with problems, real problems not like me. What happened to you? How did it come to this?

It's pasta every fucking night here. I can't live like this any more.

I miss my friends, I miss my bedroom, I miss my life and I miss you.

Please, please, please let me come home. I promise I'll behave. All I did was protect you. You can't see it, but he's not right for us. He wants you all to himself. Remember this: I won't be fourteen forever, and I'll never forget.

TO WHOEVER WANTS TO LISTEN

I'm writing this letter to anyone and everyone because there is no one.

Christmas is different here. We have a tree, but it lacks any life. I woke thinking it was any other day until I sat on my own at the table, staring at the lifeless tree. I notice under its dead branches a colourful box, making the tree even more dilapidated than before.

'Merry Christmas from all the staff.' But where are you? It's very quiet; the fridge takes centre stage with its broken Concerto Number One in Humming Minor.

Whoever receives my importune letter – will you take pity on me?

The echo is my only response, even it defers to reply.

The ominous silence is ubiquitous.

Merry Christmas whoever you are.

Yours Truly

Pariah

PLEASE REMEMBER ME

Dear Mum,

Please remember me.

Today was difficult for me because it was my birthday and I didn't hear from you. I waited by the phone hoping you'd call.

But you didn't.

I woke up really early so that I could catch the postman and see if you had sent me a card.

But you didn't.

Mum, it was a year ago today that I was taken away from you. It was my birthday. That day you forgot to buy me a toy because you were ill and I couldn't wake you up. I was hoping that you would have remembered and brought me two presents – one for last year and one for today.

But you didn't.

I will wait by the phone next year and hope you don't forget. Maybe you will bring me three toys. This year came and you forgot. I hoped you would have remembered.

But you didn't.

Last year became this year and this year became last. I waited by the door. I was waiting to see you, hoping you'd bring me a card.

But you didn't.

Each year I wait in anticipation, knowing that you are busy working. You're making money to take us both away somewhere nice. I sat patiently at the gates, hoping and praying that you'd come to collect me.

But you didn't.

Dear Mum, it's been ten years since I wrote this letter. I sat up crying in bed every night waiting for you to call and say you love me.

But you didn't.

People told me that you were bad and I should forget about you.

But I didn't.

MOURNING SCABS
OF HEROIN

I pick my scabs for relief
Warning signs indiscreet
Burning hurts, the nerves of past
Red, scorned blood, cut with glass
Pressure increase, urgent attention
Sentenced life, condemned redemption
Screeching sears, no one feels my pain
Aching jaw, from shouting strain
Silent echoes, nothing gained
Back to my room, the voice refrained
Memories trigger fearful tears
Infected arms from poisonous gear
The injection breaks the skin so weak
No space left, I use my feet.
The veins sleep through lack of light
Desperate urges I cannot fight
Temptation makes me pick my skin
Nails break, so I use a pin
Druggies fight the brown I'm craving
Crying out, but no one's saving

I WAS ONCE
A CHILD

I was neglected
I was rejected
I was abused
I was used
I was beaten
I was kicked
I was bitten
I was left alone
I was abandoned
I was spat at
I was laughed at
I was worthless
I was scared
I was cold
I was in pain
I was wet
I was starving
I was manipulated
I was provoked
I was choked
I was burnt
I was scum
I was trash
I was intimidated
I was frightened
I was calm
I was loved
I was hugged

I was liked
I was kind
I was fragile
I was all of these things when I was just a child.

TEARS AND FEARS
OF A CHILDREN'S HOME

I do not belong here
It's a tarnished life of fear and gear
Painful years, seen and spent
Lots of time to repent
Tears, fights, and arguments
The tears and the fears of leaving home
Gone forever, all alone
Reaching out to be saved
Rejected love, the words engraved
Why am I here? I'm leaving
Red eyes flare, I'm seething
Flashbacks burn from my past
Gone the years, out at last
I'm scared, though, I'm just a child
I sometimes get a little wild
The tears and fears of leaving home
Gone forever, all alone.
Crying out to be heard
Lifelong memories, all a blur
I don't want to go. Why me?
I'll be good from now on. You'll see
My time here just went wrong
Bags packed, up and gone
I'll go then, goodbye
Hope you remember me
Eat shit and die

IN LOVING MEMORY
OF MY LOST CHILD

I could see you through the gates but you couldn't feel me. You're standing lonely, on your own, staring curiously at the clouds. I see crystal eyes filled with desperate tears. Why are you left stranded by those callous foes? I shout your name, hoping it strikes a chord, but it drifts away with the wind, evaporating back to the sky, never reaching its goal. I feel your sadness in my veins. It's burning viscerally with toxic acid. The legal force field defends the boundaries of guilt, and now I can do no more.

I will never forget you exist, but you will forget I existed.

Mummy x

DEAR DAD

Dear Dad,
I'm drowning in my tears
Because I'm scared you're all alone.
1st of April, I too lost my life
Your grave is all I have,
A line on black marble,
Engraved with the heart of blood
With the sad words 'goodbye'.

If heaven had a phone, son
I'd dial right now, and call back home.
Chris, please listen to what I have to say,
I wish I could have just one more day
but I can't, Chris, I'm here, crying too.
Just think all the good times we had.

Dad, my daughter smiles with your lips
My son blinks with your eyes.
I have your heart
And with that I'm chasing my dreams
I got married; I have a beautiful wife
Do I make you proud?

It's always an awkward silence,
Saying goodbye, Dad.
Not goodbye, Chris
But see you soon, son.
I'm not alone,
I'm with you, and always will be
And the answer is yes.

ACKNOWLEDGEMENTS

Two years ago I decided I was going to write a book. I didn't know where to start or how, I just woke up one day and started writing. My objective was to write something that would encourage people to think about life: my life, their life, the life of vulnerable young children who can't defend themselves, and the adults who fall into the perils of the past and live with the nightmares of their trauma.

Writing this book gave me some internal peace. Many people from my past didn't make it, so it's only fair that I dedicate this book in their memory. We all started on the same path in life, we were all from broken homes but, somehow, I broke free and, in doing so, I survived.

I would also like to say a massive thank you to Kelly Ellis and Beth Eynon for the opportunity to tell my story, Nikki Girvan whose genius helped to shape my words and the whole team at Blink Publishing. I will be forever indebted to you. These books are so important – they save lives.

To my family and friends, my son Bobby, my daughter Antonia and my amazing wife, who has been my rock. And last, but not least, my Dad in heaven – this one's for you.

Two years later and here it is.